RELE

D1499376

THEORIES AND CONCEPTS IN COMPARATIVE INDUSTRIAL RELATIONS

STUDIES IN INDUSTRIAL RELATIONS

Hoyt N. Wheeler and Roy J. Adams, *Editors*

Industrial Conflict: An Integrative Theory
  by Hoyt N. Wheeler
Theories and Concepts in Comparative
Industrial Relations
  Edited by Jack Barbash and Kate Barbash

Theories and Concepts in Comparative Industrial Relations

Edited by Jack Barbash and Kate Barbash

University of
South Carolina Press

First Edition

Manufactured in the United States of America

LIBRARY OF CONGRESS
Library of Congress Cataloging-in-Publication Data

Theories and concepts in comparative industrial relations / edited by
   Jack Barbash and Kate Barbash. — 1st ed.
     p. cm. — (Studies in industrial relations)
   Includes bibliographies and index.
   ISBN 0-87249-580-9
   1. Industrial relations. I. Barbash, Jack. II. Barbash, Kate.
III. Series.
HD6971.T48 1988
331—dc19   88-21443
                                              CIP

CONTENTS

FIGURES

TABLES

Series Editors' Preface

As editors of the series, Studies in Industrial Relations, we are especially pleased to have Jack Barbash's volume published. It conforms perfectly to the purpose of the series—the publication of new ideas and theories capable of helping scholars and practitioners to better understand and deal with the problems of our field. It is a rare thing to find a large number of new ideas in a single volume. This book has this, along with some interesting arrangements and applications of old ideas. It also has the great advantage of providing approaches to industrial relations problems that are not only diverse philosophically, but also multinational to an extraordinary extent. We are convinced that this volume will make a lasting contribution to the field.

Hoyt N. Wheeler
Columbia, South Carolina

Roy J. Adams
Geneva, Switzerland

Contributors

W. Albeda
Chair, Scientific Council for Government Policy, The Netherlands
Jack Barbash
Professor of Economics and Industrial Relations (Emeritus)
University of Wisconsin-Madison and Visiting Professor, Graduate School
of Management, University of California, Davis, California
Brian G. Bemmels
Assistant Professor of Industrial Relations, Faculty of Business, University of Alberta, Edmonton, Canada
Nicholas Blain
Senior Lecturer in Industrial Relations, University of Western Australia, Perth, Western Australia
Jean Boivin
Professor, Department of Industrial Relations, Laval University, Quebec, Canada
R. Oliver Clarke
Principal Administrator, Organization for Economic Cooperation and Development, Paris, France
Braham Dabscheck
Senior Lecturer, Department of Industrial Relations, University of New South Wales, Australia
L.C.G. Douwes Dekker
Associate Professor of Industrial Relations, Graduate School of Business Administration, University of the Witwatersrand, South Africa
Anthony Giles
Assistant Professor of Industrial Relations, University of New Brunswick, Canada
Rien J. Huiskamp
Research Manager, Dutch Social Economic Council; Senior Researcher, Department of Economics, Free University, The Netherlands
Paul Johnsen
Professor, European Institute for Advanced Study, Norwegian School of Management, Oslo, Norway

xi

Patrick Joynt
Professor, European Institute for Advanced Study, Norwegian School of Management, Oslo, Norway

Noah M. Meltz
Professor of Economics and Industrial Relations and Assistant Dean, School of Graduate Studies, University of Toronto, Canada

Jacques Rojot
Professor in Management, Université du Maine, Le Mans; European Institute of Business Administration, Fontainebleau, France

Arie Shirom
Professor of Behavioural Sciences and Chair of Department of Labour Studies, Tel Aviv University, Tel Aviv, Israel

George Strauss
Professor of Business Administration, University of California, Berkeley

Hoyt N. Wheeler
Professor of Industrial Relations and Business Partnership Foundation Fellow, College of Business Administration, University of South Carolina, Columbia, South Carolina

Mahmood A. Zaidi
Professor of Labor Economics and Industrial Relations and Director, International Program Development, Curtis L. Carlson School of Management, University of Minnesota, Minneapolis, Minnesota

PREFACE

This volume is an outgrowth of a seminar organized by the Study Group on Industrial Relations Theory and Industrial Relations as a Field on the occasion of the Hamburg Congress of the International Industrial Relations Association (IIRA) in September 1986. We owe much to the cooperation and encouragement of the IIRA Secretary, Dr. Alan Gladstone, his colleague David Dror and IIRA President Professor Friedrich Furstenberg, who inspired the study group idea. Professor Hoyt Wheeler of the University of South Carolina was instrumental in bringing the Study Group together with the University of South Carolina Press. As a veteran in dealing with publishing houses I want to express my appreciation for the expedition and care beyond the call of duty with which the press has handled this venture. Mrs. Marion Leifer and Mrs. Marjorie Lamb of the Industrial Relations Research Association in Madison were uncommonly kind in handling study group communications. The contributors were exceedingly patient with my shortcomings and the problems of coordinating a venture among participants spread all over the globe. I hope they will think it was worth it.

My greatest appreciation, as usual, goes to my wife, Kitty Barbash, without whose collaboration, involvement and concern this task would have been beyond me.

—Jack Barbash
Madison, August 1987

INTRODUCTION

JACK BARBASH

This volume seeks to further the international dialogue on industrial relations theory. The theory embodied in these papers is somewhat more practical, more relaxed and less ambitious than the connotation that theory usually carries with it, for instance, in economics (hence the addition of the word "concepts" to the book's title).

Our theories and concepts are meant to focus on generalizations that are rather close to the underlying reality. Our theory, moreover, is not an exercise in quantitative or symbolic logic, nor does it seek to develop a paradigm of some sort.

Although, as I say, we are not dispensing formal theories here, I think that we are, perhaps, contributing to some of the prerequisites by (1) defining industrial relations in diverse contexts, (2) identifying key participants in the field who figure importantly in several papers and (3) identifying critical institutions, processes and concepts—for example, corporatism, equity, "social partnership," the public interest, systems and a "predisposition to social dominance."

If we are not bound by one theory it is just possible that common values inform our work. Our values—and here I am relying on my own perceptions rather more than on explicit allusions in the papers—seem to favor an equilibrium of power and humane constraints on the uses of that power. I think, too, that we see industrial relations operationally as the efficient and just resolution of conflict in the employment relationship. We deem this to be a worthy objective in its own right rather than a way station to some larger end. In all but a few papers, the context in which industrial relations functions is advanced capitalism in the North American–Western European tradi-

3

tion of highly structured collective bargaining in a pluralistic, democratic, welfare state.

These essays are comparative in that they are meant to yield up theories and concepts that will facilitate comparison across cultures and national lines, even where the analysis is cast in a national context. French "exceptionalism," Dutch, South African and Norwegian "corporatism," and North American "equity" are some of these commonalities. Other papers are more explicitly "cross-national."

The papers are comparative in another sense. The authors come from a variety of national, professional and disciplinary origins. By native habitat the authors are "English" and "French" Canadian, American, Norwegian, Dutch, French, South African, Australian and Israeli. Their disciplines are, variously, labor law, economics, sociology, political science, organizational behavior and, to be sure, industrial relations. By profession the authors are professors, cabinet ministers, international civil servants and practicing consultants.

The content of the papers falls into three categories: (1) case studies in a national setting that illuminate general aspects of industrial relations theory and concept, (2) theories and concepts in a more cross-national setting and (3) interconnections between theory and practice. Three and perhaps four of the papers in the first category deal with facets of corporatism—the negotiation of national economic policy between the state and the apex organizations of unions and employers.

Professors W. Albeda and Rien J. Huiskamp, in part, write on Dutch corporatism. In Chapter 1, Albeda describes the Dutch "consultation" economy in which the state and the "social partners"—unions and management—negotiate national wage policies. He distinguishes between the "great exchange"—"the acceptance by the state of the role of trade unions and employer organizations to participate in the formulation and execution of policy"—and the "small exchange," the annual bargaining process. Huiskamp, in Chapter 2, examines aspects of the "small exchange." He compares Dutch and British corporationwide bargaining structures and notes the withering of industrywide bargaining both in the Netherlands and the United Kingdom and the devolution toward bargaining with large multinational corporations. In Chapter 3 Professor L.C.G. Douwes Dekker constructs and applies a corporatist typology to South African industrial relations, particularly in the post-1979 period "where freedom of association was extended to all workers."

A sort of corporatism is at work in Norway (although professors Paul Johnsen and Patrick Joynt do not use the term) in the sense that there is "close interfacing between the legislative bodies, the unions and employers," confederations during the whole industrial era." In Chapter 4, Johnsen and Joynt "hint at a new cooperative type of management, of organization development [and] of the planning process." Professor Braham Dabscheck deals with corporatism in the course of explicating varieties of theory in Chapter 10.

The other national case in industrial relations theory is French "exceptionalism." In Chapter 5, Professor Jacques Rojot challenges the French exceptionalism thesis that France is somehow a unique case in western industrial relations. Rojot compares France to other industrialisms in respect to (1) union density, (2) "conflictual" relationship, (3) politicization, (4) "business revolutionary" unionism, (5) state intervention and (6) a mode of "economywide" bargaining—a rather milder variant on corporatist industrial relations.

The second category includes papers that deal with important concepts and theories across the industrialisms. In Chapter 6, Professor Jean Boivin delineates industrial relations as a field. Industrial relations consists of "two basic components . . . human resource management and the determination of working conditions."

Professor Noah M. Meltz (Chapter 7) argues that industrial efficiency and equity are not opposites but complements. Labor market forces have to be tempered by the more humane considerations of equity—indeed, equity can enhance efficiency. Industrial relations is, therefore, concerned with balancing efficiency and equity.

In Chapter 8, this author concludes that industrial relations is equity; that is, democratic industrial societies perceive equity as an indispensable counterpoint to the disciplines of industrial efficiency. The chapter traces the rise of equity and suggests that the equity principle may, in this period, possibly be in a state of attrition.

From diverse perspectives, Anthony Giles and Braham Dabscheck investigate the political science, so to speak, of industrial relations. Giles, in Chapter 9, finds that "industrial relations researchers have not sought to develop an explicitly theoretical understanding of the state." He identifies and critically appraises four principal "theories . . . pertaining to state involvement: (1) the public interest state, (2) the pluralist state, (3) the state as a series of social elites and (4) the Marxist class state." In Chapter 10, Braham Dabscheck reviews five approaches to industrial relations theories: the systems model, pluralism, Marxism, corporatism and the regulatory model. He rejects the idea of the state as the embodiment of the public interest "because of the problem associated with defining what, in fact, the public interest is." Finally, Dabscheck raises the question as to what management's new militancy means for industrial relations theory.

Hoyt Wheeler (Chapter 11) looks into the socio-biological foundations of industrial relations. He probes the fundamentals of human nature to get at "human behavior in the employment relationship." An innate "predisposition . . . to social dominance" underlies "the exchange of an employee's promise to obey for an employer's promise to pay."

The final category of papers examines the connections between the theory and practice of industrial relations. In Chapter 12, Oliver Clarke suggests areas for useful research on issues confronting "the advanced industrialized market economies today." The areas include trade unions and employers associations, the role of the state, conflict between industry and public policy decisions, wages and collective bargaining, changing employment patterns, labor market flexibility, structural and technology change and industrial relations in the enterprise.

Theory in the graduate teaching of industrial relations is the subject of two papers. "The prominent role of human resource management in industrial relations," Brian B. Bemmels and Mahmood Zaidi write in Chapter 13, "is what distinguishes the University of Minnesota model which is based on a systems analysis; specifically: (1) the environment, (2) inputs, (3) transformation mechanisms, (4) outputs and (5) feedback."

In Chapter 14, Professor Nicholas Blain constructs his industrial relations course on "the basis of four underlying principles": (1) rigorous definition of key terms and concepts, (2) historical context, (3) diversity of theoretical perspectives and (4) the use of theory in analyzing practice.

Professor Arie Shirom puts theory to use in Chapter 15 to develop "a diagnostic model for the initial diagnostic work on union-management relations in unionized work settings." Imbalances in union-management power relationships and their effects are diagnosed in that chapter. In Chapter 16, Professor George Strauss looks into the state of industrial relations as a field in the United States and comes away with mostly pessimistic conclusions. He seems to be saying that industrial relations as a field may be losing its market, perhaps due to institutional changes in the practice of industrial relations. Industrial relations as an academic field, Strauss argues further, is being displaced by new disciplines that are preempting large pieces of industrial relations' traditional content and students. He suggests how industrial relations can regain some of its market.

I hope I have done justice to the spirit and content of the various papers. My colleagues, however, should not be committed to the uses to which I have put their work here. They have had no chance to see it before publication. I hope they will read it afterward and approve.

I

Comparative Industrial Relations Theories in a National Context

1

Labor Relations and Neo-Corporatist Decisionmaking

W. Albeda

The view that the central theme of labor relations is the exchange embodied in the labor contract is a commonplace. The labor market is the place where labor is bought and sold. Of course, workers, as Alfred Marshall remarked in *Principles of Economics,* have an intuitive objection to the idea of labor as a form of merchandise.[1] Indeed, one important (if not the important) role of the trade unions has always been to limit the dependence of the workers on the permanent changes in the relative scarcity of labor in local or functional labor markets. The collective agreement finds its function exactly here.

In the "system" proposed by Dunlop all systems of labor relations are systems in which trade unions (and workers) and employers and employers' organizations participate.[2] The relationships among the three are more complicated than those between the traditional partners in the labor market—the employer and the union. In that case the exchange is clearly present, although nobody could overlook the power relationship that influences the two bargaining positions. The position of the government is less clear. In this paper it is my intention to show that in the case of the government the element of an exchange relationship is also present. This might be a way to explain the changing influence of the trade unions on governments and parliaments in different countries.

During the last twenty or twenty-five years in different nations attempts have been made to coordinate decisionmaking of the different power centers within a society, and to involve private organizations (i.e., employers' organizations and trade unions) in the decisionmaking of the government.

Two reasonings are employed to explain this development. 1. In socioeconomic policy, it is realized, power meets power. If the government wants

9

to develop a policy to influence important data, such as wage levels, income distribution, working time, and mobility of labor, it will find that employers and trade unions not only have strong convictions and a policy of their own, but also that they have the power to frustrate the policies of government. To eliminate the danger of conflicts it is better that the government negotiates with the social organizations. If the three powers agree, the overall control of the situation will be more complete. 2. A second reasoning says that it is becoming more and more clear that political democracy as such is not sufficient. Insofar as the government carries out a policy that has important consequences for groups of citizens, the principles of democracy imply that the way is paved for such a policy by intensive consultation of groups who are influenced by it. Consultation between the three partners concerned may thus be looked upon as the development of the socio-economic dimension of democracy.

In the first reasoning the government is more or less forced to a division of power with the strong pressure groups of employers and trade unions. It is a form of coercion, given the power of trade unions to organize social unrest and of employers to follow a course that runs against the government. In the second case the right of people to influence policy that affects their position is recognized. In the first view the government has to do it, whether it wants to or not. In the second view it is one of the ways in which a government shows its democratic conviction.

From the point of view of the social organization this development may be seen as the final result of the attempts of private pressure groups to influence the decisionmaking process at the highest level of government. The result of this development is the "consultation economy," an economic system in which three processes of economic coordination and decisionmaking—market governmental decision and consultation—function side by side and together.

THE CONSULTATION ECONOMY AS A NEO-CORPORATIST PHENOMENON

The consultation economy has been considered both as an angel of goodwill and as the villain in the beautiful play of a well-running market economy. The first option is that of the group of authors who see in "neo-corporatism" the most effective way to organize a modern market economy. In the second option, represented most clearly by Mancur Olson, the functioning of the market is frustrated by the interplay of employers' organizations and trade unions.

Olson says in a rather sweeping statement: "On balance, special-interest organisations and collusions reduce efficiency and aggregate income in the societies in which they operate and make political life more divisive."[3] In Olson's eyes such organizations tend to occupy themselves mainly with problems of distribution of income rather than with problems of production. Distributional issues as such are divisive, in the sense that they lead to often permanent divisions in society and, as a consequence, also in politics. In a society dominated by such groups more and more attention is turned away from the free market out of fear of its distributive effects.

As a consequence the potentialities of a free market for production are foregone. And, as anybody "who has given the matter a decade or more of specialised study" knows, "an economy with free markets and no government or cartel intervention is like a teen-aged youth: It makes a lot of mistakes but nonetheless grows rapidly without special effect of encouragement."[4]

Neo-corporatist authors such as Schmitter and Lehmbruch[5] are not as opposed to Olson's reasoning as it seems. Neo-corporatism has come to stand for a voluntary arrangement between the government, the employers and their organizations and the trade unions. A precondition for a neo-corporatist system is a government that is willing to compromise with the trade union movement. The position of the employers is different in the sense that the aims of the employers in such an arrangement are not as controversial as those of the trade union movement (control over wages in order to overcome inflation). Employers, therefore, will tend to participate in this kind of arrangement without difficult bargaining. It is the trade union movement that may have ideological objections (collaboration with government in a capitalist society, or collaboration with the "wrong" kind of government) or more practical problems (will members understand the arrangement, does the trade union keep its members although it accepts a policy of wage moderation).

Only a trade union movement that has no dangerous rivals and a strong centralized structure can afford to enter into such an arrangement. The centralization is necessary because only a central position permits a sufficiently broad view of the relative importance of wages in the national economy. A strong centralized structure is also necessary if the trade union wants to be a dependable partner. Member unions should not be able to operate outside the agreement reached at the central level. Union members should be committed enough to resist temptations to undermine the agreed-upon policy by exploiting local or functional labor market situations.

In Austria and Sweden such an arrangement is still effective. In the Netherlands before 1963 the centralized wage policy was based upon such an arrangement. After 1963 the conditions for the arrangement were no longer fulfilled.

WHY DO TRADE UNIONS PARTICIPATE IN NEO-CORPORATIST ARRANGEMENTS?

In principle one could imagine three reasons for the trade union to participate.

1. The trade union movement wants the same policy and has the same objectives as the government.
2. The government offers the trade union movement enough to convince it (or rather, makes it worth its while) to join the government in the elaboration and execution of its policy.
3. The government forces the trade unions to join it in carrying out its policy. In a democratic society this arrangement seems excluded.

For the government, a not-so-different kind of reasoning might be developed.

4. The government feels forced to consult the trade unions for fear of social unrest or ungovernability. The trade unions have so much power that it is impossible not to involve them in the governmental policy making and execution.
5. The government looks upon trade union involvement in policy making and policy execution as a normal democratic procedure.
6. The government has the same political outlook and priorities as the trade union movement.

Looking at these possibilities it seems clear that only the situation as described by (1) or (5) and (6) will be sufficiently stable to survive the adventures of social and economic policy making. Of course, (4) and (5) could lead to (6); (2) and (4) might lead to the ideal (1)–(6) situation.

THE CASE OF THE NETHERLANDS

In the Netherlands between 1945 and 1962 the (1)–(6) situation was, to a large extent, present. The misery and deprivation of the five years of occupation by Nazi Germany had brought the three partners together. Moreover, there was no difference of opinion regarding the necessities of developing a new economic base for expanding employment and creating a more acceptable standard of living. In the meantime, trade unions and employers agreed that a policy of rather low wages was necessary to create new manufacturing industry in a nation that had not had much experience in that field before the war.

The centralized wage policy became an interesting example of a policy carried out by the three parties. It might be useful to underline the fact that the wage policy was characterized by a strong, and at least legally, dominating influence of the government. The important decisions with regard to wage developments were taken by the government. The government, of course, was advised by employers' and trade union organizations, and would follow unanimous proposals of the two. In the not infrequent case of a failure to agree, however, it was the government that decided.

The trade unions accepted the arrangement because it brought about more employment for the longer term and wage equality between regions and industries. Moreover, the machinery set up to monitor the wage policy—Central Planning Bureau, Social Economic Council and permanent informal contacts between trade unions and government—gave the unions influence on socio-economic policy in a broader sense. The shift of power to the government was the result of a tradeoff between day-to-day involvement in wage bargaining (that the unions gave up) and becoming an important pillar in the process of policy making in the growing welfare state. The moment the unions realized that their lack of involvement in the yearly wage bargaining within industries and companies led to growing problems with the trade union movement they left the arrangement.

It is interesting to note, however, that the unions kept their important place in the decisionmaking machinery of state and society. The involvement of the trade union movement in the decisionmaking seemed to be irreversible. The reason is simple. Although there was no longer the complete consensus that formed the basis for wage policy, the participation of trade unions in the decisionmaking process remained profitable for both the unions and the government.

In the following years, between 1963 and 1970, wage setting remained free. The government tried to retain influence over the wage level. It hoped to convince the trade unions of the necessity of keeping wages in line with productivity growth. It also wanted to make room for the introduction of new social security legislation. (Every guilder used for financing social security cannot, at the same time, be used for increasing the purchasing power for workers.)

The trade unions refused to repeat their performance of 1945–1962. As a result, wages went up strongly between 1962 and 1973. At the same time new legislation and social security was introduced. Increasingly, social security benefits were linked to the development of the wage level. During the same time that the wage level was left more and more to free bargaining, it became the basis of an increasingly expensive system of social security. In 1970 trade unions had to witness their members in tight labor markets take over the initiative and increase their own wages. At this point the labor market went out of the hands of policy makers.

Under these circumstances the government called upon the social partners to come together to bargain on the central level. Although the three "partners" agreed on the necessity to limit the increase of wages, they failed to reach agreement. This led to collisions between government and trade unions. Wage freezes by the government did not really help.

An interesting interlude was the conclusion of the first and only central agreement in the autumn of 1972. The years 1971 and 1972 were marked by strikes in the building industry and the metal industry. The relationship between the trade unions and the government was less than optimal. The trade unions did not like the composition of the cabinet, which had no Social-Democrats, and they hated the wage law of 1968 with its possibility of interfering with bargaining in individual collective agreements. But the three partners were so impressed by rising inflation and unemployment that central bargaining could take place. The government had to set the stage by withdrawing its right to interfere with individual collective agreements (Article 8 of the wage law).

The central agreement, signed by employers, trade unions and the government, was an important milestone in Dutch labor relations. Neither central bargaining nor influence of trade unions and employers on government policy was new. However, the presentations of the outcome of the central bargaining process as a contract, including obligations accepted by the three partners concerned, was new. On the one hand, the deal included wages; on the other hand, government promised legislation with regard to fiscal policy, social security and government spending. The contract led to great difficulties within the social-democratic N.V.V. (Netherlands Federation of Trade Unions), which led finally to the stepping down of its chairman Harry ter Heide. A recent comment sums up the problems quite clearly: "A social-democratic trade union makes a deal with a bourgeois government. . . . [But if an] economic analysis by the trade unions shows that wage increases should be curtailed, [the] government should understand that trade unions want to have something in exchange for their cooperation."[6]

In this view there are two possible roads to the neo-corporatist strategy. One is a trade union decision to cooperate with a friendly (social-democratic) government. The other is for the union movement to enter into a (hard) round of bargaining with a "bourgeois" government.

The conclusion of this social contract (which did not prevent an unusual number of strikes in 1973) led to an interesting discussion in the Netherlands. Some authors feared the development of a trade union state—a state that would be dominated by the political power of the trade union movement. Others expressed the fear that trade unions were "domesticated" or "encapsuled" by the bourgeois society. In the Netherlands the idea of "policy exchange" has always dominated trade union thinking. Center-left cabinets (especially the Den Yul cabinet, 1973–1977) accepted the reasoning behind the policy exchange. In theory, the center-right cabinets (the preponderant case since 1967) tended to stress the common interest of the proposed policy, but were willing to enter into bargaining when possible, as in the 1973 case.

THE GREAT AND THE SMALL EXCHANGE

During the post-World War II period in the Netherlands, participation of interest groups in policy making and in the execution of policy was accepted as a normal element in the process of governing the country. It is useful, at this point, to accept the terminology of the great and the small exchange, introduced by Dutch sociologists.[7]

Great exchange is the acceptance by the state of the role of trade unions and employers' organizations to participate in the formulation and execution of policy. In the Netherlands this great exchange was performed after the war but prepared before the war. More and more the trade unions and the employers' organization were represented in state committees. Many politicians view the involvement of employers' organizations as more natural and logical than the participation of trade unions. Mixed bodies were set up where representatives of unions and employers could study possible compromises and advise the government. After the war the Social Economic Council (consisting of 15 employers, 15 unions, and 15 independent members) was organized as an official and obligatory advisory body for the government. In this connection trade unions were officially recognized as representatives of important groups within the population. And the trade unions expressed their readiness and willingness to participate in the preparation and execution of government policies. Such an attitude presupposes a certain amount of consensus. Great exchange is an expression of such a consensus.

On the basis of the great exchange, new bargaining among the three partners takes place from year to year through the small exchange. The existence of the great exchange, one might say, is reenforced and reenacted every time a new small exchange takes place.

The formal existence and continuation of the great exchange cannot be doubted since the trade unions participate actively in bodies such as the Social

Economic Council. They have maintained this position since 1945. The evidence of the yearly small exchanges is not so clear.

Between 1945 and 1963 the close collaboration between trade unions and the other two partners in the great exchange was confirmed every year in the practice of the centralized wage policy. It has often been said that the Dutch wage policy was not a good example of a great exchange in the sense that the presence of the government was too strong in this arrangement. Only the government had decisive powers with regard to wages. Trade unions and employers had only advisory roles. But the arrangement was functioning on the basis of the consent of the trade unions and the employers.

Although the great exchange survived after the wage explosion of 1962–1963, yearly rounds of central bargaining did not yield much success. A failure to reach a new "social contract" did not mean that the parties came home from the bargaining table with nothing at all. "Quasi-contracts" often played a role in decentralized wage formation, as in the legislative process.

Still, it can be said that until 1980 it was difficult for the government to develop and carry out new policies without at least a serious attempt to convince the trade unions and the employers. But during the same period the government tended to give up its attempts to convince the trade unions and decided to use its powers under the wage law to limit the wage increase. Even the center-left Den Uyl cabinet used the wage law more than once. The time of consensus was over.

In 1979 an attempt to reach a tripartite agreement for 1980 failed (the "almost" agreement). The parties were close to an agreement on a package deal including wage limitation, labor market policy and shortening of working hours. But lack of unity within the F.N.V. (the social-democrat and Catholic Dutch Federation of Labor) led to failure. The government, impressed by the negative effects of the second oil crisis, decided to use the wage law again. The most important element that led to repeated wage law use was the automatic price index. It should not be forgotten that the social security system was linked to the wages in the private sector. Moreover, there existed a system of linkages between wages in the private sector and the salaries of all civil servants, and of all workers in the semiofficial sectors. Private sector bargaining determined two-thirds of the government budget.

The aftermath of the wage freeze of 1979 (followed by a freeze in 1980) showed a basic change in the relationship between trade unions, employers and government.

CHANGES IN THE TRIPARTITE SYSTEM

It seems useful to describe this new situation for the three parties concerned—the government and the two social partners, employers and trade unions.

The Government

1. Mass unemployment since 1980 has taken the pressure off of the labor market. As a consequence it is no longer necessary to convince the trade unions to moderate their wage claims. The moderation of wage claims is enforced by the labor market. The temptation to use the power given to the government under the wage law is no longer present.

2. The financial crisis that formed one of the most visible symptoms of the crisis of the welfare state led the government to launch a policy of reduction of public spending and a correction of the social transfers that are characteristic of the welfare state. As a result, the dialogue between the state and the trade unions broke down; at least what remained of it was no longer effective. Although the trade unions continued their presence on many advisory bodies (like the Social Economic Council and the Social Insurance Council), the growing polarization of opinions among the trade unions, the employers and the government has undermined the influence of such bodies.

The management of the welfare state and its system of social security and social assistance was carried out during the sixties and the beginning of the seventies in a continuous dialogue among government, employers and unions. The correction in the system of social security and the welfare state made this dialogue no longer fruitful or effective. The formerly strong link between the political and social system became weaker and in some years was close to disappearing. But, it must be stated, the trade unions never gave up hope of convincing the government, although they now try to convince the electorate of the necessity of choosing a different majority in parliament.

3. The attempts of the government to loosen the link between wages in the private sector and the public sector led to a permanent stalemate in the process of negotiations. The civil servants' unions are very influential members of the trade union centers (in the Christian federation they have a majority, in the F.N.V. they are close to that position).

The Changing Role of the Employers

1. In a depressed labor market the power relationship between employers and trade unions is reversed compared to that of the tight labor markets of the sixties and seventies. Employers have a much stronger position in the labor market.

2. Parliament and government were impressed by the sorry state of business in the Netherlands at the end of the seventies and therefore tended to listen carefully to the complaints of the employers who, for the first time, seemed to have high credibility. The conclusion that the welfare state is in for an important change got the ear of the majority of politicians.

The Changing Role of the Trade Unions

1. The position of the trade unions is perhaps the most difficult. Their influence in the labor market has decreased. In bargaining with employers they carry not only the burden of public opinion impressed by the necessity of austerity, but they are hindered by the existence of mass unemployment. The time of convincing victories in the labor market is over. Wage bargaining had small possibilities, especially before 1984. Job bargaining (the demand for a shortening of working hours) had only limited results. Concession bargaining could not be prevented.

2. As a consequence the trade union movement as a whole lost almost 20 percent of its members between 1976 and 1986. The loss of members, of course, contributed to the loss of power.

3. As already stated, trade unions underwent an immense loss of power on the political scene. Not only the fact that their connection with the political establishment (the labor party, PvdA) dropped out of the governing coalitions after 1977, but also the change in the power relations in the labor market and the course taken by the center-right coalitions led to an estrangement of the trade unions from the political center of power.

4. It is possible that economic recovery and a possible ballot victory of the Social Democrats will lead to a reestablishment of the political power of the Dutch trade union movement. Certain factors might have a more permanent influence on the position of the movement.

a. Employment has been reduced, especially in the centers of trade union power (manufacturing industries, skilled labor).
b. We see growing employment in sectors that do not organize workers easily (service sector, high-tech, etc.).

c. We see new types of workers: The increasing participation of women takes place in the form of part-time or temporary work. Such workers do not organize themselves easily.
d. The professional and clerical workers, who are on the increase too, have no tradition of union membership.

Weakened Neo-Corporatist Structure

The Netherlands used to have a rather strong neo-corporatist structure. This implied that with regard to social economic policy the government carried on two different dialogues at the same time: (1) the dialogue with parliament and (2) the dialogue with the social partners. In the 1950s these two dialogues led to consensus. Often the parliamentary dialogue was adapted to the social dialogue. The consensus disappeared in the 1960s and even more so in the 1970s. More and more the parliamentary dialogue tended to overshadow, and even from time to time overrule, the social dialogue. Should we deplore this development, or rather accept it as a positive development?

It is difficult to deny that the corrections of the welfare state and the reduction of the budget deficit would have been impossible within the neo-corporatist arrangement. It was the severing of the political dialogue and the social dialogue that made this policy possible. And, says the parliamentary majority (and I tend to agree): Look, this policy works! The Netherlands, which had a very deep depression with more unemployment than any other European nation, is having a rather strong recovery.

The Future of Our Neo-Corporatist Arrangement

The question might be asked, in the first place, is a neo-corporatist arrangement, based upon social consensus between government and the two social partners, at all desirable? Countries such as Sweden and Austria are known for their relative success in the field of corporatist policy making. In Sweden the LO (Swedish Confederation of Trade Unions) and the social-democratic governments have for a long time been able to reach agreement on the most important issues. It is difficult to deny that such an arrangement can work and has worked for a long time in these nations. In Sweden it was based upon the always-present consensus of LO and the social-democratic cabinet. Even the short intervals of a bourgeois cabinet did not put an end to this consensus. In Austria it is based upon a compromise between the Social Democratic Party and the People's Party that functions in all realms of life where the influence is partitioned between the two. The trade unions and the employers participate in this compromise.

In most other nations such a consensus does not exist. Of course, a complete consensus or at least a majority opinion that always asserts itself and is represented by one or two political parties and the trade union movement is rather rare in a modern democratic nation. Given the fact that unions, in most cases, no longer (if ever) represent a majority of workers, it seems improbable that other nations will be able to follow this path. Especially in the case of the Netherlands, where the social democracy never managed to reach more than one third of Parliament, a consensus based on agreement between government and the trade union movement seems to be the exception rather than the rule.

This should not imply that central negotiations are not necessary or useful. The present government clearly shows the possibilities. Given the depressed state of the labor market, wage increases do not seem to be our first danger and worry. At the present time, unemployment is clearly the social evil that concerns trade unions, employers and government alike. As a consequence, although complete consensus is out of reach, partial agreement is possible. Examples of consensus include:

1. the agreement of November 1982 on economic recovery and shorter working hours, in which employers and unions expressed their common intention to give priority to the creation of employment over a possible increase of wages. This agreement involved initially only the partners in the Foundation of Labor (employers and unions), but the government later voiced its (self-evident) agreement with these intentions;
2. the agreement of 1985 to launch a program of training and retraining for unemployed workers to help them to reenter the labor market;
3. the agreement of 1986 to intensify the development of training within enterprise and in general; and
4. the central negotiations that were developed in 1987 and which may lead to a global agreement on the development of wages in the private sector, the public sector and the social security benefits.

NOTES

1. Alfred Marshall, *Principles of Economics* (8th ed., New York: Macmillan, 1948).
2. John T. Dunlop, *Industrial Relations Systems* (New York: Henry Holt, 1958).

3. Mancur Olson, *The Rise and Decline of Nations* (New Haven and London: Yale Univ. Press, 1982), p. 47.

4. Ibid., p. 177.

5. Philippe C. Schmitter and Gerhard Lehmbruch, eds., *Trends Towards Corporatist Intermediation* (London: Sage, 1979); see also Lehmbruch and Schmitter, eds., *Patterns of Corporatist Decisionmaking* (London: Sage, 1980); and T. Akkermans and P.W.M. Nobelen, *Corporatisme en Verzorgings-staat* (Leiden/Anterwerpen: Stenfert Kroese, 1983).

6. Klaus Armington, "Neo-korporatieve inkomenspolitiek" in Hans Kenan et al, *Het neokorporatisme als nieuwe politieke strategie* (Amsterdam: CT Press, 1985), p. 39.

7. Ger Arendsen and Arend Geul, "Corporatisme" in Akkerman and Nobelen, op. cit.

2

LARGE CORPORATIONS, INDUSTRY BARGAINING STRUCTURES AND NATIONAL INDUSTRIAL RELATIONS: A COMPARATIVE AND ORGANIZATIONAL APPROACH

RIEN J. HUISKAMP

This study draws together an industrial relations approach and an organizational approach. As such it is written from a distinct theoretical point of view, the interorganizational relations perspective. It is believed that such an approach is more fruitfully applied than a comparison of industrial relations systems, either representing countries or industries. This perspective is applied in a relatively new comparative framework. The subject matter of the study, developments in bargaining structures are compared in two different industries within one country (the Netherlands), while one of the two industries (engineering) is compared with the same industry in another country (United Kingdom). In this way, although keeping one of the two constant, industries and countries can vary. Keeping the industry constant one varies the countries and keeping the country constant one varies the industries.

In recent literature attention has been focused on the relationships between the bargaining structure of a country and strategies of the main actors in industrial relations. For instance, comparing the United States and Europe, Kassalow has stated that company bargaining leaves trade unions more susceptible to employers' counter strategies than industrywide bargaining. Industrywide bargaining, in his view, enables unions to maintain wages in periods of low economic growth, whereas company bargaining offers trade unions better chances for wage improvement in periods of high economic growth.[1] Streeck has argued that industrywide bargaining in West Germany is an expression of a coordinated and solidaristic union strategy, whereas company bargaining in England is the result of a fragmented and sectional union strategy.[2] The latter strategy would partly explain the predicament of the British economy and the "institutional arthritis" predicted by Olson in those countries, which, over a long, uninterrupted period, have accumulated scores of pressure groups, for example, trade unions.[3]

Empirical studies on the development of bargaining structures after the Second World War have observed a shift from industrywide to company bargaining.[4] Some authors have prophesied the "withering away" of industrywide bargaining.[5] Concentration in industry figures prominently among the variables explaining this recent shift. Large companies leave the umbrella of an industrywide bargaining unit in order to establish their own wage policy. If many other corporations follow suit the employers' association will disintegrate and trade unions will have to resort to company agreements. Also, trade unions may play an active role in the disintegration of an industrywide bargaining unit if they decide to concentrate their resources on large corporations with better abilities to pay. Therefore, the choice between industry and company bargaining is strongly related to the mutual strategies of unions and employers.

In this paper we study the impact of the development of large corporations on industrywide bargaining structures and national industrial relations and relate this impact to strategies of trade unions and employers. In the analysis a comparative approach is used. First, the impact of large corporations on bargaining structures in different industries and on national industrial relations within the same country is examined. A comparison will be made between the Dutch metalworking industry and the Dutch non-metalworking industries. Second, we look at the impact of large corporations on bargaining structures in the same industry within different countries. In this respect a comparison is made between the Dutch and the British metalworking industries.

In the Netherlands the state, unions and employers strongly supported the development of industrywide bargaining in postwar reconstruction as an essential tool of wage policy. It is an ideal case to study for the impact of large corporations on industrywide bargaining. Data is presented on the development of the number and coverage of bargaining units in Dutch metalworking and four other manufacturing industries in 1970, 1977 and 1984. All agreements and the number of workers covered in the Netherlands are registered by the Ministry of Social Affairs and Employment. The start of the period studied (1970) was dictated by the availability of the data for the first time in that year. The study concentrates on the bargaining structure of the manufacturing industry. Five industries were selected for further analysis. The chemical industry was chosen as an example of an industry dominated by single-employer agreements. Three other industries (paper; food, drink and tobacco; timber and furniture) were chosen because of their varied mixed bargaining structures of single- and multiemployer agreements. We chose the engineering industry because of its share in manufacturing employment and as a good example of an industry dominated by multiemployer agreements. The selection is representative of bargaining structures at industry level.

According to Derber, unions and employers in the British metalworking industry pioneered industrywide bargaining[6] and are presently moving toward company bargaining. Based on an earlier study of industrial relations in this industry[7] we will pay special attention to a comparison between the Dutch and the British metalworking industries. The metalworking industries in Holland and Britain were chosen for the international comparison because of the importance of these industries as pattern setters in national industrial relations and because of the work done earlier on the British metalworking industry.[8]

CONCEPTUAL FRAMEWORK

Developments in bargaining structure are traditionally described in terms of multiemployer agreements and single-employer agreements. Data are collected by the frequency of number and occasionally by coverage of three types of bargaining units: single-plant, multiplant and industrywide. This classification is not precise enough for studying the impact of large corporations on bargaining structure. For instance, a single-plant bargaining unit may reflect an agreement concluded for a small independent company or a subsidiary of a large corporation. Also, how wide is industrywide; does a bargaining unit cover a whole industry or just a branch of an industry?

We propose to introduce a new classification of bargaining units from an organizational perspective. In doing this we heed Weber's warning against the identification of "collective bargaining structure . . . with any simplified notion of the bargaining unit."[9] In order to stress the relationship between bargaining units and strategies of their constituent organizations we look at bargaining units as the expression of interorganizational relations between unions and employers.[10]

Multiemployer agreements concern interorganizational relationships between unions and employers' associations. These do not necessarily coincide with an industry as commonly defined. The metalworking industry is a prime example. It comprises many distinct branches; indeed, many observers speak in terms of "separate and distinct industries."[11] Some conclude that the real identity of the engineering industry can be determined only from the respective members of the employers' federations and trade unions, and from their bargaining relationship.[12] We classify our data on multiemployer agreements according to the various degrees to which the interorganizational relations concerned cover an industry. An industrywide bargaining unit covers a whole industry; a single-branch bargaining unit covers a branch producing a fairly homogeneous product. In between there are multibranch bargaining units that cover several branches of the same industry. In this way the classification of the bargaining units reflects the number of distinct markets covered by the unit. This classification makes it possible to observe changes within multiemployer agreements. Is there a development toward or away from real industrywide bargaining?

We also classify our material on single-employer agreements from an organizational perspective. In this case it concerns interorganizational relations between unions and one firm, corporation or division, Dutch-owned subsidiary, foreign-owned subsidiary and small independent firms.

The classification of single-employer agreements is based on an empirical study of the concentration in Dutch manufacturing during the sixties and seventies.[13] Instead of the traditional study of concentration ratios in industries Koot opted for a distinction between corporations, divisions, semidependent subsidiaries, dependent subsidiaries and small independent firms. The criteria for classifying companies on this scale were ownership, the presence of management functions (such as sales, product development, etc.) and the possibilities of a company to influence market behavior of other companies in one or two industries.

It was not possible to classify our agreements in the five categories of companies as defined by Koot. It was, however, possible to distinguish between agreements of corporations and divisions, agreements of subsidiaries and agreements of small independent firms. Agreements of subsidiaries could be classified as being either of Dutch or foreign ownership. Foreign-owned divisions are classified under corporate/divisional agreements. This concerns large Dutch corporations taken over by foreign companies, but still to be regarded as corporations in the terms as defined by Koot. By and large, most company/divisional agreements are multiplant and most subsidiary or small firm agreements are single-plant.

Loveridge has stated that the study of single-employer agreements in terms of single- or multiplant has obscured changes in ownership of firms, and we add organizational consequences, "in any of the analysis of industrial relations."[14] Our new classification allows us to observe changes within single-employer agreements that reflect just that: Is an increase in the number of single-employer agreements related to small companies or to large corporations establishing their own bargaining unit? Are agreements decreasing in number as a result of bargaining being increasingly carried out at the corporate level?

As we said before, the interorganizational perspective is introduced in order to extend the analysis beyond collective bargaining units as such. Bargaining units only reflect formal bargaining structures. A company or its workers may determine (part of) their own wages without establishing a formal bargaining unit. They may do so in contravention of or in accordance with the rules established by the constituent parties to the agreement. Differences between negotiated wage rates and actual earnings will provide some evidence for the degree to which unions and employers' associations are able or willing to make these rules binding and enforceable among their members' organizations.

We will also look at the organizations themselves, as constituent members of the interorganizational relationships. Employers have a decisive influence on the bargaining structure. They have to decide on both the decisionmaking structures in a corporation and the establishment of employers' associations. To control labor costs the employer may decide to integrate subsidiary bargaining units into a corporate unit. Unions may stimulate such a development because it helps them in their efforts to centralize their organizational structure, or because it may equalize terms and conditions with better paying subsidiaries.

So, union policies and organizational structures are relevant. Is their membership based on particular industries or on sections of workers within different industries? What is the position of lay officials at company levels? The wage policy pursued is of utmost importance: Is the wage policy solidaristic, embracing all workers in an industry, or sectional and directed to certain groups of workers or sections of an industry? There could also be a tendency for agreements within one industry to be interlinked because one union or set of unions coordinate their wage policies in different bargaining units; or perhaps the agreements are interlinked in terms of pattern-setters and pattern-followers. These linkages, mainly depending on trade union organization, may involve bargaining units of several industries. Such a coherent set of bargaining units is called a bargaining domain.

The conceptual framework developed in this paragraph can be visualized in a simple model (Figure 2.1). Variables such as the particular industry characteristics, concentration of ownership and bargaining domains are situated in an "outer layer" and influence the interorganizational relations, shaping a historical context for union and employer strategies. Those strategies, in turn, influence each other as well as variables such as concentration of ownership and the boundaries of bargaining domains. In the core of the model

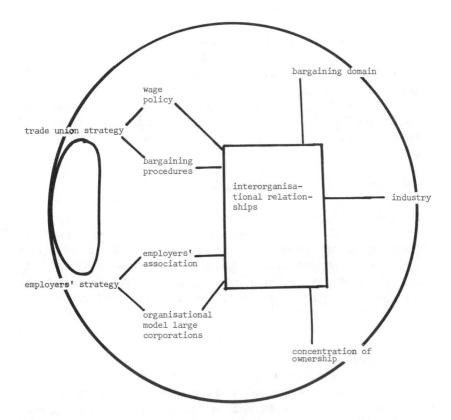

Figure 2.1. Industry characteristics, interorganizational relationships, union and employer strategies.

we can also find that those constituent organizations shape the interorganizational relationship through wage policy and the corporate decisionmaking process. Within the Dutch case we concentrate mainly on analyzing the outer layer, whereas the core is examined in detail in the Dutch-British comparison.

COMPARISON BETWEEN DUTCH METALWORKING AND NON-METALWORKING INDUSTRIES

Windmuller has identified three hallmarks in postwar Dutch industrial relations: consultation, centralized industrial relations and the crucial government role.[15] Consultation in Dutch industrial relations has a wider meaning than collective bargaining. At the national level it often results in national agreements or guiding principles for collective bargaining at industry or company level. The government plays an important role in these consultations. During the postwar reconstruction period the government stimulated the making of multiemployer agreements. These agreements could be made legally binding for all employees working in the industry covered by the agreement. Postwar multiemployer agreements increased in number and coverage up to the early 1960s. Thereafter there was a merger wave in industry, which peaked at the end of the decade.

Number and Coverage of Bargaining Units

Developments in the metalworking industry will be compared with developments in the four selected industries in terms of number and coverage of bargaining units. The results are presented in Table 2.1. Between 1970 and 1984 the number and coverage of bargaining units formed by small firms decreased in nearly all selected industries. Already in 1977, their role in the bargaining structure is of marginal importance. Notable is the increase of bargaining units established by corporations and divisions, perhaps not so much in numbers as in coverage. In the metalworking industry there has not been much change since 1970, but in all other industries (except timber and furniture) the importance of the corporate/divisional bargaining unit has increased. The number of Dutch-owned subsidiary bargaining units in the metalworking industry is negligible. In all the other industries (except paper) there has been a considerable decrease. Bargaining units established by foreign-owned subsidiaries are clearly on the increase. But again, this is not reflected in the metalworking industry.

Looking at the development of multiemployer agreements it is evident that again there are large differences between metalworking and the other industries. Metalworking is the only industry with an industrywide bargaining unit. In one industry (paper) only single-branch bargaining units are in existence. In the three other industries, during the period 1970 to 1977, the decrease in number and coverage of multibranch bargaining units seems to be less than among the single-branch. However, between 1977 and 1984 the coverage of multibranch bargaining units also diminished strongly.

As to former Dutch-owned subsidiary bargaining units, we find that they have been integrated into corporate/divisional bargaining units. The same process occurred in the case of small firms overtaken by other companies. The growth of coverage in corporate/divisional bargaining units does not originate

Table 2.1. Number and Coverage of Bargaining Units in Dutch Non-Metal and Metalworking Industries 1970–1984

Unit	1970 Number	1970 Coverage	1977 Number	1977 Coverage	1984 Number	1984 Coverage
		Chemical				
Corporate/divisional	11	23.949	17	46.502	22	54.060
Dutch-owned subsidiary	32	5.480	17	3.398	14	2.392
Foreign-owned subsidiary	27	6.156	39	7.940	49	9.131
Small firm	32	2.843	18	2.095	11	1.799
Industry-wide	—	—	—	—	—	—
Multi-branch wide	—	—	1	2.600	1	2.600
Single-branch wide	3	3.125	1	200	1	200
		Timber and Furniture				
Corporate/divisional	3	3.440	2	2.763	1	1.800
Dutch-owned subsidiary	8	805	3	140	4	345
Foreign-owned subsidiary	1	600	1	300	4	957
Small firm	23	1.424	21	1.304	10	505
Industry-wide	—	—	—	—	—	—
Multi-branch wide	3	35.000	4	38.000	4	28.500
Single-branch wide	8	11.300	4	10.025	3	10.950
		Food, Drink and Tobacco				
Corporate/divisional	9	9.385	13	28.117	15	29.091
Dutch-owned subsidiary	15	3.485	6	1.707	8	1.190
Foreign-owned subsidiary	8	1.871	12	3.383	14	2.757
Small firm	25	2.820	22	2.254	14	2.549
Industry-wide	—	—	—	—	—	—
Multi-branch wide	5	70.000	5	61.500	5	55.000
Single-branch wide	17	75.445	13	52.716	12	52.770
		Paper				
Corporate/divisional	1	1.700	3	8.118	7	6.803
Dutch-owned subsidiary	4	1.340	6	1.520	5	1.138
Foreign-owned subsidiary	1	135	2	352	4	996
Small firm	6	1.345	4	753	4	973
Industry-wide	—	—	—	—	—	—
Multi-branch wide	—	—	—	—	—	—
Single-branch wide	6	12.150	6	13.150	6	8.500
		Metal Working				
Corporate/divisional	2	67.340	4	69.371	4	74.080
Dutch-owned subsidiary	3	964	1	500	2	1.017
Foreign-owned subsidiary	—	—	—	—	—	—
Small firm	4	606	1	216	1	200
Industry-wide	2	410.000	2	400.000	2	469.300
Multi-branch wide	1	50.000	—	—	—	—
Single-branch wide	4	8.800	3	9.400	2	68.000

Source: Huiskamp, 1983.[16]

exclusively from this process of integration. Some corporate/divisional bargaining units have increased the number of workers covered because of the integration of two of those units in the wake of a merger. In some instances a corporation has decided to conclude its own agreement during the period studied.

Of the former single-branch bargaining units some were dissolved, but most of them were integrated or merged into multibranch or industrywide bargaining units. This trend becomes even more visible if we take a look at the years before 1970, which we do only for the multiemployer agreements. The results are presented in Table 2.2. The bargaining structure of the paper industry is a notable exception, because none of the single-branch bargaining units have merged in either a multibranch or industrywide bargaining unit. In the metalworking industry not only single- but also multibranch bargaining units were integrated into the industrywide bargaining units.

In both the metalworking industry and the non-metalworking industries there is one clear trend: Smaller bargaining units have either been fused or integrated into new or existing bargaining units. Some have even disappeared. This trend also occurs among single- and multiemployer agreements, even where only a few agreements are present; among the multiemployer agreements in the chemical industry and the single-employer agreements in engineering. In this respect, however, there are two differences. In metalworking the integration of bargaining units had already come to an end before the period we study.

The second difference concerns the size of the bargaining units. The bargaining units in the engineering industry are considerably larger than those in the non-metalworking industry, even after the process of integration in the latter. There are basically three large bargaining units in this industry. These are the huge corporate bargaining unit of Philips (coverage 77,000) and two industrywide units, one for artisan establishments and one for industrial establishments. With the exception of Philips, no other large corporations have established their bargaining unit in this industry.

Changes in the Rules of Agreements

Most multiemployer agreements in the non-metalworking industry are standard agreements. In the case of a standard agreement, the relative change in the negotiated wage rates strictly applies to all wages under the agreement. Companies are not allowed to pay less or more than increases settled on.

In the metalworking industry the agreement for industrial establishments is formulated in terms of a minimum agreement. This means that under the

**Table 2.2. Development of Multi-Employer Agreements
in Selected Industries, 1950–1984**

Scope	Year				
	1950	1960	1970	1977	1984
	Chemical				
Industry-wide	—	—	—	—	—
Multi-branch wide	—	—	—	1	1
Single-branch wide	4	4	3	1	1
	Timber and Furniture				
Industry-wide	—	—	—	—	—
Multi-branch wide	2	3	3	4	4
Single-branch wide	12	10	8	4	3
	Food, Drink, Tobacco				
Industry-wide	—	—	—	—	—
Multi-branch wide	3	4	5	5	5
Single-branch wide	23	17	17	13	12
	Paper				
Industry-wide	—	—	—	—	—
Multi-branch wide	—	—	—	—	—
Single-branch wide	6	8	6	6	6
	Metal Working				
Industry-wide	1	1	2	2	2
Multi-branch wide	2	2	1	—	—
Single-branch wide	10	3	4	3	2

Source: Huiskamp, 1983.[16]

agreement, companies are allowed to pay more, but not less than the agreed change in the wage rate.

In Table 2.3 increases in negotiated wage rates and earnings over the period 1972 to 1983 are presented for the metalworking industry and three of the selected non-metalworking industries. The difference between earnings and wage rates is traditionally explained in terms of wage drift. In this instance wage drift is not only corrected for overtime but also for changes in the composition of the labor force (age, skill and sex) and of the industry. Wage drift minus this "structural" drift provides us with an indicator of "pure" drift.

If we compare the industries we notice the following: Pure drift in the metalworking industry is the same as in the chemical industry, but there is a sharp contrast with the food, drink and tobacco industry and the timber and furniture industry. Pure drift is negligible and even negative in the latter two industries. In other words, there are no additional increases to negotiated

Table 2.3. Average Yearly Changes in Wages and Wage Drift, 1972–1983

Industry	Wages		Wage Drift	
	Negotiated Wage Rates	Earnings	Structural Drift	Wage Drift
Food, drink, tobacco	8.1	8.6	0.6	− 0.2
Timber, furniture	7.1	7.5	0.3	0.1
Chemicals	6.7	8.5	0.8	0.8
Metal working	6.7	8.0	0.5	0.8
Total manufacturing	7.0	8.3	0.7	0.5

Source: Centraal Bureau voor de Statistick (CBS), Der Haag, 1985.

wage rates at company level other than just structural drift. At the same time, in these industries, the increase in the negotiated wage rates are much higher than in chemicals and metalworking. There seems to be a clear correlation between the level of negotiated wage rates and pure drift. The more wage rates increase, the smaller pure drift appears to be. How is this to be explained?

In standard agreements unions negotiate relatively high wage rates, as at the company level no increases are allowed. In a minimum agreement unions can afford to bargain for a relatively low increase, because under the rules of the agreement a fresh round of negotiations is allowed to take place at company level.

Companies in the food, drink and tobacco industry and the timber and furniture industry seem to follow the rules formulated by unions and employers' federations very precisely. There are indications that a number of small firms pay below the negotiated rates.

In the chemical industry, where single-employer agreements prevail, we did not expect an earnings gap to occur. However, the oil and other chemical companies are concentrated in the Rotterdam area, where the Shell agreement is the leader. Many of the neighboring firms raise their rates just above the rates agreed on by Shell, without any formal agreement. In this way, the corporate agreement of Shell functions like a minimum agreement in the bargaining domain of the process industry.

A change of the engineering agreement from a standard into a minimum agreement took place during the second half of the sixties because of the growing need of the mostly larger companies to establish their own wages and conditions.[17] In the bargaining structure of this industry we have not witnessed an increase in corporate/divisional and foreign-owned subsidiary bargaining units over the period studied as large companies have been capable of determining part of their own wage conditions without breaking away from the industrywide bargaining unit. A process of accommodation occurred through a change in the rules governing collective bargaining.

Centralization in Bargaining Structure and National Industrial Relations

Unions, government and employers' associations in the Netherlands fostered the development of multiemployer agreements after the war. Some of these agreements have developed into centralized bargaining units, gobbling up smaller agreements. The increase in company bargaining has not caused a rupture in Dutch industrial relations because the formation of large corporations fitted neatly with national industrial relations features, that is the centralization of many single-employer agreements into the corporate/divisional bargaining units.

This integration reflects the organizational process of upgrading and downgrading within corporations as described by Koot.[18] Studying corporate structure in the 1960s and 1970s in the Dutch manufacturing industry, Koot depicted two developments representing the same phenomenon. The first was the development of firms into corporations or divisions with either control of ownership or the presence of management functions and the possibility to influence market behavior. It is a process of promotion on the corporate ladder.

The second was a process of downgrading by firms, first losing their control over ownership and in due course most managerial functions, ending up as a mere production facility. Some firms kept control over their ownership and their management functions, but being mostly small, could not influence market behavior. Along with functions such as research and development and marketing, some years after a takeover, local management lost its power to conclude collective agreements to central management.

The centralization of decisionmaking had been initiated by management, although unions could also play a crucial role. In a study of large corporations in the Netherlands and West Germany carried out in the seventies, Bomers found that unions favored bargaining at corporate level in home-based multinationals and at subsidiary level in foreign-based multinationals.[19] Evidently our data show an increase in both corporate/divisional and foreign-owned subsidiary bargaining units. Obviously, unions looked for the best possibility to exert influence on corporate decisionmaking in their homeland.

In the metalworking industry, with the notable exception of Philips, the existence of corporations has not led to the establishment of corporate bargaining units. Instead, the unions and the employers association concerned agreed on a second wage round at company level.

In other than metalworking the presence of corporate/divisional bargaining units seems to relate to the absence of a centralized industrywide bargaining unit as it exists in engineering. In this respect it is very important whether an industry constitutes a bargaining domain in its own right, such as the metalworking industry, or is part of a bargaining domain together with other industries. The paper industry is part of the bargaining domain of the printing industry. In the printing industry single-employer agreements are totally absent and the bargaining structure has been dominated from a very early point in its history by an industrywide bargaining unit. This agreement in the printing industry acts as wage leader and, with only single-branch bargaining units in the paper industry, room is left for the establishment of corporate/divisional bargaining units. A similar process occurred when the timber and furniture industry was linked up with the building industry. If the bargaining structure of an industry is part of a wider bargaining domain, its multiemployer agreements are prevented from developing into an industrywide bargaining unit. This, in turn, leads to a niche for corporate/divisional bargaining units.

In the chemical industry, part of the bargaining domain of the process industry, multiemployer agreements stopped at an early stage as the postwar expansion of this industry coincided with the concentration of ownership. Corporate/divisional and foreign-owned subsidiary bargaining units were established before the interorganizational relations between unions and employers' associations were developed on any scale. If such relations do not cover a whole industry before the concentration of ownership occurs the establishment of corporate units is likely to take place.

In the food, drink and tobacco industry no industrywide agreement came into existence. This industry is very heterogeneous, more than the industries studied (there is no common raw material). Some branches of this industry are covered only by multiemployer agreements and others only by single-employer agreements. But again, our arguments about concentration and interorganizational relations between unions and employers are also valid on the level of branches. Take for instance the tobacco industry: This industry consists of two branches, cigars and cigarettes, both completely foreign-owned. In the cigar industry small companies were taken over and developed into degraded subsidiaries, while in the cigarette industry Dutch corporations were taken over at a later stage and still have a measure of independence. The interorganizational relations between unions and the employers' association stem from a very early date and covered the cigar industry only, while in the cigarette industry no such relations came into existence before the concentration of ownership occurred.

The process of concentration does not necessarily lead to the establishment of parent companies in an industry. We have mentioned the process of upgrading and downgrading at company level. There is, however, no reason why such process should not occur at industry, or more likely, at branch level.

It is quite possible that whole branches of an industry consist of downgraded subsidiaries. A parent company may never have been established in such a branch and the multiemployer agreement may never have been challenged. Indeed, many subsidiaries of corporations are still covered by multiemployer agreements.

A last remark concerning the formation of large corporations refers to the process of deconcentration of ownership or decentralization of decisionmaking. Some large corporations went bankrupt after 1977, especially in the paper industry and in the timber and furniture industry. Most of the subsidiaries were taken over by other (foreign) corporations and some of them again became small independent companies. In both industries our classification of bargaining units makes it possible to trace this process. Between 1977 and 1984 there is an increase in foreign-owned subsidiary bargaining units and some reversion to small company bargaining units. According to our 1984 data there is as yet no tendency in large corporations toward a renewed autonomy for local management.

The conclusion is that large corporations have had a clear impact on Dutch bargaining structure. At the industry level the relationship between multi- and single-employer agreements is still quite varied and complex because of differences in the development of interorganizational relations between unions and employers, differences in the process of concentration and in the relationships between those two processes in their historical development.

Nevertheless, in all industries and corporations management and unions have shown a remarkable consistency in their strategy to establish company bargaining units; integrated and concentrated bargaining units, reflecting organization processes, both within corporations and trade unions. Integrated and comprehensive multiemployer agreements coexist with similar single-employer agreements.

The centralization in bargaining structure has led to an intermediate level of large bargaining units, which have become the foci of Dutch national industrial relations. One could even wonder whether the sets of interorganizational relations around these trendsetters have not replaced the Dutch national industrial relations system as such. In this sense we also feel that methodologically a systems approach to industrial relations has to be replaced by an interorganizational approach. In studying the impact of large corporations on different industries within the same country, we have come across the importance of trade union and employers' strategies. By comparing the same (metalworking) industry in two different countries, the Netherlands and Great Britain, the attention will be focused on those strategies.

COMPARISON BETWEEN DUTCH AND BRITISH METALWORKING INDUSTRIES

According to Derber, the British industry pioneered the development of industrywide bargaining.[20] A comparison between Dutch and British bargaining structures in engineering runs into problems relating to the similarities and differences between the two metalworking industries. For the Netherlands, most bargaining units are formally established and the results of the bargaining process are generally applied in the companies under the agreement.

In Great Britain, however, formalization and standardization in collective bargaining does not exist on this scale in the engineering industry. There has always been a tension between bargaining at the central level and at the local level. In the earlier stages of industrial relations in metalworking, this tension was reflected by national industry bargaining versus regional district bargaining. Bargaining above the level of the company originally took place at the district level. For a short period, around the time of World War I, industry bargaining appeared to become the dominant mode of wage determination. Shortly before and especially after World War II company bargaining developed rather quickly.[21] The tension between central and local bargaining was reflected through industry bargaining versus company bargaining and at a later stage also within companies between corporate/divisional bargaining and plant bargaining.

As a consequence of local bargaining being transferred from district to company and especially plant level, industrywide bargaining led only to minimum agreements concerning wages and conditions. The bargaining pattern was irregular; meetings took place only when deemed necessary. Can one speak of a bargaining unit in the sense of procedural rules and substantial outcomes applicable to most companies as in Dutch engineering? If British engineering did pioneer industrywide bargaining it certainly did not do so in terms of formal bargaining units. In recent years, especially during the 1960s and 1970s, the proportion of standard earnings accounted for by the rates negotiated in the industry agreement dropped drastically. Increases were agreed on in company bargaining by shop stewards. Without the formal establishment of company bargaining units, a two-level bargaining structure came into operation at industry and company levels.

Many large corporations broke away from the industry agreement and established their own annual agreement. In order to prevent the extinction of the industrywide agreement the unions and the employers' federation agreed on a new variant of the minimum agreement. In this new variant the minimum does not function as a floor, giving rise to a second wage round at company level, but as a safety net. In a minimum agreement workers receiving more than the minimum rate have their wages increased in such a way that parity between their company rates and the industry rates is at least reestablished. The floor raises everybody standing on it. Under the minimum safety net agreement the change in the industry wage rate applies only to those companies in the industry whose workers are paid the minimum.[22] In this way, there is no automatic link between the industry rate and the company rate. Management has more freedom to establish its own wages. The industry agreement functions as a safety net. Companies will drop into the net if wages have come down to the minimum.

Brown and Terry documented this change in the British metalworking industry. More recently, however, Elliot has stated that the industry agreement in metalworking is moving back from a safety net to a floor position. Due to the weakening of their domestic bargaining positions in the wake of the economic crises, workers try to base their increases on and above increases in the industry rates.[23]

Changes in the bargaining structure are not restricted to changes in the relationship between company and industry bargaining, but also occur within company bargaining. Because of reforms mainly induced by management, bargaining has moved in some companies from subsidiary (plant)-level to divisional or corporate level. In other companies this is not the case. Studying large corporations in British engineering, Loveridge has stressed "the longevity of the . . . federal corporate structure" in contrast to corporate centralism in other countries.[24]

Whereas the industry agreement in British metalworking has taken a position between a minimum floor agreement and a minimum safety net agreement, the Dutch engineering agreement hovers between a standard agreement and a minimum floor agreement. If additional negotiations in Dutch engineering companies take place at all, they are carried out within a detailed set of procedural rules laid down in the industry agreement. Increases above industry rates are very precisely determined by domestic job classification schemes, which are not basically different from the scheme in the multiemployer agreement. The domestic increases are negotiated between the company and the

national (regional) fulltime union officials with shop stewards either not being present at the negotiations or attending only as observers.

Union and Employers' Strategies

We observe more company bargaining units and more plant bargaining in
British than in Dutch metalworking. Both industries are covered by an industrywide bargaining unit. However, the way in which the rules, agreed to
by the parties, are applied in the companies differs. In Holland unions and
employers' federation either enforce the rules or the procedures and deviation from these rules is strictly formulated. In the United Kingdom the rules
are neither strictly applied nor extended for special application at the plant
level.

Metalworking industries share many commonalities in their technical-
economic structure, such as the work process, the composition of the labor
force, the raw materials and labor to capital ratios. Nevertheless, the industry
is very heterogeneous in its product markets and there have always been large
differences between growth sectors and stagnating sectors with different
abilities to pay wages. Indeed, the industry is often defined in terms of the
interorganizational relationships between trade unions and the employers'
association. As these constitute a bargaining domain in their own right, we
are in a position to compare interorganizational relations rather than industries. In both industries one set of interorganizational relationships covered
a substantial part of the industry before the concentration of ownership
occurred.

Looking at the strategies of the constituent organizations within this
historical context, it is of crucial importance whether or not the trade unions
favor uniform wage rates. Is there an emphasis on the protection of the lower
paid, restraining members' demands in the companies with a better ability
to pay? An industrywide agreement is a better instrument for comprehensive, solidaristic wage policy than a single-employer agreement. A minimum
agreement acting as a safety net does allow for larger variations in wages
among members in different firms. If the industry agreement is pushed into
a marginal role, lower paid workers, especially those in small firms, will be
worse off.

In Dutch unions the bargaining function has been monopolized by the
fulltime officials. This is very precisely laid down in the rules and organizational structure of the unions. In British unions plant bargaining by lay officials has occurred for a long time and this has also been supported by important sections of the paid officials. In this respect there are also important

differences with unions. For instance, in the British engineering union (AEUW) the right wing is in favor of a more solidaristic wage policy and the left wing is in favor of bargaining in the stronger sectors and plants of the industry. The metalworking industry especially—heterogeneous, but covered by one set of interorganizational relations—offers many opportunities for sectional bargaining. The unions' strategy is the outcome of the position of both political wings in the decisionmaking processes. Although in Britain the left wing was dominant in the sixties and seventies, in the Netherlands the solidaristic policy holds the majority in the unions.

For this reason, from the beginning of this century, the organizational structure of the Dutch unions did not allow for an independent position of shop stewards. Whether such a formal organizational structure will be maintained depends very much on the strategies of the employers' federation. Does the employers' federation prefer to negotiate with paid officials or are they in favor of recognizing lay officials? Is the employers' federation concerned with a standard wage rate throughout the industry? Historically in the Netherlands employers have concentrated on a standard wage rate to be negotiated with paid officials and to be applied at company level. This strategy has been more difficult to implement in the sixties and seventies because of the increasing differences between large corporations and small companies. These differences also became stronger and stronger in the British Engineering Employers' Federation and has resulted—as in Dutch metalworking, but to a greater degree—in a further relaxation of the rules of the industry agreement.

The development of corporations adds, in the first instance, to decentralization in the bargaining structure, but the development of their own internal organizational structure acts, in the second instance, as a force towards centralization. Whereas in Holland both management and union officials initiate and stimulate this process, in the United Kingdom this process of centralization is more haphazard, due to the organizational structure of trade unions (the position of shop stewards at plant level) and of companies (management at plant level). It is also possible that there are differences between Dutch and British managers such as those between German and British managers. German managers use their discretionary powers less than their British counterparts, even within formal centralized decisionmaking structures.[24]

CONCLUSION

If we compare the impact of large corporations on the bargaining structures of the Dutch non-metalworking industry, the Dutch metalworking industry and the British metalworking industry, the result is as follows. The concentration of ownership during the 1970s has led to changes in the relationship between industry and company bargaining. It led to the establishment and growth of corporate/divisional and foreign-owned subsidiary bargaining units in most Dutch non-metalworking industries and a relaxation of the rules of industry bargaining in the Dutch metalworking industry. In the British engineering industry it led to both. The shift from industry to company bargaining does not necessarily represent a decentralization of the bargaining structure. The integration of bargaining units within large corporations represents a centralization, reflecting the development of decision-making within large corporations in the wake of the actual mergers. In Holland, the large corporation as a new focus for the development of interorganizational relationships between unions and employers fits in very well indeed with the centralized and comprehensive nature of Dutch national industrial relations. One could say the large corporation as a non-voluntary hierarchy of companies has replaced the employers' association as a voluntary arrangement. In British engineering this integration is less obvious due to different strategies of employers and unions toward crucial issues such as corporate decisionmaking, wage policy or internal union structures.

With the aid of our conceptual framework we have interpreted the changes in bargaining structures as changes in interorganizational relationships and related these to historical-structural developments and to strategies of trade unions and employers. The simple model presented here needs further elaboration and the inclusion of other variables such as government strategy.

NOTES

1. Everett M. Kassalow, "The Future of American Unionism: A Comparative Perspective," *The Annals of the American Academy of Political and Social Science,* May 1984, pp. 52-63.
2. W. Streeck, *Industrial Relations in West Germany: A Case Study of the Card Industry* (London: Heineman, 1984), pp. 143-145.
3. Mancur Olson, *The Rise and Decline of Nations* (New Haven and London: Yale University Press, 1982), p. 41.
4. D. R. Deaton and P. B. Beaumont, "The Determinants of Bargaining Structures: Some Large Scale Evidence for Britain," *British Journal of Industrial Relations,* July 1980, pp. 202-216; W. E. Hendricks and L. M. Kahn, "The Determinants of Bargaining Structure in U.S. Manufacturing Industries," *Industrial and Labor Relations Review,* Vol. 35, No. 2, 1982, pp. 181-195.
5. W. Brown and M. Terry, "The Changing Nature of National Wage Agreements," *Scottish Journal of Political Economy,* Vol. 25, No. 2, June 1978, pp. 119-133.
6. Milton Derber, "Strategic Factors in Industrial Relations Systems: The Metalworking Industry," *Labour and Society,* 1976, No. 2, pp. 18-28.

7. M. J. Huiskamp, *Shop stewards en arbeiderszeggenschap een onderzoek naar arbeidsverhoudingen in de Britse metaalverwerkende industrie* (Alphen aan den Rijn: Samsom, 1976).

8. Ibid.

9. A. R. Weber, "Stability and Change in the Structure of Collective Bargaining" in L. Ulman, ed., *Challenges to Collective Bargaining* (Englewood Cliffs, NJ: Prentice-Hall, 1967), pp. 13–36.

10. C. Lammers, "Industrial Relations from an Interorganisational Perspective: A View from the Continent," in A. Thomson and M. Warner, eds., *The Behavioural Sciences and Industrial Relations* (Aldershot: Gower, 1981), pp. 32–43; Thomas A. Kochan, "Determinants of the Power of Boundary Units in an Interorganisational Bargaining Relation," *Administrative Science Quarterly,* Vol. 20, No. 3, 1975, pp. 434–452.

11. M. Derber, op. cit., p. 20.

12. S. W. Lerner and J. Marquand, "Workshop Bargaining, Wage Drift and Productivity in the British Engineering Industry," *Manchester School of Economic and Social Studies,* No. 1, 1962, pp. 15–60.

13. W. Koot, "Concernvorming en zeggenschap over ondernemersbeslissingen" in A. W. M. Teulings, ed., *Herstructurering van de industrie* (Alphen aan den Rijn: Samsom, 1978), pp. 114–137.

14. R. Loveridge, "Centralism Versus Federalism: Corporate Models in Industrial Relations" in K. Thruley and S. Wood, *Industrial Relations and Management Strategy* (Cambridge: Cambridge University Press, 1983, pp. 170–193).

15. J. P. Windmuller, *Labor Relations in the Netherlands* (Ithaca, N.Y.: Cornell University Press, 1969), pp. 434–441.

16. M. J. Huiskamp, "De cao-structuur van de Nederlandse industrie," deel 1, 2, en 3 in *Economisch Statistische Berichten,* 1983, pp. 131–137, 154–158, 180–184.

17. J. De Jong, *Het Nederlandse systeem van arbeidsverhoudingen* (Rotterdam: Universitaire Pers, 1974), pp. 55–77.

18. W. Koot, op. cit., pp. 117–122.

19. G. B. J. Bomers, *Multinational Corporations and Industrial Relations: A Comparative Study of West Germany and the Netherlands* (Amsterdam: Van Gorcum, Assen, 1976, pp. 128–138.

20. M. Derber, op. cit., pp. 18–28.

21. M. J. Huiskamp, op cit., pp. 73–78.

22. W. Brown and M. Terry, op. cit., pp. 124–125.

23. Ibid.; R. F. Elliot, "Some Further Observations on the Importance of National Wage Agreements," *British Journal of Industrial Relations,* No. 3, Vol. 19, 1981, pp. 370–375.

24. R. Loveridge, op. cit., p. 191.

25. J. Child and A. Kieser, "Organisation and Managerial Roles in British and West German Companies, An Examination of the Culture-Free Thesis" in C. J. Lammers and D. J. Hickson, eds., *Organisations Alike and Unlike, International and Interinstitutional Studies in the Sociology of Organisations* (London: Routledge & Kegan Paul, 1979), chap. 13.

3

THE CONCEPT OF CORPORATISM FROM AN INDUSTRIAL RELATIONS PERSPECTIVE —————

L.C.G. DOUWES DEKKER

Cooper defines corporatism as the "sharing of influence by the State and the primary economic organizations through joint decision-making in certain of the traditional autonomous spheres of each party, as a means of minimizing crisis and conflict in society. Such activity can be found at any level of societal organizations, though clearly, national-level practice is most relevant to this discussion,"[1] (i.e., the discussion of the interrelationship between the policies that unions and employers seek to pursue and those of the government). The nature of the institutional arrangements between the organized expression of capital and labor is part of the continuing debate about South Africa's future socio-economic cum political order. Corporatist arrangements have strategic implications for federations of unions and employers' associations in the allocation of resources to their respective societal goals. The concept of corporatism should not be discredited before debating the structural and process implications underlying the alternative forms of the relationship between a state and the industrial relations subsystem.

Three articles on the relevance of corporatism for South Africa have been published. Prinsloo suggests that the "coming corporatism" implies political control and administrative regulation by the state. He expresses the hope, however, in his concluding comment that this threat could provide an opportunity for the black unions to enter the heart of the state apparatus and bring about transformations.[2] Pretorius presents a relevant and, as yet, singular source of historical and factual information about past tripartite practices. In terms of this question regarding the likelihood of state or societal corporatism in the future, Pretorius does not identify the role that bilateral agreements could play to ensure the latter alternative.[3] In his analysis of the interaction of private and public decisionmaking, Brand makes no mention of the implementation of policy matters, the concept of corporatism, the relevance of unions and employers or the imperative of mandates from constituencies.[4] This is significant considering Brand's past responsibilities with the Prime Minister's Economic Advisory Council (PEAC). Does this suggest that only a consultation process occurred in the deliberations of the PEAC proceedings? The purpose of this paper is to analyze the alternative arrangements of different forms of corporatism and to raise certain questions pertaining to the South African situation.

Analysis of formal and informal consultations and negotiations between capitalism and the state in South Africa from 1924 to 1939 suggests that a relationship of mutual advantage was forged.[5] The state was assured of revenue by capitalism through economic growth and in return suppressed black labor, which facilitated capital accumulation. Legitimacy for order and control in that society came from the cooperation through cooptation of white labor, as a result of protection of artisan status and reservation of jobs for white workers. The industrial council system reinforced the cooptation as white unions gained benefits for their members at the cost of black workers who were not represented on that joint body. The symbiotic relationship between capitalism and the state continued after World War II. But capital started to question the instruments of control over black labor; that is, (1) from the late 1960 decade, legalized job reservation was criticized because it caused skilled labor shortages, and (2) since the early 1980s, influx control and the pass system were criticized because they threatened the social order, denied mobility of black labor and the process of urbanization. However, the legal removal of these two instruments of control, namely, the exploitation color bar and the job color bar, does not in itself lead to a more equitable distribution of wealth and does not enable organized labor to influence national socio-economic policy.[6] That is, the symbiotic relationship can be and is still continued. Is this the best option for capital to promote? Will black labor accept that?

Freedom of association was only extended to all workers in South Africa in 1979. This late development places responsibility on the leaders of the federations of employers' associations and unions to learn from the institutional arrangements developed by other societies. They need not work through the anguish of the power play that typified the early stages of experimentation in industrial relations of those countries, but can build on those institutional achievements. This is essential because South Africa has to face two unique challenges with their own power play. These challenges are needing to cope with (1) the expression of rights to organize, bargain collectively and take industrial action in a shorter period of time than allowed for elsewhere and (2) the race factor in future institutional arrangements. The leaders of capital and labor owe it to their constituents to gain a sound perspective of the scope and limits underlying corporatism so that considered choices can be made within the organizations through which they express themselves.

The legitimacy crisis of the present South African government comes at a time when union federations have emerged whose potential power and relevance demand societal expression and involvement. The degree of societal influence of organized labor in the future will depend on the specifics of the role responsibility that can be developed from their relationship with federations of employers' associations in the form of bilateral agreements and with the government of a post-apartheid society. The basis for negotiating trade offs to meet respective goals is laid during the crisis period. The ongoing debates about different governmental systems will benefit from accepting the likelihood that existing linkages between the current government agencies and organized labor and capital interest groups will survive the reform process to a certain degree.

In the past, primarily white interests were served. This same structure can serve the interests of all race groups, provided the power balance between union and employers' associations is strengthened and a process of joint decision-making is instituted. If capital accepts that its past and current symbiotic relationship with the state is not sufficient for a future South Africa, then it has to enter into negotiation through its employers' associations with union federations. The compromised agreements would lead to formulation of joint social policy requirements that any future government has to heed. If such negotiations are formulated, union and employers' association federations could establish a labor market board and provide consensus mechanisms crucial to legitimatizing the new state. The achievement of such a situation, which requires strategy considerations by the three parties, constitutes the strength of societal corporatism.

CHARACTERISTICS OF CORPORATISM

The essential characteristic of societal corporatism is the emphasis on voluntary participation by the parties. The parties enter it with caution, have to retain their mandated link to their constituencies, and can and do withdraw and participate only if the trade off makes sense. The institutional arrangements that coerce the unions and employers to serve the ends of the state are excluded from the definition of societal corporatism. The possibility of authoritarian or totalitarian control by the state over the labor market parties is a reality and has to be guarded against.

Lehmbruch draws a further distinction, namely that between sectoral corporatism and corporatism. In many countries sectoral corporatism emerged when various agricultural organizations gained a representational monopoly and privileged access to government, that is, sectoral corporatism refers to a specific interest group that gains advantage for its members. Lehmbruch's analysis suggests that if sectoral corporatism has operated in a country, then it is easier for the development towards societal corporatism to occur.[7]

Most countries develop forums where organized capital and labor meet with government agencies. These tripartite bodies deal with specific social policy issues—housing, job creation, unemployment and other insurance against loss in income, public transport services and other community issues. Such tripartite committees offer various forms of participation to the leaders of unions and employers. These private sector representatives can facilitate the implementation of a social policy, advise on specific problems or be involved in actual policy decisionmaking processes. In the latter, more comprehensive form of participation, the representatives regulate their conflict of interest through trade offs in order to influence policy issues. The oft-quoted example is price and incomes policy, but in fact this emphasis has ignored influences on other policy areas mentioned above. The involvement of the parties to the labor market in implementation of social and other policy matters can involve other interest groups. When expenditure on social issues required by the joint agreement of the labor market parties reaches such proportions that public finances and the national economy are affected, however, tripartism changes into corporatism and the labor market parties become the crucial interest groups because they control essential resources. Such possible transformation illustrates the developmental aspect of corporatism and highlights the following features of such state-societal institutional arrangements.

(1) The centralized interest organizations of capital and labor (the federations) are strengthened and developed into peak associations that possess a near representational monopoly.

(2) Peak associations can demand or are granted privileged access to government, and institutional linkages emerge between them and the public administration with significant effects on resource allocation and, hence, wealth distribution.

(3) A social partnership emerges between the organized expression of capital and labor on the basis that the regulation of conflict between these groups

influences and coordinates the formulation and implementation of government policy.[8]

CUMULATIVE SCALE OF CORPORATISM IN CERTAIN COUNTRIES

The features of corporatism discussed above along with the implications of possible developmental stages provided Lehmbruch with measures to refine cross-national research and establish a cumulative scale.[9] The illustrative purpose of Lehmbruch's cumulative scale of corporatism has been extended to include examples of countries falling into the category of state corporatism, that is, those institutional arrangements controlled and directed by the state. The forms of societal corporatism expressed in various countries are as follows.

Pluralism, found in the United States, Canada and New Zealand, is characterized by a predominance of pressure group politics and lobbying of parliament and government agencies by fragmented and competing interest groups; a low degree of effective participation by unions in policy making, and primarily plant-based collective bargaining. Concerted incomes policy is not even considered.

Weak Corporatism, found in the United Kingdom and Italy, is characterized by participation of federations of labor and capital in formation and implementation of socio-economic policy, but only with certain limited sectors of policy or specific stages (consultation or implementation) of the national policy-making process; plant-based collective bargaining; and nationwide bargaining only with certain companies or for a specific economic sector. Concerted incomes policy is difficult to implement or maintain.

Medium Corporatism, found in Belgium, West Germany, Ireland, and Denmark, is characterized by features similar to weak corporatism in respect to national policy processing; collective bargaining on nationwide and industry levels; and only temporary success with concerted incomes policy.

Strong Corporatism, Austria, the Netherlands, Sweden, and Norway, is characterized by effective participation of federations of labor and capital in policy formation and implementation across those interdependent policy areas that are of central importance to the management of the economy and have social implications, for example, employment creation, inflation control and social security provisions.

Two other types of societal corporatism, concertation without labor and state corporatism, are not included on Lehmbruch's scale. **Concertation without labor** is found in Japan and France. The weakness of the organized labor movement in France enables cooperation between governmental bureaucracies and big business to dominate the national planning process. **State corporatism** is found in communist countries, for example during the fascist regime in Spain, and the years of Salazar's control over Portugal. The last two totalitarian countries were tolerant of a degree of private ownership and private enterprise, but freedom of association was denied and the participation by persons representing employers (economic) and workers (social) in tripartite bodies was by state selection; that is, the so-called union or employer bodies were created by or kept as auxiliary and dependent organs of the state.[10] After the restoration of democracy and freedom of association in Spain and Portugal independent federations have been established and in Spain societal corporatism has emerged. In the post-independence period of African countries, the unions or their federations increasingly became an administrative arm of the state, but collective bargaining was retained in some countries, Kenya for example. These various developments suggest that the specific dimensions differentiating state and societal corporatism have to be identified. Are there structural characteristics that differentiate between these forms?

Inducement Versus Constraints

Certain comparative differences between societal corporatism and state corporatism can be identified from studies of developing countries. The intriguing characteristic of societal corporatism is that the voluntary participation of the autonomous federations of capital and labor with government agencies gives legitimacy to the functioning of the state. What is the nature of the hold of state corporatism over the parties? How can it be denied?

The analysis by Collier and Collier[11] of the nature of state corporatism in Latin American countries identifies characteristics useful in evaluating possible shifts from state to societal corporatism. The focus of their analysis is on the union movement and not on employers' associations. Only under complete dictatorships are employers' associations, which express the right of employers to associate, threatened.

The International Organisation of Employers (IOE), is a nongovernmental organization dedicated to the defense of free enterprise. It is the umbrella body of national employers' associations recognized by the International Labour Organisation (ILO). During recent years the IOE has concentrated considerable activities and efforts to promote and protect employer organizations in Latin American countries. The nature of agrarian reforms, nationalization and state intervention are identified as endangering the operation of market economy principles. It is to be noted that the IOE supports freedom of association, tripartism and bilateral agreements between federations of unions and employers' associations. Its ongoing activities demonstrate that employers can also lose their right to associate. Is this a message for employers' associations in South Africa?

The following organizational needs of unions are used in the Collier and Collier analysis: to recruit and retain members, to be recognized as legitimate representatives of workers in their dealings with other interest groups and to be assured of a stable source of income. In their cross-country analysis the authors analyzed the advantages that state assistance implies, for example, financial subsidies and recognition. Such inducements are offered by the state if it wants to be in a position, when necessary, to control or constrain the wage demands of unions or the use by unions of industrial action. Two scales measuring high and low levels of inducement as well as constraints in the labor laws of each Latin American country were developed. The degree of inducement was scored by examining labor laws for the following provisions:

> Registration and the privileges this confers; right of association and protection against employer harassment, unfair labor practices, monopoly representation of a single union in a sector, majority unionism, compulsory membership (e.g., sanction of a closed shop), subsidization of unions (e.g., stoporder provisions); and paid educational leave provisions.

Under the heading "constraints" the labor laws were examined and scored in terms of provisions for:

> controls on leadership and goals of unions (e.g., political party affiliation), regulation of collective bargaining (e.g., imposition of decrees on substantive aspects of agreements and strike actions through provisions for cooling-off period, and compulsory arbitration requirements), provision for state monitoring and intervention in internal union affairs (e.g., auditing of financial records, regulating expenditure of funds, and criteria for suitability of leadership as well as dissolution of unions).[12]

The two scales of inducement and constraints assist in the evaluation of degrees to which a society tends towards state or societal corporatism. Societal corporatism is marked by high inducements and low constraints and a voluntary relationship between the parties where the legitimacy of the state is dependent on seeking the involvement of these labor and capital parties in socioeconomic policy issues. State corporatism involves both high inducement and constraints on the operation of unions as well as dependency by the employer groups and unions on the state for their continued existence. As government bureaucracies are loath to give up control, societal corporatism only emerges after a crisis or when the labor market parties have entrenched their autonomy and entered into bilateral agreements.

Bilateral Agreements

Bilateral or basic agreements to regulate the industrial relationship between federations of unions and employers' associations can facilitate a move away from state corporatism or counter the move towards it. It would appear that, if the federations of capital and labor decide to control their own relationship voluntarily and accept self-restraints because of negotiated trade offs achieved in respect to their societal goals, the state will have little or no justification to interfere. That is, the two labor market parties forge a basic constitution for the working life of that country.

The operation of a basic bilateral agreement covering the "rules of the game" of labor-management relations ensures the autonomy of the organizational expression of capital and labor in their relationship to the state. Bilateral agreements can only be entered into if the two parties accept each other's legitimacy and the leaders respect each other. The parties are required to endorse certain values and must have developed, through experience of trial of strength and organizational development, a degree of power balance in their interaction. Jointly negotiated and fair procedures, which endorse due process, are one index of power balance.

Basic or bilateral agreements range in scope but the procedures would provide for issues such as levels and scope of collective bargaining, role and function of shop stewards, power to facilitate joint consultation in the workplace to prevent unilateral management action regarding such aspects as personnel practices and the production process, the nature and purpose of third party intervention, disclosure of information, and responsibilities for an influence on technological change. Another power index would be provision in the collective bargaining procedure for industrial action (strike or lockout) should a deadlock be reached.[13] Commitment to the use of procedures would reflect endorsement by the constituents of both parties to such values as fairness, industrial justice, equity, good faith, self-determination, incrementalism, representivity, compromise, peace obligation, due process, and mutual survival. These commitments and endorsements would imply acceptance of self-constraints and deny the need for state-imposed constraints. The basic agreement would provide the inducement that would normally be used in state corporatism to force unions into submission. That is, in acknowledging the role of power balance self-restraints and endorsement of values, the parties undertake to develop a relationship pattern based on cooperation (while allowing for adaptation) rather than antagonism.

Countries moving towards societal corporatism would entrench freedom of association, civil liberties and private ownership in their national constituency. If freedom of association in the industrial relations sense is only protected by labor legislation it faces the danger of being diluted when another government comes into power. The American labor movement has referred to this as the "legislative snare." The basic agreement would clarify the respective rights and obligations and provide for the necessary checks and balances to prevent abuse of the powers of freedom of association.

PRECONDITIONS FOR CORPORATISM

The above analysis of the various forms of corporatism should provide the leaders of unions and employers' associations with some insight into this phenomenon and particularly alert the parties to the ways in which the state can shape institutional arrangements to serve its own ends. The historical analysis of developments in a number of countries reveals further characteristics that can best be regarded as preconditions for corporatism.

The historian Maier analyzed societies in which corporatism emerged and developed both in its weak and strong forms. He went beyond the national characteristics of countries in order to determine why leaders of capital and labor negotiated procedures to direct their behavior and what social priorities were agreed on. Those priorities included the objectives of economic stability, the imperative of export performance, importance of reasonable profit margins, critical need for investment, the necessity for environmental protection and, specifically, joint agreements on social policy.[14] The following preconditions are based on Maier's analysis:

(1) The prevalence of a social democratic ideology, which accepts the view that the roles of the state and the market are interwoven. That is, employers in their collective expression accepted the regulatory function of jointly agreed active labor market policies.

(2) Acceptance by the leadership of the federations of unions and employers' association that power is an expendable commodity and not a fixed

sum and structurally determined. That is, shared power and responsibility through collective bargaining decisions provide potential processes to reach agreement on programs of action and resource allocation that can be of benefit to both sides.

(3) Perception among the unions that their federations can, through their own organizational base, influence political decisions without having to rely solely on a political party. If unions are to be involved in social policy decisionmaking, the trade off implications include some degree of wage restraint in return for the social security benefits, full employment policies, and community upliftment. This strategy does not exclude links between the union federations and a social democratic-oriented political party, but ensures autonomy of the labor market.

(4) Societies in which unions are not seen as a threat but are accepted, in particular, by employers as a legitimate and essential institution.

(5) Emergence of a crisis situation such as war or necessity for reconstruction of society. These situations brought the parties together for a period and resulted in agreement on collective bargaining and social policy priority criteria.

(6) Related to the precondition regarding a state of crisis is the awareness among the parties of their vulnerability in the face of complex forces including (a) reaction to the effect of hyperinflation and its impact on jobs (unemployment), loss of markets, decrease in living standards and falling profit margins (economic dimension); (b) awareness of the destruction resulting from violence in communities and the implication for quality of life in a society when democratic processes are denied and totalitarian practices emerge (political dimension); (c) awareness among business tycoons that they should pull their punches lest they repeat past mistakes, for example, wartime collaboration with authoritarian state in maintaining armaments industry (leadership dimension = capital); (d) reaction to the intrusion of political divisions among union leadership and threat of unions allowing themselves to be subordinated to political parties (leadership dimension = labor); and (e) the effect of the denial of freedom of association and implication for individual rights of unilateral decisionmaking (industrial relations dimension).

(7) Emergence and existence of democratic and cohesive industrial relations federations of unions and employers. The phasing-in of union achievements in relation to political party victories is crucial. Corporatist arrangements did not take root in countries where the socialist party achieved electoral success or mobilization before the union movement gained victories for collective bargaining.

(8) A historical tradition of strong government acknowledging the bilateral agreements between the federations who are accepted as social partners. The

federations, as labor market parties, exercise restraint over industrial action in order to influence broader social goals.

(9) Federations of employers and unions who have had experience of joint declarations or bilateral agreements through which respect and a power balance has emerged, can deny state interference and can demonstrate to constituents that such arrangements do not imply a loss of autonomy or necessarily collusion.

(10) A society that endorses social policy. In analyzing the development of social policy, Berenstein[15] concludes that an important stage in that evolution was acceptance that the rights of man include (a) static protection and maintenance of what the individual has already acquired, property rights, and (b) the dynamic aim to alter the individual's situation by assisting him to acquire the right to something not possessed—social rights.

The above historical preconditions can best be regarded as variables that are likely to influence the degree to which corporatism will emerge in a country. If the parties have some knowledge of these preconditions their awareness becomes an intervening variable and the dimension of their propensity to participate becomes the crucial precondition. Propensity implies both willingness and ability. These qualities depend on the stature of the leadership, their ability to cope with role conflict, and cohesiveness of the organizations they represent. Federations of unions and employers are democratic in nature and, hence, awareness among the constituencies about the alternative institutional arrangements or degrees of corporatism the labor market parties become involved in is crucial. The extent of statesmanship among the leaders is of vital importance to facilitate setting up agenda items and structured attitudes towards working together. Hence, the processes whereby that leadership participates in corporate structures should be discussed.

PROCESSES

The analysis by Cooper[16] of countries with societal corporatism suggests that the institutional dialogue between government, labor and capital was achieved most effectively if joint decisionmaking and bargaining rather than consultation or concertation was entered into. What are the characteristics of these processes? First, the process of consultation suggests a two-way exchange of information in which each party represents its position on an issue(s) and discusses these with the other party. Second, the process of concertation differs from consultation in that it is usually initiated by the government with a view to decisions being taken on a specific issue. This process is also referred to as "state induced collaboration."[17] Concertation is meant to involve education by the parties leading to an appreciation of needs and problems of each other, thereby promoting a willingness to exchange opinions and to reach an agreed perception of the general or public interest.[18] Third, the process of joint decisionmaking requires the parties to share responsibility for the decisions. It also implies that bargaining is involved as the agreements deals with a future policy in the form of a package arrived at through trade offs regarding national economic and social policy priorities. Cooper's analysis of five countries suggests that consensus is only achieved when the parties are involved in joint decisionmaking and not consultation. The scope for this process is dependent on power and respect as qualities of the relationships entered into and maintained by the labor market parties. Consensus on a policy issue does not necessarily represent agreement on what constitutes the general interest. That is, bargaining is entered into by union and employers' associations and the compromise of trade offs is considered, because "each party can see that any alternative policy would be likely to be less desirable than the agreed package from the point of view of its own interest and that each party has enough confidence in the means by which the policy package will be implemented, to go ahead with the agreement."[19]

An important facet determining the degree of corporatism that emerges in a country is the extent to which the process is facilitated by systematic structures established by either legislative requirements or joint agreements. Unstructured participation to attend to a specific issue in deadlock or to seek clarification before formal declaration of a deadlock is also necessary to supplement more formalized negotiations. The leaders on both sides have to cope with role conflict, that is, competing response tendencies that require different role performances. Union leaders in particular experience tension between (a) the dependence on employers, because only through interaction can prime union objectives be achieved, and (b) democratic need of accountability towards membership and, hence, necessity to remain independent. Unstructured and off-the-record exchanges are inevitable consequences of role conflict and therefore the safety net of formal negotiation with open agendas and report-back mechanisms is crucial to prevent collusion.

Lehmbruch[20] suggests that the ability to influence national socio-economic policy implied in the process of joint decisionmaking results in the willingness by both parties to underutilize their economic power. Thus, power of industrial action that parties can express in collective bargaining to promote sectional and sectoral interests in a segment of the labor market is exchanged for direct political influence on the national level—but political influence through separate structures, such as in a union, not through a social democratic-oriented political party. This feature of corporatism suggests that the success of national level institutional arrangements is dependent on collective bargaining operating at least on a sectoral (possibly nationally or regionally) and not on a plant-based level. Countries either classified as pluralist or with weak corporatism emphasize plant-based bargaining.

Table 3.1 highlights some of the variables that leaders would have to consider when formulating a strategy to fill out all the levels of the industrial relations system and not concentrate only on plant-level action and negotiation. Workers join unions for a number of reasons including the material benefits, job security, identification with a cause, and promotion of societal goals. Union leaders have to determine the strength of the latter incentive among members and the likelihood of satisfying it through the union as an independent organization. Such crucial decisions relate to the use and, through self-restraint, possible curtailment of economic power.[21]

AND SOUTH AFRICA?

The above insights might guide the labor market parties in South Africa in their attempts to consider the "how" of working together. The dynamics of the reform that South Africa is experiencing will inevitably thrust unions and employers' associations forward into crisis and into ad hoc contact on community issues.[22] Certain tactical allegiances are already emerging and, if built upon, can demonstrate the value of getting on with the job at hand. From the grass roots level they offer important experiential learning curve exposures. The boycott weapon has brought employers' associations to the negotiating table. Should they not negotiate with union leaders who are also community spokesmen?

But will labor market parties be taken seriously—and what of other interest groups? The analysis of corporatism in other countries suggested that the respective governments regard the social partners as prime actors in their social planning and implementation programs. This has occurred because of the control these organizations can exercise over the key resources of capital and labor. The labor market parties, are, therefore, placed in a quite different category from other interest groups because of their ability to exert pressure on governments or simply to frustrate the initiatives of those governments.[23]

The following observations and propositions were noted about the South African situation in 1986 when this chapter was being written. First, a suffi-

**Table 3.1. Levels of Working Together and Potential
for Integrated Industrial Relations Subsystem**

Level		Variables	
		Potential Organizational Expressions of capital and labor	Key Content of Agreement or Negotiations
State	6	Consultation or joint decision making between labor market parties and government agencies through tripartite bodies	Tripartite deliberation on socio-economic issues and social policy on basic needs
National	5	Federations of unions and employers' associations establish joint forum or labor market board	Basic bilateral agreement on industrial relations procedures and socio-economic trade-offs
Industry/ economic sector	4	Union and employers' associations for a specific industry establish joint body to facilitate collective bargaining	Collective bargaining agreement on wages, working conditions, social security funds and specific issues
Regional	3	As per 4 or 5	(a) As per 4 but on regional level (b) As per 6 but on regional level
Holding company or division of conglomerate	2	The conglomerate prefers to have a lobby input into level 6 without labor. Workers are represented on company board	Holding company or division enter with union into procedural agreement or guidelines
Plant	1	Management and shop steward committee can establish joint consultation besides negotiating committee	Procedural recognition agreement—substantive agreement supplementing or in addition to 4

Note: The extent to which capital and labor are active on all levels is dependent on the degree to which corporatism is accepted. Variables that influence the utilization of all levels include: that country's constitutional support for freedom of association; propensity of employers' associations and unions to consider trade-offs on the nature of the socio-economic order; extent of legislative or basic agreement support to empower certain processes, e.g., co-determination and joint consultation; relationship between labor market parties and political parties; levels at which trial of strength, collective bargaining expressed, etc.

cient number of preconditions are emerging in the South African society to provide a conducive environment in which the key federations of unions and employers' associations can consider guiding South Africa's post-apartheid society towards a weak or moderate form of corporatism. This is imperative because the governmental responses to township uprisings can lead to state corporatism. Second, the requirements of the joint decisionmaking process will not be readily adopted by existing government agencies, which will prefer the consultation process. Third, divisions in union federations and employers' associations are considerable. Societal corporatism will not satisfy all their respective goals for a post-apartheid society. But initiatives can, for a sufficient number of unions and employer associations, become a factor in generating national cohesiveness on both sides, but in particular, the labor movement. Fourth, the reform of the industrial council system by rebuilding on its self-governance principle provides a base for the development of bilateral negotiations between sectoral union federations and employers' association. In certain situations this might require drastic restructuring.

Finally, since 1976, capital has strengthened its symbiotic relationship with the state (e.g. through the Urban Foundation) and attempted to promote an ideology of unfettered free enterprise (Free-Market Foundation and Project Free Enterprise). These trends militate against bilateralism and will strengthen the emergence of state corporatism through interference in union affairs and inducements promoting certain union groupings.

South Africa has reached a stage in its industrialization and urbanization that can provide a takeoff into mass housing schemes, social security benefits and other programs. Such social policy activities, if programmed through trade offs resulting from bilateral negotiations, will provide meaningful involvement for both parties and tangible improvements in the quality of life of workers, and reestablish legitimacy in our society. Admittedly, the continued role of existing tripartite bodies will be questioned. But ingenuity can come out of proposed bilateral negotiations.

Societal corporatism reinforces democratic values and processes in other than the political arena. The costs of corporatism include the time of leaders, commitments by the respective organizations and the risk of losing autonomy through both cooptation and collusion. The risks are justified because basic bilateral agreements force capital and labor to take each other's interests into account by having to consider their respective concerns about industrial relations and the future socio-economic order. The intra-organizational bargaining within each part will be a significant process and, in fact, could result in two clear divisions in both the divided union movement and employers and their associations. This will bring home to employers that they should exercise the right to associate and the need to establish their solidarity. It is because of these dynamics, tensions, role conflict dilemmas and organizational strains that the bilateral agreements are the first step toward societal corporatism.

The leaders of the labor market parties cannot let the opportunity slip by and allow South Africa to be plunged into state corporatism. The cumbersome but essential long-term task of considering the scope of forging a basic constitution for working life and gaining experience in exercising shared responsibility can now be started. The efficiency concerns of capital and the emphasis on values and due process by labor can, through ingenuity of the leaders, be incorporated in the structural and process requirements of worker participation expressed at various levels of interaction between their respective organizations.

NOTES

1. M. Cooper, *The Search for Consensus* (Paris: Organisation for Economic Cooperation and Development, 1982), p. 68.

2. M. W. Prinsloo, "Political Restructuring, Capital Accumulation and the 'Coming Corporatism' in South Africa," *Politikon,* Vol. 11, No. 1, 1984, pp. 20–42.

3. L. Pretorius, "Interaction Between Interest Organizations and Government in South Africa," *Politeia,* Vol. 1, No. 1, 1982, pp. 1–30.

4. S. S. Brand, "Die Process van Partikuliere en Openbare Besluitneming, *S.A. Journal of Business Management,* Vol. 14, No. 2, 1983, pp. 80–87.

5. D. Yudelman, *The Emergence of Modern South Africa* (Westport, CT: Greenwood Press, 1983), p. 288.

6. L. Douwes Dekker, "Trade Unions: Collective Bargaining Agent and Social Partner," 1986 (to be published), p. 22; L. Douwes Dekker, "Aspects of the Labour Market," in J. Matthews, ed., *South Africa in the World Economy* (Johannesburg: McGraw-Hill, 1983), p. 271.

7. G. Lehmbruch, "Concentration and the Structure of Corporatist Networks," in J. Goldthorpe, ed., *Order and Conflict in Contemporary Capitalism* (Oxford: Oxford University Press, 1984), pp. 60–80.

8. Ibid., p. 61.

9. Ibid.

10. P. C. Schmitter, "Still the Century of Corporatism?" *Review of Politics,* Vol. 36, No. 1, 1974, p. 102.

11. Ruth Berns Collier and David Collier, "Inducements Versus Constraints: Disaggregating Corporatism," *The American Political Science Review,* Vol. 73, No. 4, 1979, pp. 967–968.

12. Ibid., pp. 82–83.

13. L. Douwes Dekker, *The Right to Strike,* Research Paper No. 5, Johannesburg, Centre for Business Studies, University of the Witwatersrand, 1985, p. 49.

14. C. Maier, "Preconditions for Corporatism," in J. Goldthorpe, ed., *Order and Conflict in Contemporary Capitalism* (Oxford: Oxford University Press, 1984), pp. 39–59.

15. A. Berenstein, "The Development and Scope of Economic and Social Rights," *Labour and Society,* Vol. 7, No. 4, 1982, pp. 393–407.

16. M. Cooper, op. cit., p. 77.

17. L. Panitch, "Recent Theorisations of Corporatism: Reflections on a Growth Industry," *British Journal of Sociology,* Vol. 31, No. 2, 1980, pp. 159–187.

18. M. Cooper, op. cit., p. 13.

19. Ibid.

20. G. Lehmbruch, op. cit.

21. L. Douwes Dekker, *The Right to Strike,* p. 49; L. Douwes Dekker, "Trade Unions: Collective Bargaining Agent and Social Partner," p. 22.

22. L. Douwes Dekker, "Who Constitutes the Private Sector," *Business Alert,* No. 40, Johannesburg, Centre for Business Studies, University of the Witwatersrand, 1986, p. 13.

23. J. Goldthorpe, "The End of Convergence," in J. Goldthorpe, ed., *Order and Conflict in Contemporary Capitalism* (Oxford: Oxford University Press, 1984), p. 324.

4

THEMES IN THE HISTORY OF
INDUSTRIAL RELATIONS IN NORWAY

PAUL JOHNSEN AND PATRICK JOYNT

The traditions and results of industrial relations development in Norway are rooted in the country's history. Therefore, there are a number of traits in the development of industrial relations that are different from the development and characteristics of other countries.

Some international influences have had little or no impact on Norwegian industrial relations through the years, and others have had a conspicuous effect on the whole industrial environment, both internally and externally. The 300 years under Danish rule, until 1814, left a country of highly urbanized, small societies, but still united and with an extremely nonaggressive mentality in spite of foreign rule. The coming of the industrial state, which was as late as this century, demonstrated a socially and psychologically homogeneous population with historically built-in tolerances towards ambiguities. Until after the turn of the century, Norway had all the characteristics of what we today call a developing country.

The country is geographically elongated, with a scattered population. Agriculture, fisheries and other self-supplying occupations have dominated most of the districts both inland and along the coast. In 1980, although Great Britain had 52 percent of the total workforce employed in industry, Norway had 23 percent, and jobs were concentrated in a few urban areas.[1] The help-to-self-help traditions are deeply rooted in Norway and have only diminished during the last two decades, due to the rapid rise of the well-developed welfare system.

Norway was among the last European nations to adopt old age pensions. The Netherlands and Sweden introduced pensions in 1913, but Norway did not pass a national pension scheme until 1936.[2] In 1934 newspapers wrote in favor of not following the extravagant financial dispositions of the neighboring countries in Scandinavia.[3]

A stronger national unifying mentality grew during the years under Swedish rule (1814–1905). As a consequence, it is probable that this national self-determination process did have an impact on internal relations in Norway. There may, therefore, be an underlying cultural disposition for the evident cooperative industrial relations practices that exist in Norway. Historically, investment in conflict-oriented industrial relations strategies is almost nonexistent. The gradual escalation of national resources has been accompanied by an adapted trust in egalitarian solutions. Hence, conflicts as alternatives to arbitration are relatively few in the industrial relations history of Norway.

The consensus traditions have produced a number of strong impacts on the collective systems. The main bargaining partners, the Norwegian Employers' Confederation (NAF) and the Norwegian Federation of Trade Unions (LO) have cooperated within a number of areas of traditionally conflicting interests, including training, safety, industrial democracy, research, and statistics. There are obvious advantages in the traditional cooperative strategy, such as minimum loss of man-hours caused by disputes, maximum opportunities for egalitarian systems, creativity with the maximum use of human potentials uncontaminated by prestige and status differences, and minimum social obstructions in professional development and careers.

On the other hand, the egalitarian tradition may have had a homogenizing and nondeveloping influence as well. The agreement to start the socio-technical experiments in the 1960s had such a gravitating impact on industrial thinking that management development has, to some degree, been neglected in the country. The reason that management processes have been highly undernourished in Norwegian companies derives partly from the autonomous group paradigm accepted nationwide. That paradigm was authorized by the two dominant, opposing organizations in Norwegian industry. This does not, however, suggest a deliberate and general repression of the belief in managerial competence and the necessity for managerial capacity. This is a field that has become urgently discussed in Norway during the last few years, and research in the field of increasing managerial competence is about to be escalated. In some respects top and operating management positions were strengthened during the initial phases. Middle managers were neglected here, but experience, especially in the intensive technologies, has shown the need for these vital positions. There are other signals in our time; among others are the relatively new competitive situation between labor unions and the willingness to go on strike in the new growth areas such as offshore personnel and different groups within the civil service.

Culture is an implicit factor in this analysis, as we will argue that certain Norwegian traditions, values, attitudes and behavior have had a major impact on the Norwegian industrial relations system. We have also laid the foundation for assuming that the model used in this analysis is a cooperation model rather than a conflict model.

A HISTORICAL REVIEW

The first relevant act within the field of industrial relations was passed by the Norwegian Parliament on June 27, 1892. This was 96 years after the passage of the first British act for protection of child workers in the cotton and wool industry. The Norwegian Act of 1892 had a wider scope, however, because it dealt with such aspects as general inspection in industry, limitations of working hours and employers' responsibility for accidents.

The latest Work Environment Act of 1977 demonstrates a consistent trend (from 1892) towards a higher degree of safety, security and good working conditions generally for workers in all kinds of enterprises. The latest act is, however, unique in more than one respect.[4]

• It represents general improvement in a number of areas such as safety, working hours, and physical working conditions.

• It introduces *subjective* measures of satisfaction with work and working conditions. These measures are based on both contemporary research and agreed-upon values and standards as much as on previously negotiated agreements between the parties involved.

• It gives instructions for work planning with a requirement that the workers who will be affected by the plans when they are put into action are involved in the planning.

The law implies inspection of and judgment on the working standards both from internal and external bodies. In addition, the law guarantees the double role of production and personal and academic development. This is very much in harmony with the social-technical traditions in Norway.

In Norway there has been a close interface between the legislative bodies and the unions' and employers' confederations during the whole industrial era. On occasion, the main organizations in industry have arrived at agreements on improved conditions for workers before Parliament has been prepared to pass new laws within the actual field. Which institution came first has varied through the years as improvements have been made.

The Norwegian Federation of Trade Unions (LO) was founded in 1899. The Norwegian Employers' Confederation (NAF) was founded only one year later, in 1900, and in today's program motivates its existence with the demand for "solidarity." This illustrates both the thinking and the cooperative tradition in Norway.

NAF's objectives are

1. to maintain good and lasting relations between employers and employees, to endeavor to avoid labor disputes and to solve disputes when they arise;

2. to advise the members of the Confederation concerning wages and working conditions and assist them during conflicts with the employees or their organizations;

3. to promote cooperation between Norwegian employers and assist in establishing associations among them; and

4. to deal with social questions that are of significance to the undertakings, and with other matters of mutual interest.[5]

LO's introductory section of the Program of Action adopted by the Congress in May, 1981, states that the Norwegian Federation of Trade Unions (LO) will

1. protect the trade union and the financial, social and cultural interests of workers;

2. help to develop the democratic form of government, to defend freedom and the protection provided by law;

3. increase the influence of workers on decisions made in all sections of working life and strengthen economic democracy;

4. work for an active economic policy that protects full employment and a varied pattern of population distribution, curtail the rise in prices and ensure an even distribution of incomes in order to encourage a social trend towards a higher quality of life;

5. retain public responsibility for the joint tasks of society and develop satisfactory services for various groups;

6. work for equality of status between the sexes, women and men being given equal opportunities to exercise their rights within the organization and in the community as a whole;

7. work for the freedom and independence of the trade union movement; and

8. promote international cooperation.[6]

It is beyond the scope of this paper to go into detail concerning all the legislation dealing with industrial relations in Norway. Rather, we will highlight

Table 4.1. Legislation Related to Union Representation on Enterprise Committees

	Basic Agreement	Representation	
Year	Committee	Management	Union
1945	Production Committees, Cooperation on Technology	50%	50%
1966	Company Cooperation Committees	50%	50%
1973	ACT		
	Enterprise Assembly	2/3	1/3
	Board Members	2/3	1/3
1977	ACT		
	Work Environment Committees	50%	50%
	Special Committees	50%	50%

some of the interesting points in the development. Representation has been a key factor in the democratic-oriented legislation, as Table 4.1 shows.

THE BASIC AGREEMENT

The basic agreement between LO and NAF dates back to 1935, and is known as the "Labor Charter." LO calls it "the prime element in all collective agreements between these organizations." There are no serious objections to this description. The LO/NAF Basic Agreement has no doubt formed the pattern for all later agreements between unions and employers, including the civil service. The respect for this charter has been great. It consists of three main parts.

Part A. This part establishes "the right to organize, negotiate and the obligation to maintain industrial peace for the duration of the Agreement."

Part B. This part is known as the "Cooperation Agreement," and deals with various rules for organizing industrial cooperation.

Part C. Supplementary agreements are set up in this part. Among these is the Basic Agreement for data-based systems (of 1978). Possibly the most important of these supplements is the agreement on development of the work organization, which includes resources from LO/NAF for conferences, scholarships and job analysis projects. Otherwise, this part gives details of such aspects as duration, joint regulations and procedures for solving disputes.

Paragraph 9, Part A of the Basic Agreement is of interest. This paragraph gives working guidelines for cooperation between the employees and management within single departments. This paragraph deals with some of the same practical as well as psychosocial fundamentals for sound and mutually satisfactory work conditions. It describes the necessity for identification by the individual employees with the company, and why this is an inevitable foundation for effective production. In order to obtain this identification it is important to have suitable forms of discussion for solving common problems and questions, both for the individual employee and for the company's officials.

The paragraph also aims at the best utilization of each individual's potential and describes in detail how formal and informal behavior can promote this utilization. As in the phrasing of the Work Environment Act, the managers and management responsibilities are also underlined in Paragraph 9: "The management must discuss with the shop stewards," "The management must as early as possible discuss plans for expansion, reductions or changed conditions of importance for the workers."[7]

It is possible that industrial relations in Norway, as illustrated by these examples, has a traditional habit of avoiding major problems in industry, and this tradition is maintained by laws and agreements.

The cooperation part (Part B) of the Basic Agreement shows in detail how the parties have agreed on organizing coexistence strategies in enterprises and departments. In addition, the parties combine the Part A regulations (about rules, rights, voting procedures, etc.) with a psychological reasoning on the importance of good communications between management, employees and shop stewards.

As we shall see later, this "communication culture" in Norwegian enterprises seems to work well, and may be the major cause for good relationships. In addition, the low differentiation of status, wages, socio-economic background of the actors in the different groups and similar unifying traditions are of vital importance when it comes to problem-solving, reductions of antagonism and increased mutual understanding. The national culture may have expressed itself through the authors of the agreements and influenced the negotiators and actors at any given time.

As we have pointed out previously there has been a mutual influence between the legislation and the negotiation bodies as far as industrial conditions are concerned, and the relationships between the different actors have been undramatic through the years. Sometimes the organizations have reached new agreements that have been turned into law after some time. At other times a law comes first and sets the scene, for example, for the representative systems in the controlling bodies of the enterprises.

In 1947 the main organization (LO/NAF) agreed to establish "production committees" in the larger companies.[8] The 1966 revision of the LO/NAF Basic Agreement turned these committees into "general company and work environment committees." Subcommittees, called department committees, were also established.[9] The leading motive for these company committees was *cooperation.*

An NAF publication states: "Both legislation and agreements in these fields and also the internal development work of an undertaking are included in the term 'democracy in industry,' "[10] Some comments are necessary here. Initially there was a definite resistance from the employers' (NAF) side to the election of workers' representatives on the boards. Only two of eight representatives in a committee "that gave advice on industrial democracy in 1964" voted for workers' representation on the boards. Both research and employers' opinions have advised against such representation as a means of increased industrial democracy. Arguments from the "Cooperation Research Group" included "Practical experience and results from new research have given us a gradually stronger feeling that the core of the problem is this: If one does not obtain a higher degree of personal influence on the concrete, daily level— then one cannot expect any real influence from the majority of the employees in the broad company political questions."[11]

In this light, it is interesting to quote from a speech given by Prime Minister Einar Gerhardsen (Labor Party) on December 9, 1961.

> From 1945 it was said in the common program for our political parties: The task for our enterprises and all economic activity in our country is to provide work for all and increased production; and through fair distribution of the end results—give good living conditions for everybody. . . . In each company, advisory production committees will be established, consisting of workers and employers, in order to increase the interest in forwarding the most effective production, a good work environment and occupational training. . . . Some of these bodies work very well, and we can see great and positive results of their work.[12]

All experience shows that this side of industrial relations has been followed up during the 23 years since Gerhardsen's speech. The reorganization of the internal cooperative bodies in each company has been done quite undramatically. The resistance from the employers' side to the elected workers' representation on the board of directors dwindled and turned into general agreement. Workers' representation in these bodies are now mostly regarded as strengths. The criticism that comes up now and then aims at the professionalization of the boards in general and not at the workers' representation. There is full agreement on the fact that workers' representation on the boards and similar organs have made the relations between employers and employees better, and that the information exchange between otherwise quarreling parties has improved.

It is interesting to note how the politicians act in this arena of cooperation. Within one field of the discussions about general conditions in industry, the democratic right to influence the working conditions, there never has been any difference of opinion. The following are two examples from speeches of political opponents.

> 1. The right to use one's own capabilities in creative work, the right to be taken notice of, the right to influence and forward one's own intentions, is fundamental in our culture.[13]
> 2. Under all circumstances must we give increased attention to the qualifications, human competence and attitudes among those who shall represent the interests of the employers and employees, as well as those who represent the national interests in company bodies.[14]

The first statement was given in a 1962 speech by the president of the Norwegian Association of Industries, later Minister of Industrial Affairs in a conservative government, S. W. Rostoft. The second statement is taken from Prime Minister Gerhardsen's speech at a conference on industrial democracy in 1961.

A commission was established in 1963 to propose actions for the introduction of industrial democracy in Norwegian companies. In 1964, when the well-known industrial democracy research project started in Norway, the leaders of the project, Einar Thorsrud and Fred Emery, wrote in their first book: "Our time is characterized by mutual respect between the parties in industry. They are more capable of dealing with questions with greater differences of opinions, in objective ways, than ever before." The year 1964 must be recognized as a milestone in the development of industrial relations in Norway. Until that year industrial relations had been characterized by the "agreements of 1945 on productivity councils in each company and the open information contact between the representatives of employers and employees" and "peaceful negotiations, formal and informal ways of cooperation between workers and managers in the majority of enterprises."[15]

After the year 1964, the public attitudes turned towards the innate problems of industrial democracy as a dimension in itself, and a problem area of greater importance than the operational participation between manager and workers. Most research within the industrial relations field in Norway has been done on the premises of the workers' unions, the labor movement and the labor party ideology. There has been literally no objection to this perspective. On the contrary, the Employers' Confederation has cooperated actively both in the research bodies—like the Cooperation Council (LO/NAF)—and in the adoption of the industrial democracy paragraphs in the Act of 1973 (for limited companies). Thus, 1964 became a notable year because of the great attention gained by the LO/NAF industrial democracy project, which was started at that time.

Another research project on the "Workers' Collective" was reported on in 1967 by Sociology Professor Sverre Lysgaard.[16] The project was carried through in a paper factory not far from Oslo. The focus was set on the tendencies for workers to react to the total work situation as a workers' collective and not as individuals. The ambitions of the research group were modest in 1954 when the project started. They wanted to study the work, the communications system and the individual cognitions of the total company situation. The findings directed the research group's attention to the tendency of workers to talk about "me" and "them" within the same company of 735 employees. The defense of workers against technical and economic claims was then studied more in depth, especially the workers' collective as a sociological institution, how it develops its own norms and how these are expressed in the daily job situations. Some characteristics of the workers' collective are the traditional tendency to set production standards of their own, not to exceed the present work pace level, how to mark differences between the workers and employers/manager/experts, how to notice when a colleague crosses the border to "the other side," how to stick to the safe group, and how to follow rules for communication and cooperation (a) within one's own group and (b) with "the others" outside one's own group.

The notable side of this research project is hardly the sociological analysis of individual and group dynamics. These are studied and reported in a number of ways before and after 1960. But Lysgaard's theory, more than many others, points to the systems of cognition and behavior as a function of those basic values that are internalized in the actor (employee) often as a result of the internal environment of the company. He points out the fundamental collision between the company and its employees. The decisions based on the technical and economic system are characterized by being unsatisfactory, one-sided and uncompromising. Characteristics of the workers in relation to these decisions will be insufficient, complex and wanting safety, as suggested in Figure 4.1.[18] The Lysgaard theory of the workers' collective is a rather basic theory, and so were the observations made of different values linked to the company and the individual objectives.

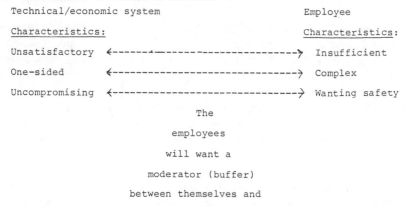

Figure 4.1. Characteristics of the workers in relation to decisions.
(Source: Sverre Lysgaard, *Workers' Collectives* (Oslo: University of Oslo, 1967.)

The experienced manager and shop stewards have openly exchanged views on this conflict of interests during the whole postwar period. The parties in industrial negotiations never had any doubt about the existing collectives within companies and the differences in expressed views, based on one's own group values.

In spite of this cognition, the Norwegian opposing parties seem to have had a fundamental trust, or at least not sufficient evidence for not trusting the other party in finding peaceful solutions to existing problems. During the radical, political period of the 1960s, Norway also had revolutionary tendencies in some groups of employees, but these tendencies were usually viewed as revolutionary, academic influences on workers' unions and other organizations. Some of the strikes in the 1960s and 1970s were led by ex-students who had left the university in order to assist the uneducated workers in their battle for equality. Even in Norway, the climate was such that this assistance was accepted, and a number of companies had severe internal unrest between 1968 and 1975.

The Lysgaard theory and research are products of the distance between academic and company realities. The mapping of the various "contexts of action" for management and workers has, however, brought a gradually deeper understanding of the psychological and sociological realities of working life. In that light, Lysgaard's research has given the most valuable contribution to the industrial relations knowledge level of any research done in Norway.

The other field experiments in the industrial democracy research project have given very mixed results to the body of experience concerning Norwegian industrial relations problems. The autonomous group experiments were terminated in nearly all cases and the companies returned to groups led by managers as soon as the researchers left the company.[19] The focus on the sociotechnical balance in planning and daily work, however, has been strengthened even more in the years after 1964. And the legal situation today is a totally different one as a consequence of this research and its political influence on the Company Acts of the 1970s. In that respect, the industrial democracy research in Norway has been a strong political power factor in the industrial relations movement.[20]

In a lecture to the Norwegian Polytechnical Association on March 3, 1980, Professor Thorsrud talked about "the organizational innovation that did not come, and the one that ought to come." Here he reflects on the ideas of the organizational perspectives in industrial democracy research: away from uniform organization models, away from the highly specialized structures in industry, away from one-man one-role systems, away from closed career systems and away from hierarchical information systems and similar organizational systems in order to obtain meaningful working conditions for workers in industry and other enterprises.[21]

Prior to concluding this section, we will briefly describe the procedures for solving work conflicts in Norway, or the "peace duty" as it is often called. Paragraph 6 in the Norwegian Act on "Work Conflicts" states that a dispute between an employer and a local union shall not be solved by strike, lockout or any other forcible means. The peace duty demands that the parties negotiate, and if they do not reach an agreement locally, the main union and employer's association must try to finalize the dispute. If that does not happen the dispute is forwarded to the Labor Court, or conciliation is used. This implies that a strike or lockout is legal only in connection with tariff adjustments, where conflicts of interest are not solved by negotiation, mediation or during four days after notice of work stoppage is given. After that, the Parliament (Stortinget) may pass a special act to settle the dispute by a compulsory wage board. The parties can also choose to agree on the use of a voluntary wage board.

In reality, nearly all legal conflicts in Norway are settled through negotiations. However, there has been a recent increase in conflict of interests; this year within the civil service, otherwise competing unions went into a united strike after mediation without results. There have been occasional illegal work stoppages in the offshore areas, which seem to give signals of a harder negotiation climate than in the past. Figures 4.2 and 4.3 summarize the procedures used in solving industrial relations conflicts.

1. Negotiation

Notice of termination of the collective
agreements. Exchange of demands. Negotiations are started.

The negotiations are unsuccessful.   The negotiations are successful.
Collective notice of termination.   Proposed new agreement adopted
The State Conciliator is notified.   through balloting, and a new col-
                                            lective agreement is established.

2. Mediation.

Temporary restriction on work stoppage.
The State Conciliator summons the parties.

The mediation is broken off, or the   The mediation proposal is put
mediation proposal is rejected through   forward and is adopted through
balloting. Work stoppage may take   balloting.
place 4 days after the end of mediation
or 4 days after the mediation proposal   A new collective agreement exists.
has been rejected.

The Storting may pass a special act
providing that the dispute shall be
settled by compulsory wage board/
arbitration.

Voluntary wage board/arbitration.

Figure 4.2. Negotiation and mediation.

PRESENT INDUSTRIAL RELATIONS STATUS IN NORWAY

Norwegian companies have benefited from the cultural inheritance and the
tradition of modest and equitable social conditions in industry. In spite of
what radical criticism has stated about the Norwegian industrial situation,
the wage differentiation is roughly a one to three relationship between average
workers and top management wages. This illustrates the distribution of
economic resources in the country as being fairly equal, especially when taking into account the marginal tax of 80 percent on top wages.

A rapid and marked increase in better educated employees—about 50 percent of the population pass a degree equivalent to high school or A-level in
the English educational system—has also resulted in an increase in offers of
higher education for fully employed workers and increased activity in in-
company training. This has also made it possible to recruit managers from
all social levels, which was not the case earlier. The equitable wage situation
and the broader professional/managerial recruitment basis has broken down

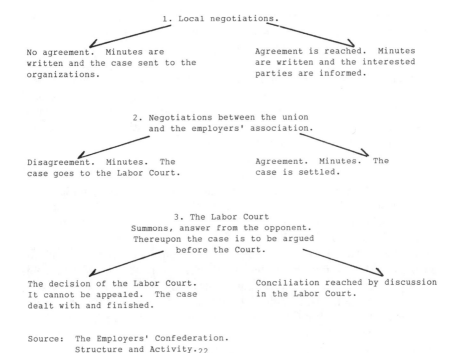

Source: The Employers' Confederation.
          Structure and Activity.22

Figure 4.3. Legal disputes.

many status differences that in previous years made industrial relations synonymous with negotiations about rights and money.

There has been discussion about the difficulties in recruiting managers because of the strain and lack of benefits for managerial actors. Today there is a greater tendency to hear complaints from first line, middle and middle-top managers that they have less influence and information in their jobs than the shop stewards. In other words, the movements for a higher degree of worker democracy and participation has brought symptoms of a pattern of balance in favor of the representative system in industry, and, consequently, in favor of the labor union representatives in relation to the responsible managers and company officials. There are hardly any voices against this in-company development, but the one-sided attention to the previously less privileged groups has in many managers' eyes led to possible understimulation of their role and total situation. This is also a possible problem combined with the pressure for higher efficiency and more claims for managerial responsibility, especially when it comes to productivity, competence, profitability and full employment.

This new balance pattern between the enterprise and employee goals has turned the question of industrial democracy into less of a socio-cultural problem and more into a question of using the human potentials, creativity and cooperation for survival in future. Joynt, in a ten-year comparative study of motivation factors in four countries found that Norwegian managers were the only group of managers who placed the desired motivational factor—good relationships with colleagues—among the top five motivational factors. It is constantly number one, and part of the explanation may be the new balance in favor of representation from the unions.[22]

A research project conducted by the Norwegian Productivity Institute in 1981 and 1982 gives a great deal of information on the activity within the internal company committees installed by law or according to the Basic Agreement between LO and NAF.[23] This research project was a follow-up of a previous project conducted between 1973 and 1975, and was done on behalf of the Federation of Trade Unions (LO) and the Employers' Confederation (NAF) before the revision of the Basic Agreement in 1982. As a frame for the project, the research group studied the organization of the different committees/bodies; the activity and contact between management and workers, formally and informally; organizational development and environmental work; and a general evaluation from both management and the workers' representatives of the importance of the different forms of cooperation and disagreement within the various areas of cooperation.[24]

Within industrial companies more than 90 percent had established company cooperation committees prior to the 1977 act, which demanded the establishment of work-environment committees with equal membership from workers and management. One of three companies combined these bodies after 1977, but three of four companies kept the bodies separate, as both parties found that they supported each other. All the companies with more than 100 employees had established work-environment committees as demanded by the 1977 act.

Even though the Basic Agreement states that department cooperation committees should be established (and not must be established) in addition to company cooperation committees, 73 percent of the industrial companies with more than 500 employees had such committees. About half of the companies reported that they have installed special proposals procedures for employees, and 60 percent of all companies reported the use of workers in time-limited project committees. Every fourth company has established special education and training committees.

In addition, a great number of the companies reported that they have found different ways of having contacts between the parties, from mostly informal contacts to regular meetings each week between management and shop stewards; 29 percent reported daily informal conferences between management and shop stewards. Looking at the activity and contact between management and workers, 86 percent of the companies reported that they had negotiated at least once during the last 12 months, and of these, 56 percent had negotiated more than 10 times, mostly about wages and working hours, but also to a great extent about other problems, which included accounts which have been on the agenda in 86 percent of the companies; work environment and welfare questions, discussed in 70 percent of the companies; recruitment, employment, and training, discussed in about half the companies; and layoffs or reductions of personnel, which have been discussed in 30 percent of the companies.

The decision process in the committees is of interest. To vote on proposals for a decision in vital cases should be a normal event. This does not happen. However, in 84 percent of the companies the decisions are taken on the basis of consensus in the committees.[25]

On the basis of having cooperation committees of different kinds and representation on the boards of directors, there were a series of different, organized activities, such as special organizational projects, quality circles, regular job talks between manager and employee, and invitations to workers or workers' representatives to management meetings. There are positive and negative views among both managers and shop stewards concerning these activities, but informal participation in line management meetings seems to be acceptable, when this does not bind one of the parties to responsibilities outside their normal scope of work or to their function as elected representatives. Kalleberg studied the different phases of the legal obligations as stated in the Work Environment Act of 1977, and found that most of the firms had organized their legal activities properly, and that training as required by the act and other agreements was being done.[26]

The necessary mapping of work conditions as required by the act was done in 45 percent of the companies with 150 or more employees and in less than 20 percent of the companies with fewer than 150 employees. An action program, which is also required by the act, was done in less than 10 percent of all the companies.

This brings us to an interesting dilemma. What do you do with those who break the law, but are in the clear majority? Gustavsen and Hunnius address this issue in addition to making a strong argument for the use of subjective measures in national legislation.[27] The last word has not been said, but it would appear that many organizations are giving the law lip service as far as the organizational development aspects are concerned. There is a great deal of debate in both Sweden and Norway as to whether job satisfaction can be legislated.

Kalleberg, in his conclusions, pointed out that of the companies with problems in the work environment, close to half of them felt it was difficult to find a positive solution to the problem. Twenty-five percent felt they did not have the necessary expertise and an additional 25 percent felt that a solution to the problem would result in a decrease in productivity.[28]

Another aspect of the entire focus here is the centralization of much of the industrial relations system in Norway. The Industrial Democracy in Europe (IDE) report of 1981[29] showed that Norway had one of the most centralized industrial relations systems in Europe. Little was done at the local level and negotiations often resulted in national agreements. As we mentioned earlier, there are signs that Norway is moving away from a centralized model to a decentralized, many-faceted one. There are many who feel that the spirit of cooperation rather than conflict may be lost in this process.

CONCLUSION

Generally speaking, the present industrial relations situation in Norway is very realistic, in the sense that tension is not connected to power or status but rather to competence and existence. Legal innovation was a task of the 1970s, and the basic agreements and the acts are presumably in full accordance with all the actors involved as well as the actual situation in each company. The task at the moment is to make the legal claims and the agreed-upon organizational patterns work in practice. The aim for all seems to be, basically, the ability to compete in a world market and keep the rate of unemployment as low as it is, presently around 5 percent.

We feel that Norway has been fortunate in having the necessary "slack" nationally because of water energy and the "black gold" (oil) from the North Sea. This slack, as well as cooperation, has propelled Norway to the top as far as the Standard of Living Index is concerned. In many respects, a new type of management, of organization development, of planning process, is hinted at in this paper. This is only the beginning, and we feel strongly that much more work should be concentrated in this area.

NOTES

1. T. S. Kuhnle, *Verlferdsstaten* (Oslo: University of Oslo, 1983), p. 25.
2. Ibid., p. 27.
3. "Valg; Norge," *Aftenposten,* October 15, 1934, p. 1.

4. The Work Environment Act, 1977.

5. Norwegian Employers' Confederation (NAF), *Program,* 1985.

6. Norwegian Federation of Trade Unions (LO), *Programme of Action,* May 1981.

7. LO-NAF, *Agreement of 1982.*

8. LO-NAF, *Agreement of 1947.*

9. LO-NAF, *Agreement of 1966.*

10. NAF, *Program,* 1985.

11. E. Thorsrud and F. Emery, *Industrial Democracy,* Cooperation Research Group (Oslo: University of Oslo, 1964), p. 1.

12. Speech by Prime Minister Einar Gerhardsen (Labor Party) on December 9, 1961.

13. S. W. Rostoft, President of the Norwegian Association of Industries, Speech, 1962.

14. Gerhardsen, *op. cit.*

15. Thorsrud and Emery, *op. cit.,* p. 1.

16. Sverre Lysgaard, *Workers' Collective* (Oslo: University of Oslo, 1967).

17. T. Allan, Notes from visit to MIT, by Paul Johnsen, 1971.

18. Lysgaard, *op. cit.*

19. G. Bolweg and P. Moxnes, *Opplaeringsmetoder I,* (Oslo: University of Oslo, 1982).

20. Agreement between the Labour Organization and the Employers Conference, Hovedavtalen, 1982, p. 4.

21. Einar Thorsrud, Lecture, "Bedriftsdemokrati," at Norwegian Polytechnical Association, March 3, 1980.

22. P. Joynt in Patrick Joynt and Malcolm Warner, eds., *Managing in Different Cultures* (Oslo: Universitetsforlaget, 1985).

23. J. Bjornstad, *Bedriftsinternt samarbeid* (Oslo: University of Oslo, 1982).

24. LO/NAF Research project, 1973–1975.

25. Ibid.

26. R. Kalleberg, "Metodei Forskning" in Torodd Bergh, ed., *Deltakerdemokratiet* (Oslo: University of Oslo, 1983).

27. Bjorn Gustavsen and Gerry Hunnius, *New Patterns of Work Reform* (Oslo: Universitetsforlaget, 1981).

28. Kalleberg, *op. cit.*

29. Industrial Democracy in Europe-International Research Group, *Industrial Democracy in Europe* (Oxford: Clarendon Press, 1981).

5

THE MYTH OF FRENCH EXCEPTIONALISM ——

JACQUES ROJOT

Among western European countries, France and its system of industrial relations have often seemed to be a puzzle to observers. As has been pointed out by Frederic Meyers, "Most of the literature in English about French trade unionism and the French system of industrial relations describes it as some sort of abnormality, an exception to most generalizations about trade unionism and industrial relations." Meyers then tries to explain differences and uncover similarities through following the historical development of French industrial relations.[1]

Starting from the same point, we plan to follow a different process. If the French model of industrial relations is indeed an exception, then questions must be raised as to the validity and even the possibility of a theory of industrial relations. A fully developed, totally accepted general theory of industrial relations has not yet been constructed. Many partial theoretical efforts do exist, as well as broad explanatory schemes with a more general scope, including Cox's web of rules, Barbash's collective management of conflict, and Dunlop's system.[2]

If such efforts are of general explanatory value one of two things must be feasible: either they can account for or explain the particularities of the national systems in general, and the French one in particular, or these particularities have been overstated or misunderstood.

Indeed, no industrial relations system in any given country is exactly similar to any other one. That in itself would make it an exception, as Meyers rightly points out.[3] Historical developments, economic factors, the political environment and the prevalent social system uniquely shape each national set of industrial relations. Actually, chance often plays a part in that shaping process as was rightfully pointed out by John Niland, when discussing the role of arbitration in Australian labor relations.[4] Within these specification and national differences the question remains: Can theory explain these differences or, in the specific case of France, have these differences been misunderstood or amplified to such a degree that they make the French situation look like an exception?

It would be fascinating to follow the first approach, and we shall use it sparingly and in a very limited way in the following developments. In our view this constitutes a "second step" of some kind. What we plan to attempt here is to try to demonstrate that the so-called exceptional characteristics of the French system are not really so but, at the most, constitute extreme points on a range of characteristics shared by industrial relations in most western developed countries.

Our analysis will be limited to the region of the world roughly encompassing western Europe and North America. We do not plan to arrive at a general theory of the development of industrial relations as it was attempted by Kerr et al., within the frame of industrialization.[5] Actually our attempt is much more modest than trying to build theory.

Our goal is simply to bring the elements of an answer to the point raised by Meyers: How different is France?[6] We shall draw on some elements from a paper written ten years ago,[7] and add several new issues.

Our method will consist of exploring, one after another, the various aspects of French industrial relations generally advocated as making France a different case, and then examining the extent to which such aspects are really different, or the reason why they can be expected to be different within generally held assumptions in industrial relations theory.

A common source of error may be found in the use of a sometimes difficult tool, the comparative method. French industrial relations were often singled out as different on the basis of country-by-country comparisons. The limited usefulness of such comparisons was early pointed out by Dunlop who advocated studies limited to given industries from country to country. He proceeded to such analysis across seven countries in the bituminous coal and construction industries.[8] Walker, Shalev and others concurred and a limited number of very interesting studies following such a method were produced.[9] Since then, the largest bulk of comparative analysis had been carried on primarily on a country-by-country basis.[10] This presents several problems, including the risk that a writer can be so familiar with his own national subject that he really cannot convey an understandable content to the reader because too many hidden assumptions exist that are supposed to be known or shared by all. There is the risk of using words that are apparently the same but have different meanings in different countries (e.g., works councils and arbitration); and there is a risk of describing legal institutions devoid of actual live content, for instance mediation and conciliation in France. In the absence of truly comparative studies as defined by Meyers,[11] which would involve France, this factor may go a long way in explaining why industrial relations in France are considered to be different.

Within this framework we shall proceed, first, with one of the factors most commonly held as an exceptional characteristic of French industrial relations, the low rate of organization. At present the rate of organization is estimated to be around 15 to 20 percent, down from the 20 to 25 percent of some ten years ago. Two issues must be separated here; first, the fact that the rate of unionization is decreasing, and second, whether unionization is lower in France than in most western industrialized countries.

The fact that the rate of unionization is decreasing hardly makes France an exception and need not be discussed here, whatever its intrinsic interest. It is a fact, however, that the rate of unionization has always been low. F. Sellier, on the basis of elaborate calculations, has reached the conclusion that a rate of 20 to 25 percent constituted a constant of French trade unionism.[12] It is true that unionism is lower than in countries such as Belgium or the Scandinavian nations but it is also true that it is not of a much different order of magnitude than countries such as the United States (30 percent), West Germany (35 percent), and the Netherlands (32 percent). Union membership does not constitute an exception but can be explained with one of the elements of industrial relations theory: The reasons for joining unions has been widely explored and need not be reopened here.[13] What is important to remember is that we find different types of attitudes among union members towards joining unions and different reasons for an individual to actually join a union. On a worksite different groups can be carved out of the population of employees. These groups include leaders, local union officers and shop stewards; militants who are those taking active part in union work such as propaganda and attending meetings without being in formal leadership positions; sympathizers who have a favorable point of view of the union but stop short of taking active steps towards organizing a union shop, or of being involved in union activities within a union shop;[14] followers who would enjoy union benefits such as job security and high wages, but would rather not pay union dues; and finally, individuals neutral or hostile to the union.

The same group categories can be found in the United States, France, and Italy—even if not always strictly comparable—as one might have guessed. Therefore, starting from plant level this allows for another way of looking at rates of unionization. We can define two extremes of the range. In a union shop at a given worksite in the United States, United Kingdom and Denmark, the rate of unionization across the bargaining unit would be 100 percent including everybody, even the workers neutral or hostile towards the union. At the opposite end is a situation in France where all factors playing against organization are present. Here the union members would include only the leaders and the most militant activists who, by French law, could not be prevented from representing a union on the shop floor. On the other hand, in the United States or Canada there would be no union at all because of the "all-or-nothing" rules.

What, now, are the factors that can play against unionization, or conversely in favor of it? Clearly, prominent among them and underlying our preceding remark is the legal system. U.S. labor law provides for carving out a bargaining unit and then granting, mostly through election, exclusive jurisdiction to a given union. This provides for an "all-or-nothing" system. The U.K. system also allows for the legal possibility for a given company or plant to remain nonunion. Conversely, in most European continental countries labor law provides for a different system: The union(s) cannot be legally prevented by the employer from setting foot on the shop floor. Once established, however, it is up to the union to gather members; it is not protected from the efforts of competing unions and not given exclusive jurisdiction, and often no union security provisions exist (with the exception, in cases such as Denmark or the United Kingdom, and in fact in certain sectors of industry in other countries, the law notwithstanding, custom establishes an equivalent system). Therefore, they cannot be prevented from existing, but have no guaranteed membership. In some countries only one dominant union exists for a given category of employees, as in West Germany and the Scandinavian countries.

However, the influence of the legal system should not be overestimated. With totally opposite kinds of labor laws in respect to union security, exclusive jurisdiction, union presence on the shop floor and bargaining units, the United States and France present rates of organization hovering around the same figure, 18.5 percent.

Many other factors must be taken into account, such as the actual influence of antidiscrimination laws, benefits linked with union membership (such as joining a union-run social security system as is the case in Belgium), costs of joining (union dues paid by the employer in Belgium) or nonmonetary terms (career prospects for union members may be more or less blocked, as may be the case in the public sector in some countries), benefits reserved to union members and not applying to nonmembers (such as the coverage by collective agreements).

Membership can be expected to be low when joining a union means only the obligation to pay dues because benefits are by law available to all, whether members or not. A history of bitter opposition by employers is another disincentive. Conversely, in a country where joining a union involved gaining some benefits granted only to union members, such as education and social security, where union dues are paid by the employer and with a tradition of limited by actual cooperation between management and unions, the rate of organization can be expected to be high.

We did touch upon another factor commonly considered to differentiate French industrial relations from the main trend, and put it in a category with Italy sometimes—more recently—with Spain and Portugal. This has been expressed as the excessive politicization of unions or the absence of business unionism.

On the first level it has often been postulated that French and Italian industrial relations are of a conflictual nature as opposed to the more consensual or cooperative nature of other countries in the western world. But a basic element of industrial relations theory generally implies that industrial relations are conflictual, or power-centered by their nature. The mechanism of and the unavoidability of it have been postulated and demonstrated, the most recently in a coherent and systematic manner.[15] Those two positions can be usefully combined in one view in such a way that French (and Italian) industrial relations fall within the general range of possible industrial relations models, in positions that certainly are specific, but no more so than the U.S position, for instance.

Our notion of conflict is not deterministic. It is, therefore, not Marxism's predefined and unavoidable class conflict that renders industrial relations and organizational behavior conflicts useless. We do not subscribe in any way to a deterministic theory of history, nor do we offer or subscribe to any general theory of society.

The conflict we refer to here is the basic conflict in an industrial society between those who plan and those who execute, those who prepare and arrive at decisions and those who carry them out. This basic conflict is, by the way, independent of the ownership of the means of production. Rather than taking place between employers and workers, it is better defined as taking place between management (in a very restrictive sense) and employees (in a very extensive sense). Rather than being a conflict centered on the ownership of the means of production it is a conflict centered on the allocation of the resources from production, on the allocation of power to influence it and on the logic—economic versus social—of the actors.

First, this conflict is of a permanent nature and inherent to industrial society. It is a conflict of a limited nature. This conflict cannot be suppressed but

it can be managed and channelized through the processes of industrial relations including, but not limited to, collective bargaining. Second, the conflict
is not of an absolute nature. None of the actors want the total disappearance
of the others. Employees need management and management needs the
employees. This is the case regardless of how much they disagree on the allocation of resources, the decisions to be taken or their reciprocal influence.

One could wish for the disappearance of the private owner of the means
of production, for instance, but one must agree that there should be a given
mode of running large productive organizations whether the goal toward which
they are aimed are agreed to or not, and whether the acceptability of the mode
of running them is shared or not—even if this creates built-in resentment.
It has to be done.

Therefore, it is conflict, but limited conflict. We can borrow the concepts
of precarious partnership or incomplete antagonism from Schelling.[16] When
earlier discussing Dunlop's concept of the ideology of the system, the binding element of the system, by such a concept of precarious partnership that
allows at the same time for the nature of industrial relations as "power relations" and the necessary acceptance of each other by the actors.[17]

There is no more a fully cooperative system of industrial relations than
there is a totally conflictual one. However, the mixture of conflict and cooperation varies inside each model of precarious partnership. This is the case at
the national level but also at the regional, industry, or even company and
plant level where, within one given national framework, enormous differences
and discrepancies coexist.

What tilts each model towards a more cooperative or conflictual attitude—
that is, in operational terms, towards a position more or less favorable to the
institutionalized means of solving or managing the basic conflict—is the
reciprocal ideologies of the parties. We are no longer discussing here the
ideology of the "system" but the perceptions held by each actor, which determine the attitude of one actor towards another. Clearly this sort of ideology
varies case by case, as influenced by such things as history, customs, and social
patterns.

Ideology also varies in time and according to circumstances and is not set
and fixed once and for all in all cases. For instance, the peaceful and "codeter-
mining" German labor movement has recently led a bitter strike for the
35-hour week in the metalworking industry. The "Swedish model" did not
prevent Swedish employers from demonstrating in the streets against wage
funds. Conversely, the "radical" French unions cooperated to quell the distur-
bances of May 1968.

The employers' ideologies should not be forgotten. They can be outlined around three axes. First, is the attitude regarding the right of the union to exist at all; in other words, the legitimacy of the other party. The gamut here ranges from the view that unions are a useful tool of a democratic society to the view that they should be outlawed because they are willing agents of a foreign power bent on destroying the natural way of life. It is interesting to remark at this point that the more extreme attitudes on this point are not held by European employers or by French employers but by U.S. employers. Very few French employers, if any, would publicly take a position against the existence of unions and question their right to exist as spokesmen of labor. Many U.S. employers make no secret of this position on ideological rather than practical grounds.

The second axis relates to the right of the union to be represented in the workplace. Here again there is a range of attitudes. For instance, from 1945 to 1968 the official doctrine of French employers was that unions were perfectly acceptable, outside of the plant, at industry or national level, but not on the shop floor. The third axis is, within the former two, what should be the rights and privileges of the union on the shop floor against what should be managerial rights. Whatever the opinion existing on the other two axes, it is at the third that conflict is unavoidable.

The unions' ideology can also be described along several axes. At the core is the point that all labor movements in western developed societies share the same origin: They were all born out of the industrial revolution as protest movements against the fate that industrialization had reserved for them. Whatever the country, the prevalent ideology or the speed of economic development, unions were born, grew and prospered as organizations against a state of things, reacting and demanding. Since then, all labor movements share a common basis that is the foremost reason for their existence and is still best expressed in the classic words, "more, more now!" Conflict with management over the allocation of scarce resources from production is unavoidable.

Beyond that common basis, differences exist among labor movements on the other axes. First, regarding the rules according to which "more" is or is not allocated towards labor, all labor movements have used and do use economic and political means of action including the strike or threat to strike and the lobbying and pressure for legislation favorable to employees.

Second, labor movements differ according to the value they give to the rules—these rules being the laws and customs according to which industrial relations are played. All labor movements want to win "more" according to these rules. At one extreme of the range are the labor movements for which the set of rules requires a minimum degree of consensus, for instance, proceeding through the court system of the legislative system only. At the other extreme are the labor movements for which the existing rules have no intrinsic value whatsoever,[18] no more than the process through which they are changed. Only the results count and the present rules are nothing more than the fledgling result of a balance of power, always subject to change and to influence by whatever means.

The third axis is the long-held view of society by the unions. A labor organization cannot reduce its activities to try to achieve only "more, more and more now" for its members. Although successful in the short term this would be self-defeating in the long term. Therefore, unions have a model— implicit or explicit—of a social design favorable or acceptable to their members as well as long-term policies to achieve this objective. This long-term objective and the means to reach it can be more or less compatible with the views held by management and society in general. Here also there is a range of possible attitudes. In this instance the U.S. labor movement is more the exception than the rule. As Meyers points out, all western European movements have been and theoretically remain anticapitalist.[19] The belief in the capitalist ethic makes the U.S. labor movement a special case, different from any western European labor movement.

All European labor movements, including the French, can be understood in terms of these three axes, which seem to represent a more operational concept than the fruitless opposition between "business" and "revolutionary" unions. There are no longer any really revolutionary unions, at least in western developed economies. No French union, for instance, advocates an overthrow by force of the prevalent capitalist economic system. The unions, however, differ in degrees of radicalism, which may be a more useful concept than revolution. That is, they differ in the value that they grant to the existing rules of industrial relations, the prevalent processes by which they function and their long-term objectives.

A revolutionary union is to some extent a contradictory proposition. In its principal purpose—improving wages and working conditions of the workers—the union by its own action tends to lessen the need to overthrow the existing political and economic system. At the same time, it improves the working of the system. But if a union is truly revolutionary it has for its primary goal the overthrow of the system. A truly revolutionary union, therefore, should not strive to improve the lot of its members. But in this case it would have few members outside political activists. To be efficient in whatever goal it pursues a union needs to be powerful, to have members or followers in large numbers. In order to reach that goal it must improve the condition of the workers, outside and in addition to the goals of a few political activists. Therefore, in being successful a labor movement cannot be truly revolutionary; and in order to be efficient it needs to be successful. The revolutionary union is thus in a quandary. This was illustrated by the position briefly held and then abandoned in the late nineteenth century of the anarcho-syndicalist trend in French labor, which opposed collective bargaining and statutory labor laws improving hours and conditions for they were against the true long-term interest of the working class. Marx and Lenin[20] both underlined the natural "trade unionist" trend in the labor movements which renders short-term gains illusory and risks losing sight of the true way to freedom for the working class.

The French labor movement is said to be political or politicized more than any other existing labor movement. Here, again, a clarification of concepts is needed and, again, we can place the French model of industrial relations inside a framework able to accommodate other national industrial relations models. Actually, we could make a good case for the French unions being considered as much less political than the other western European labor movements. Clearly the French unions have no institutional links with political parties whereas in the United Kingdom or in Sweden, for instance, such institutional ties exist between the Trades Union Congress and the Labour Party, on the one hand, and between the LO (Swedish Confederation of Labor) and the Social Democratic Party, on the other hand. A member of the union can be an automatic contributor to the political party or even become a member of the party through the political affiliation of the union section. The French unions' lack of any institutional relationship between union and party goes beyond what some would call window-dressing, given that links of another nature (personal, for instance) do exist. Actually, there is a deep defiance of French unions towards political parties rooted in history and illustrated in the famous Charter of Amiens of 1906 when the labor movement asserted its independence from all political parties.

We must go beyond the level of the paradox. One can safely say that no union is or can be nonpoliticized or nonpolitical. A union claiming to be apolitical merely says that it has a political stand different from others.

The explanation rests with the definition of political. In a first definition, the fact that a union is political may mean that its action has results with a political impact. Here by definition all unions are indeed political. All union action is political action in the sense that it has an impact on the essential elements of society: Strikes, agreements, organization have an effect on the organs of the state. For instance, when a union pursues a given wage policy, be it in favor of low wages, wage solidarity or exacting maximum employers' ability to pay, it automatically takes a political stand, for the results will affect the wage and income distribution in society.

In a second definition, political may be understood no longer at the level of results but as a means, that is, as a type of action necessary to reach certain results. It is the choice between economic and political means of action, between trying to obtain results through negotiating and the pressure of the strike or through statutory law. At different times in their history union movements have favored one or the other. There is no example of a union that does not use political means of action such as lobbying parliament and government or pressure upon political parties to obtain results such as statutes favorable to labor's interests. These results may affect different shares, including benefits for employees such as social security, minimum wage laws or statutes favorable to union action and to the union as an organization per se (for example, tax exempt status, recognition provisions and security provisions). A union represents a potentially powerful source of support and votes for a party. Currently, no union leadership anywhere neglects to use this form of action. It has certainly been a primary tool for the French labor movement. The U.S. labor movement also "rewards its friends and punishes its enemies" at poll time and wields a powerful influence through its Committee on Political Education (COPE).

At a third level, we should consider the links between unions and political parties. We have already pointed out that the French labor movement has no institutional link with any political party, contrary to what takes place in other countries. Many more institutional links do exist, however, between the various union centers and various political parties. They may be of a personal nature, as when the same individuals sit on the executive of both organizations, or of an ideological nature, as when union and party support the same or related aims. The U.S. labor movement falls into this same category. Although theoretically independent of any political party, as the French union centers are, the movement often has noninstitutional links with the Democratic Party, with which it shares more goals than with the Republican Party.

It is probably at a fourth level that the politicization of the French unions can be considered different. It is true that France (since 1921), Italy, Spain and Portugal have strong noninstitutional links to the Communist Party.

That is probably the only characteristic that presently sets the French labor movements apart from the northern European labor movements. It is not its links with political parties, which is the rule in western Europe. It is not the fact that those political parties are parties to the left; in other western

European countries this link exists between socialist or social democratic parties and unions. But it is the fact that the link exists with a Marxist party of a more radical anticapitalist ideology than other parties of the left. Here we probably can agree with many authors in the fact that it is a result of history.[21] Most of the leaders and militants of the French labor movement have shared a radical, antigovernment, antiemployer militant impulse. Historically this sentiment was expressed through an indigenous form of anarcho-syndicalism. After World War II it was expressed through adherence to a communist ideology.[22]

There are, however, new, marked changes. The French Communist Party did not liberalize but, on the contrary, stepped back into a strategy of hard core doctrine. Its influence, nonetheless, was steadily decreasing everywhere in the late 1970s and 1980s in terms of votes. The French Communist Party has passed from over 20 percent to less than 10 percent of the vote in political elections.

In France, like in many other countries including the United States, the percentage of unionization has decreased severely overall. Deep changes have been taking place in the French labor movement. These include a relative decrease in the influence of the CGT (General Confederation of Labor), the union center linked to the Communist Party, but growth and stability in the influence of the other centers, among which the CFDT (French Democratic Federation of Labor) shifted in 1978 from its movement towards the left to a reunionization strategy. Figures illustrate that trend.[23] It should be noted that they are influence figures taking place in an overall context of reduced membership.

Another point on which French industrial relations has often been held different is the role played by collective bargaining. Although it existed illegally, it came to play an important role only after the popular front government of 1936. A similar case could be made, however, for the influence of the 1935 Wagner Act on collective bargaining in the United States.

Unlike the United States, though, collective bargaining in France has for a long time only been related to industrywide bargaining. This is not an exception in western Europe where this is also the case, for instance, in West Germany and the Netherlands. A brief move towards plant-level collective bargaining appeared in the early 1970s facilitated by a change in the labor law. But by the late 1970s plant bargaining had slowed down; an employer spokesman might have compared this type of agreement to the extinction of prehistoric animals. For a limited number of cases plant- or company-level agreements played a promising and exemplary role. For instance, the Renault agreement initiated the fourth and subsequently the fifth week of paid vacation.

Since the late 1940s French industrial relations fostered a sui generis system of economywide bargaining outside of, and even against the existing legal framework. Union centers and employers' associations negotiated agreements on retirement pay, dismissal and continuing education. In this way categories of nonindustrial employees were covered who would otherwise not have been, under a simple extension by decree. Conversely, the government could have proposed a statute to the Parliament that would enact a set of principles and an invitation to employers' associations and union centers to negotiate further the practical application of the principles.

It is a fact, however, that plant and company bargaining and union power at the shop level remained underdeveloped in comparison to several western European countries. But an act of the government of the left, brought to power in 1981, created in 1983 a new duty to bargain both at plant and industry level. At plant level this duty is yearly and the negotiations must bear upon actual wages and working conditions. It is only a duty to bargain and no sanctions or definitions, for that matter, have been provided by the law. This followed a finding in a government report that about three million wage earners were not covered by any collective agreement, although they were protected by a minimum floor of statutory protective labor law, discussed elsewhere.[24]

French industrial relations lacks laws pertaining to settlement of interest disputes, the role of works councils, adjudication of rights disputes by labor courts and reinstatement for wrongfully dismissed employees. But these lacks did not seem to us to be enough of an "exceptional" nature to warrant discussion. Similar shortcomings are to be found, albeit probably not together, in several other western developed countries, giving witness to our premise that all national industrial relations models are, in a sense, unique.

NOTES

1. Frederic Meyers, "France," in Albert A. Blum, ed., *International Handbook of Industrial Relations, Contemporary Developments and Research* (London: Aldwyck Press, 1977), p. 170.

2. Robert W. Cox, "Approach to a Futurology of Industrial Relations," *Bulletin of the International Institute of Labor Studies,* No. 8, 1971, pp. 139–169; Jack Barbash, *The Elements of Industrial Relations* (Madison: University of Wisconsin Press, 1984); John T. Dunlop, *Industrial Relations Systems* (Carbondale: Southern Illinois University, 1958).

3. Meyers, op. cit., p. 170.

4. "Industrial Relations in Australia," Address to the San Francisco Industrial Relations Research Association, March, 1986.

5. Clark Kerr, John Dunlop, Fred Harbison and Charles Meyers, *Industrialism and Industrial Man* (Cambridge: Harvard University Press, 1960); and Clark Kerr, John Dunlop, Fred Har-

bison and Charles Myers, "Postscript to Industrialism and Industrial Man," *International Labor Review*, 1971; also Clark Kerr, John Dunlop, Fred Harbison and Charles Myers, *Industrialism and Industrial Man Reconsidered* (Princeton: Princeton University Press, 1975).

6. Meyers, op. cit., p. 202.

7. Jacques Rojot, "Syndicats Français et théorie de Relations Industrielles," *Revue Française de gestion*, Paris, Sept.–Oct. 1977.

8. Kenneth F. Walker, "The Comparative Study of Industrial Relations," *Bulletin of the IILS*, No. 3, Nov. 1967.

9. See the following: Michael Shalev, "Industrial Relations Theory and the Comparative Study of Industrial Relations and Industrial Conflict," Paper presented at the *5th Congress of the International Industrial Relations Association*, Paris, Sept. 3–7, 1979; Clark Kerr and Abraham Siegel, "The Inter-Industry Propensity to Strike, An International Comparison" in Arthur Kornhauser, Robert Dubin and Arthur Rose, eds., *Industrial Conflict* (New York: McGraw-Hill, 1954); Everett Kassalow, "The International Labor Field," *Bulletin of the International Institute of Labour Studies*, No. 5, Nov. 1968, and Everett Kassalow, *Industrial Relations, An International Comparison* (New York: Random House, 1968).

10. A remarkable exception, but with a markedly legal accent, are the comparative studies published in the University of Leuven's *Comparative Industrial Relations Bulletin*.

11. Frederic Meyers, "The Study of Foreign Labor and Industrial Relations" in Solomon Barkin, William Dymond, Everett Kassalow, Frederic Meyers and Charles Meyers, eds., *Comparative Industrial Relations* (Madison: IRRA, 1967).

12. François Sellier, *Communication to the 4th Congress of the International Industrial Relations Association*, Geneva, Sept. 6–9, 1976.

13. See for instance, Neil Chamberlain, Donald I. Cullen and David Lewin, *The Labor Sector* (New York: McGraw-Hill, 1980), pp. 123ff.; Thomas A. Kochan, *Collective Bargaining and Industrial Relations* (Homewood: Irwin, 1980).

14. In a survey of the United States the number of people who would vote for a union was found to be 30 percent.

15. Barbash, *Elements of Industrial Relations*, p. 130.

16. Thomas C. Schelling, *The Strategy of Conflict* (Oxford: Oxford University Press, 1970).

17. Jacques Rojot, *International Collective Bargaining: An Analysis and Case Study for Europe* (Deventer: Kluwer, 1978), Chapter 1.

18. The idea is developed from remarks by J. D. Reynaud in an unpublished paper, 1973.

19. Meyers, "France," p. 203.

20. Karl Marx, *Wages, Prices and Profit* (1891 reprint, Peking: Foreign Language Press, 1975), p. 78; V. I. Lenin, *What Is to Be Done* (1902 reprint Peking: Foreign Language Press, 1975), pp. 137ff.

21. See for instance Meyers, "France," pp. 172–173.

22. Ibid., pp. 194–195.

23. INSEE adapted in Michel Despax and Jacques Rojot, *France*, Vol. 3., Roger Blanpain, ed., *International Encyclopedia of Industrial Relations and Labor Law*, 2nd ed. forthcoming.

24. Ibid.

II

GENERAL THEORIES AND CONCEPTS IN COMPARATIVE INDUSTRIAL RELATIONS

6

INDUSTRIAL RELATIONS: A FIELD AND A DISCIPLINE

JEAN BOIVIN

Industrial relations may be considered either empirically or analytically. The empirical method examines a series of phenomena that is associated with the practice or the art of industrial relations, while the analytical method implies a systematic organization of the knowledge related to these phenomena, which eventually leads to the "discipline" of industrial relations.

THE PRACTICE OF INDUSTRIAL RELATIONS

Empirical Definition

In practice, industrial relations can be defined as the "management of labor problems in an industrial society."[1] The modern industrial context comprises the following factors.

1. a given technology;
2. important investments in human and material capital;
3. cost discipline, that is the technique or method used for economizing on the costs of resources in order to achieve an acceptable return on investment;
4. a disciplined labor force, that is men and women at work who by education, training and culture are responsive to efficiency techniques;
5. organization, meaning structured associations of people and the attendant rules to administer the technology, investments and labor force;
6. a good dose of economic uncertainty; and
7. the presence of the state, which plays a regulatory and interventionist role.

The management of labor problems implies the development of theories, techniques and institutions for the resolution of conflicts arising from work relations. These conflicts are normal, not pathological, in an industrial society. They arise out of the permanent interaction of management efficiency, work security and public policy. Industrial relations, therefore, may be viewed as a series of interactions or processes taking place in every organization, and generally within society, as shown in Figure 6.1.

The constituent elements, which will require more specific explanation are: (1) cost discipline; (2) the work society; (3) bargaining, which is the result of the interaction between (1) and (2); and (4) state regulation and intervention.

Cost Discipline

Cost discipline is the systematic organization of basic decisions related to the operation of the enterprise (planning, management, control) according to some standard of profitability or its equivalent.

When limited to the labor sector, cost discipline includes (a) the professionalization and specialization of vital functions such as labor market administration, work performance, collective bargaining, and morale-building; and (b) the development of controls needed to keep the labor sector in line with the broad economic guidelines of the enterprise.

Work Society

Work society protectivism is the natural response of the worker to cost discipline and the resulting tensions of (a) subordination, (b) competitiveness, (c) monotony and drudgery, (d) exploitation and (e) economic instability. The acronym PEEP (price, effort, equity, power) describes well the special interests that the work society seeks to advance. Indeed, what the work society wants is to lessen as much as possible the efforts required of its members.

The union is a special kind of work society that is more formal and broader in scope. Its goal is to be an effective bargaining agent and as such it undertakes such activities as the recruitment of new members, bargaining and strike action. Worker proneness to unionism depends upon the following factors: (a) individual bargaining power, (b) the threat that cost discipline presents to a worker, (c) the work group's ability to mount a collective response, (d) the employer's ability to counter that response, (e) the various ways in which society and the economic milieu favor or discourage cost discipline and the creation of work societies, and (f) the personal characteristics of the workers.

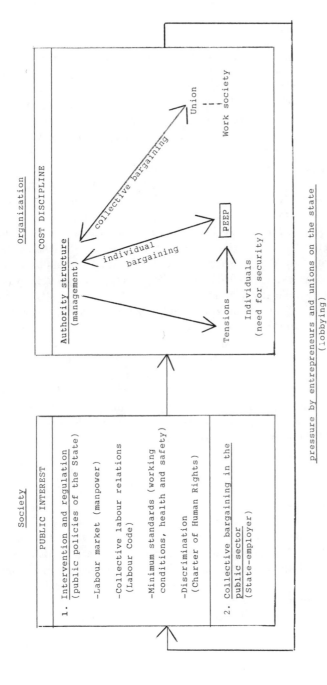

Figure 6.1. Practical dynamics of industrial relations.

Bargaining

Bargaining is the method generally used by management, the work society and the union to resolve conflicting interests. Each party goes to the bargaining table because it needs something that the other party can give it. Management needs the efficient labor of its employees, and the work society and the union both want an acceptable level of PEEP in return for efficient labor. Generally, it is the prospect of losing what each side needs from the other that brings them to bargaining.

Bargaining is a relationship involving both cooperation and conflicts. The parties have a common interest in maximizing their total revenues, but they differ in how these revenues should be divided into wages and profits.

Nonunion groups can often bargain as effectively as union groups. Although the work society may not possess the formal aspect of a union, it can limit production through absenteeism, tardiness, indiscipline or again, by the most powerful sanction of all, leaving the job. When workers organize as a union and refuse to work, it is called a strike. The strike, latent or real, is now the foundation of collective bargaining.

The parties bargain not only with each other, but internally as well. These parties are not monolithic. Opposing internal interests exist within each party and these must be resolved in order to present a unified front to the other party.

In union-management collective bargaining, the efficiency-security tension is partly resolved by a collective agreement. In North America, such agreements have a fixed term of usually two to three years. Furthermore, acceptance of the agreement by the management means that the union agrees not to strike during the period of the agreement. The agreement or contract contains the rights of the employees and the union and represents the level of the work society's PEEP.

Role of the State

The state plays two roles in industrial relations, first as a representative of the public and second as an employer (see Figure 6.1). Its areas of intervention are (1) the labor market (e.g., full employment, occupational training and placement offices); (2) minimum standards for working conditions (wages, working hours) and occupational health and safety; (3) labor relations (e.g., regulation of collective bargaining—the labor code); and (4) human rights.[2]

INDUSTRIAL RELATIONS AS A DISCIPLINE

Several authors are of the opinion that industrial relations cannot be inter-preted by a strict analytical system. Neil Chamberlain, for example, states that

> The boundaries of industrial relations are obscure and the reasons for drawing them not easily rationalized. The field sprawls and the territory . . . takes in a polyglot lot of inhabitants with diffuse and often separate interests . . . all the way from people with very real and operational prob-lems of a how-to-do-it nature . . . to people whose interests are global in scope and abstract in focus.

For George Shultz, "Industrial relations is problem-based. It is not a disci-pline in itself, but rather draws on many disciplines for theory and technique to understand and help solve the problems arising in the work place, the labor market and at the bargaining table."[3]

Despite all these dark opinions on the possibilities of industrial relations, there are two reasons for the development of a more generalized foundation. The first is that industrial relations is an active field of study dealing with many of the critical problems of our society. An attempt should be made to develop analytical methods for studying these problems, which permit both practitioners and scholars to have common reference points in order to see their work as part of some larger whole. At this stage of its scientific develop-ment, the very limited theoretical pretensions may even have some scientific value; they can keep the level of generalization close enough to reality to enable practitioners and scholars to see some connection between them. The second reason is that no other field adequately covers the territory.

The Object of Industrial Relations

Despite the fact that this undefined field appears to encroach upon other disciplines such as sociology, psychology, economics, law and even history, it is, nevertheless, the only one to deal with both the economic and the social, and the individual and collective relations existing between the various pro-duction agents within the plant, the enterprise, the industry and the entire economy.

Wherever work is done in market or state-run economies, in industrial, or in developing countries, such relations take place at different hierarchical levels. As mentioned in the previous section, the need for efficiency and work pro-tectivism makes these relationships inevitably conflictual. The notion of "relations," or again what people label as "exchanges," is the real pole around which the study of industrial relations turns.[4]

Relations can be those maintained by various organized groups, or can be the individual and informal relations within organizations. They can also be those between the different regulatory agents in the market place or the economy, if they have an impact upon the work being done in organizations.

The Special Interdisciplinary Approach of Industrial Relations

Since industrial relations can be studied from the angle of many different disciplines, does this mean that the study is just the juxtaposing of those aspects of these disciplines that relate to work? We do not think this is the case and therefore agree with Dimitri Weiss who states that "industrial relations is more an interdisciplinary field that is situated at the *crossroads* of several disciplines, and is not a merger of several disciplines."[5]

Only a unified interdisciplinary approach will enable us to understand a field that includes such different subjects as collective bargaining, collective agreement administration and grievance settlement, wage determination, fringe benefits, employer and union organizations, manpower, human resource management, minimum working standards, industrial health and safety, the quality of working life, state labor policy and industrial conflict.

Although the field of industrial relations overlaps a certain number of pre-existing disciplines, it is distinct from those it overlaps and is, therefore, studied as a separate discipline. Thus, we can consider industrial relations not as a basic science, but as a derived field of knowledge, where elements borrowed from many disciplines (economics, sociology, law, psychology, labor history, political science and administration) are used to study a particular series of work-related problems.

Persons who receive an industrial relations education should be able to grasp the numerous implications of a work situation. Whereas the specialists in law, economics, psychology or even administration tend to favor the object of their particular field of study, industrial relations practitioners must be able to grasp all the many implications of the problem at once. For this reason a minimum knowledge of the basic principles of law, sociology, psychology, economics and administration are required.

Now that we are in a position to give the industrial relations field a narrower definition, Gerard Dion's definition becomes particularly useful. The field of industrial relations is

> a coherent body of knowledge with links to different disciplines (sociology, economics, law, psychology and the history of work, political

science, administration), which enable a person to understand, explain, plan and organize economic and social relations, whether individual or collective, formal or informal, structured or not and which arise or are formed within the enterprise, the firm, the sector, or in the economy as a whole, between workers, employers, their representative organizations, and the state, and related to their situation, needs, and rights, and the goals sought for the production of goods and services.[6]

The Two Basic Processes of Industrial Relations: Human Resource Management and Labor Relations

The above definition is extremely general and refers to a series of phenomena that are observable. One way of making it more operational is to look at the two basic components of industrial relations: human resource management and the determination of working conditions, generally called "labor relations." These components refer to the key elements at the origins of industrial relations in all industrialized or developing countries, which include cost discipline and the work society that develops in reaction to the tensions created by the need for management efficiency.

Human Resource Management

Human resource management comprises all the means, activities and programs advanced by organizations to acquire, maintain, develop, deploy and use in an efficient way, the persons doing or susceptible of doing productive work.

It is not the creation of capitalist enterprise, as all organizations, whether socialist, cooperative, union, public, parapublic or private, need to efficiently manage their human resources. Moreover, human resource management involves all the persons in a given organization, both staff and workers.

Human resource management also exists at the societal level and can be found generally in public policies for the labor market. When an efficient administration and distribution of human resources is lacking, several economic and social objectives become seriously compromised. Basically, a free-enterprise system contains many obstacles that may impede or hinder the socio-economic development of society and its individual members. It is then up to the state to intervene in order to correct and prevent imbalances. Its major tool is often manpower policy.

Certainly the principle of efficiency does not call for the same methods, nor does it have the same consequences when applied to a specific organization or to a society in general. In the first instance, only two agents—managers and workers—are involved, while in the second, a third agent—the state—is involved.

If industrial relations is studied using the principle of efficiency, the focus is on human resource management. From this point of view industrial conflict is always present, but the approach used seeks to defuse conflict so that the organization (or society) can reach its objectives.

Labor Relations

The second basic component of industrial relations is the establishment of working conditions in organizations. This is labeled labor relations and deals with all the phenomena and activities involved in drawing up the rules for work, which are of two types: the substantive rules to determine the conditions for carrying out work (wage scales, standard daily or weekly hours, fringe benefits, etc.), and the rules to determine the procedures to be used for amending or enforcing the substantive rules.[7]

According to Clegg, there are six ways of determining the rules for work. Although collective bargaining is the one most often studied and most widely known, it remains only one of these ways. Other ways to determine rules for work are (1) unilaterally by the employer, a common procedure when there is no union; (2) unilaterally by the union, a method not widespread in North America, which is found most often in Great Britain; (3) legally by the legislature, as in the development of minimum standards; (4) through customs and practices in force in organizations; and (5) through consultation, as is the case in the public sector in the United States, where several employers (municipalities, school boards, etc.) are obliged by law to meet and confer with representatives of their employees. This latter method is midway between collective bargaining and unilateral determination by the employer.

When labor relations is considered as a rule-making process, the reference is to a complex series of agreements involving all the customs, practices and rules that the parties accept as a *modus vivendi*, and that the legislator either tolerates or enforces. Such agreements or contracts can be concluded between two individuals, termed individual labor relations, or can be managed, negotiated and dispensed by the representatives of the workers, in which case the term is collective labor relations.

A Problem of Semantics

Labor relations encompasses many elements found in human resource management. It goes without saying that all organizations must have rules on how work is to be done, whether the employees are unionized or not. It is in this sense that we speak of labor relations as being part of human resource management. Once the employees are unionized, the method used to establish working conditions, such as the collective bargaining process, is much more visible and is a very important part of the life of the enterprise.

Human resource management and labor relations differ in that each is initiated by one of the two opposing needs at the center of industrial relations: the need for management efficiency or the need for work society protectivism.

The important concerns of labor relations are the phenomena used to create Barbash's PEEP, which is the determination of the *price* (wages and working conditions) that the organization must pay to compensate the physical and mental *effort* of the members of the work society who want to be treated with *equity* and who will not hesitate to use their *power* to be better protected. This is the reason reference is often made to the conflicting dynamics of labor relations. When the members of the work society decide to use their power, they are interacting with management, whose actions are going to be dictated by management efficiency.

The concepts underlying PEEP cover a vast territory, as they apply not only to union enterprises but also to nonunion enterprises, where working conditions are left to management. There are also more or less formal work societies found even at senior levels (an example is the organization of senior staff in a civil service organization). PEEP also takes into account the presence of the state, which is responsible for ensuring a minimum level of PEEP within organizations, especially where employees have little or no power.

The broad impact of the activities related to PEEP probably explains why some authors have always considered industrial relations and labor relations as synonymous. This could also be because the field of industrial relations developed at the same time the union movement (the chief concern of which is PEEP) experienced rapid growth. Also of note is the fact that Hugh Clegg, a well-known researcher in the field, has stated that "collective bargaining is so important that it covers almost the entire field of industrial relations."[8]

We must, however, correct this error and insist on the fact that the phenomena linked to human resource management extend beyond the scope of the activities for determining an adequate level of PEEP in enterprise, despite their importance.

An example is the selection of personnel. Should the activities related to recruitment and selection (interviews, tests, competitions, etc.) be considered part of the field of industrial relations? We believe they should. We would, however, be most surprised to find the selection of personnel included in the traditional definition of labor relations.

Although the field of industrial relations is concerned with the entire relationship between efficiency and protectivism, labor relations operates only within the latter component of this relationship. This is the reason these two concepts cannot be considered as synonymous: The whole cannot be defined by one of its parts.

The Three Agents in Industrial Relations

The two basic processes—human resource management and labor relations—bring together three agents: organizations and their managers, employees and their work society (which can be a union) and the state. Since sufficient explanation has been given on the role of the first two (employers and employees) within the process of human resource management and labor relations, it is now time to introduce the third partner, the state, the role of which has become increasingly more important in modern industrial relations.

In a neo-liberal pluralist society, the state represents and defends the interests of society and adopts the laws and regulations for this purpose. The role of the state, therefore, is to make efficient use of all of its human resources.

As previously mentioned, the state manages human resources chiefly by adopting policies to correct the imbalances in the labor market and to complement larger economic policies. The state, however, is only one of many human resource managers in the economy, and therefore it must make certain that other managers give their human resources adequate working conditions. This means adopting public policies on the minimum conditions for such items as wages, working hours, and vacations, and also for occupational health and safety. Some of these policies are also to eliminate job discrimination. Even if human resource management in our capitalist societies is left largely to private sector employers, the state still attempts to guarantee minimum standards to workers.

Another important role of the state is to determine the legal framework and the rules to be used by the other two agents once collective relations have been established within an enterprise. This is the entire scope of the labor legislation governing collective bargaining and the settlement of labor conflicts.

Its last role, which is very different from the others, is to take care of its own industrial relations. Since the state is also an employer, it must, like other employers, develop a system to manage its human resources and to establish the working conditions of its employees. When the work society of its employees decides to form a union, it must engage in formal collective labor relations. This results in the dilemma of the state-as-employer versus the state-as-legislator. This dilemma is virtually inevitable, because the state as an employer may decide that its collective labor relations will be subject to the same rules as any other employer; and as a legislator may decide at any time to suspend, change, or ignore the regulations to ensure the common good.[9]

Nevertheless, even if the state is the ultimate power in society one must not think that its role in industrial relations is limited to an objective intervention on behalf of the common good in each of the areas just mentioned. In practice, state power is carried out by individuals who are continually being lobbied by different interest groups (including companies and unions) and who have their own interests to consider, even if only to be reelected. Public policies then are adopted within this special context and, in the final analysis, it is the possible impact on votes that often influences their orientation.

Thus the lobbying and the political action carried out by the other two agents are just as important as collective bargaining in understanding the dynamics of the industrial relations system. The purpose is to influence public policies to meet one's own ends, regardless of whether these policies affect labor markets, minimum standards or the process of collective bargaining.

The Three Areas of Study in Industrial Relations

Because the two basic processes—human resource management and labor relations—bring the three agents together, there is often the compelling need to divide industrial relations into three areas of study: human resource management (HRM), labor relations (LR) and public policies on work (PPW).

Dividing the subject into three areas of study does not mean that all the phenomena found in industrial relations must necessarily be classed in any one of these areas. For example, there is no need to ask oneself if a program to improve the quality of working life (QWL) (or courses on the QWL within an industrial relations program) belongs either to human resource management, labor relations, or public policy on work. What has to be considered is the purpose or orientation of the program (or courses). If the purpose is linked to the goals of the enterprise, then the activity can be considered as human resource management; if the union's purpose is to make it the object of collective bargaining, then it is definitely labor relations activity; and finally, if the state wants to make such programs available to enterprise, then we are dealing with a public policy on work.

It is possible, up to a point, to fit an activity into all three areas. Take QWL as an example. If a company decides to launch such a program and wants to actively seek the union's cooperation, and if the two parties join to solicit available assistance from the government, then how do we class this activity?

The difference between the three areas (HRM, LR, and PPW) may sometimes be difficult to establish, and for this reason, this very functional method of dividing the industrial relations field must not be considered as a hard and fast method or as an extremely precise guide. The divisions are just a useful reference tool to make it easier to understand that industrial relations phenomena are initiated by organizations that want to manage their personnel effectively, by work communities trying to obtain the best possible working conditions or by the public authority, which may have a number of reasons for its interventions.

In the case of public policies, it may be just as difficult to separate those that belong within the framework of industrial relations (with reference to labor matters) from those belonging to other contexts, (economic, social, educational, legal and cultural). A useful, but not infallible criterion for separating public policy on work from other public policies is to see if the policy being studied was designed for a work situation, or if its effects on labor are only indirect. It is true that all public policies could affect the workplace. For example, an increase in interest rates (economic policy) could cause a slowdown in investment, which, in turn, would have a negative influence on economic activity. Reduced economic activity means higher inventories, which lead to layoffs, and therefore the need for the state to create manpower policies (part of the industrial relations field). Also, this does not take into account the larger problems for unions, who will have to bargain for job security clauses. Taken alone, an increase in interest rates cannot be considered as a public manpower policy, since it did not originate from a diagnosed labor market need, but rather from a general public need (such as to fight inflation).

Public policies on work are usually direct and selective, while other public policies are more global. The former are short- and medium-term, and the latter are long-term policies that have only an indirect impact on work.[10]

The Systems Approach

Any discipline that aspires to becoming a science must meet the key condition of being able to be "systematized." According to Larouche and Déom, "Modern sciences or disciplines (data processing, communications, social service, robotics . . .) along with older disciplines (chemistry, biology, mathematics, physics . . .) adopted the systems approach in order to be able to integrate knowledge related to the object of study and to develop some capacity to forecast variations in this object."[11] Industrial relations has also had to take the same direction.

The elements of a system are defined as either dependent or independent variables. There are also intervening or moderating variables. The dependent variable is the base of the system and also the object of the system or the output that must be explained or studied. The independent variables, or inputs, are those that can explain the dependent variable or variables of the system.

As for the intervening or moderating variables, these are special descriptive variables that have an intermediary role in the causal relationship between the dependent and independent variables. An intervening or moderating variable is influenced by one or more independent variables and, in turn, influenced one or several dependent variables. Thus, in the relationship x-y-z, x is an independent variable, y is an intervening variable, and z is a dependent variable. Also of importance to industrial relations is the "circular causality of the variables" or what we call feedback. This means that the dependent variables can also be considered as independent variables that, in turn, will become dependent variables: the relationship between the variables creates circular causal links. This, of course, implies the presence of another characteristic that is just as important: the dynamic rather than static character of the system, meaning that it must account for change. Finally, the systems are generally considered as being "open," meaning that they can be influenced by the environment in which they are found.

Any society can be seen as having several systems, including a system of industrial relations. Other systems are the ecological system (natural resources, geography, climate); the economic system (product market, labor market, money market, technology); the political system (legislative and executive powers); the legal system; and the social system (social structures, public opinion pressures). These systems taken together constitute the environment that surrounds the industrial relations system: an environment that has a direct influence on the inputs in the system (see Figures 6.2 and 6.3).

As mentioned before, the industrial relations system brings three agents into play that are the inputs of the system and are influenced by different environmental contexts. Each of these agents has objectives, a value system, and a certain degree of power that allows it to organize and to develop its own orientations.

The interaction of these three agents brings the two basic processes, human resource management and labor relations, into play. These processes can be considered as two activities able to convert the inputs into outputs, or, again, to transform the independent variables into dependent variables. Human resource management and labor relations can therefore be considered as intervening or moderating variables.

In the process of human resource management there are just as many elements established by organizations to acquire, maintain, develop, deploy

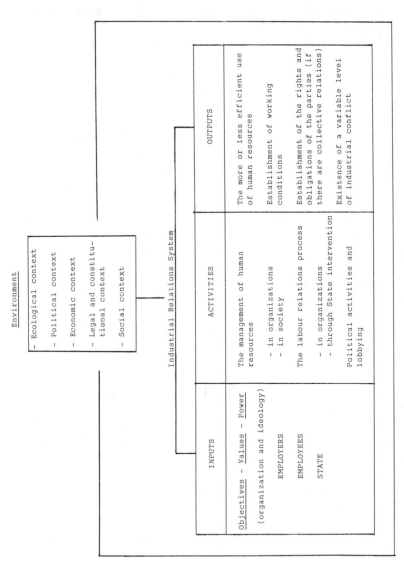

Figure 6.2. Diagram of an industrial relations system.

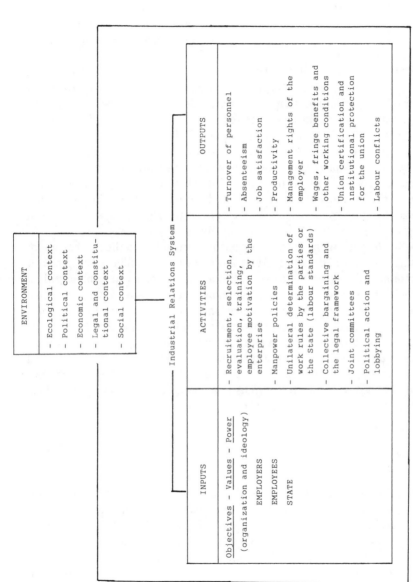

Figure 6.3. Detailed description of the industrial relations system.

and to use personnel doing or capable of doing productive work effectively (recruitment, selection, training, personal incentives, etc.) as there are established by the state to facilitate operations in the labor market (services to the unemployed, occupational training, subsidies for companies to create or maintain jobs, etc.).

Collective bargaining and everything related to it are certainly among the elements to be considered in the labor relations process, both from the point of view of the parties and that of the state. Also to be considered are all the other methods of establishing rules for work, which are (1) unilaterally by the employer; (2) unilaterally by the union; (3) legally by the legislator; (4) using the customs and practices in force in enterprises; and finally, (5) by the employer in consultation with the employees and their organizations. To the two basic processes must be added lobbying and the political action mechanisms for converting inputs into outputs, used by employers and organized employees to influence state policies in order to further their own interests.

Finally, the dependent variables or outputs are linked to the two basic processes and are defined within industrial relations, particularly the turnover of personnel, absenteeism, worker attitudes, productivity and management rights with respect to human resource management, wages, fringe benefits, and other working conditions, as well as union recognition, institutional protection of the union and labor conflicts. It should be noted that the outputs include not only the elements related to individuals, but also those respecting union or employer organizations. Once the outputs are identified for a given moment, the feedback or circular causality of the different relationships makes it possible for the outputs to act as independent variables, which influence the environment and other factors.

SUMMARY

Industrial relations can be defined as the management of labor problems in an industrial society. Implicit in such management is the development of theories, techniques and institutions to resolve the conflicts arising from work relations. These conflicts result from the permanent interaction of management efficiency, worker protectivism and the public policies developed by the state. The two processes that come into play because of this inevitable interaction between management efficiency (whether at the level of the organization or society in general) and the need for worker protectivism are human resource management and the establishment of working conditions. In North America this is called labor relations.

By human resource management we mean all the activities or programs promoted by organizations and the state to acquire, maintain, develop, deploy and use effectively the persons doing or capable of doing useful work. And by labor relations we mean all the phenomena and activities related to the establishment of the rules for work. These rules are of two types: the substantive rules, which determine working conditions and the procedural rules, which determine the steps to be taken to change or apply the substantive rules.

These two basic processes bring together three agents: the organization and its managers, the employees and their work society (union) and the state. The latter is involved in human resource management through its policies, which seek to correct the imbalances in the labor market. It also adopts policies for the purpose of establishing minimum conditions for wages, hours of work, health, safety, and job discrimination. The state also determines the legal framework and the rules for the two other agents. Finally, since the state is an employer, it must, like other employers, develop a human resource management system and set the working conditions for its own employees.

If the empirical presentation developed previously is now examined from an analytical or academic viewpoint, we see that industrial relations includes three areas of study: human resource management, labor relations and public policies on work. Also, when the systems approach is applied to industrial relations, each of the agents is seen to have goals, values and even a certain degree of power, which allow them to organize and to evolve their own philosophies. The interaction of the three gives rise to two types of activity that convert inputs to outputs. Among the outputs are the turnover of personnel, absenteeism, worker attitudes, productivity, management rights, working conditions and conflicts.

NOTES

1. Jack Barbash, *The Elements of Industrial Relations* (Madison: University of Wisconsin Press, 1984), p. 3. The comments that follow on the practice of industrial relations are taken from the introduction to his volume, pp. 3–8.

2. In *The Elements of Industrial Relations,* Barbash adds the following areas of state intervention: price stabilization and social security. We believe that these are outside the scope of industrial relations as such, even if they do have a direct influence on the field. We consider these areas of state intervention to be instead part of the economic and social contexts.

3. Neil Chamberlain, "Issues for the Future," *Proceedings of the Industrial Relations Research*

Association, 1960, p. 101. George Shultz, "Priorities in Policy and Research for Industrial Relations," *Proceedings of the Industrial Relations Research Association,* 1968, p. 1.

4. E. Gosselin, "Perspective nouvelles des relations industrielles," *Relations industrielles,* Presses de l'Université Laval, Québec, 1967, Vol. 22, No. 2, p. 1984.

5. Dimitri Weiss, *Relations industrielles* (lére ed. Paris: Editions Sirey, 1973), p. 26 (emphasis in original).

6. This definition was inspired by the one found in the *Dictionaire des relations du travail* (Québec: Presses de l'Université Laval, 1986, 2nd edition), p. 405. It should be noted that Gerard Dion applies this definition to the concept of labor relations, which he considers to be synonymous with industrial relations. See section in this paper on **The Two Basic Processes,** for a contrary opinion.

7. Hugh A. Clegg, *The Changing System of Industrial Relations in Great Britain* (Oxford: Basil Blackwell, 1979), pp. 1-2.

8. Ibid., p. 5.

9. This dilemma is even more obvious in democratic parliaments of the British type, where legislative power (except in the case of minority government) is controlled at the executive level.

10. For more detailed discussion on this subject, see J. Sexton, C. Leclerc and E. Déom, "Politique de main-d'oeuvre et politiques publiques," *Relations industrielles,* Québec, les Presses de l'Université Laval, 1980, Vol. 35, No. 1, pp. 3-17.

11. V. Larouche and E. Déom, "L'approche systématique en relations industrielles, *Relations industrielles,* Québec, les Presses de l'Université Laval, 1984, Vol. 39, No. 1, pp. 114-143.

7

INDUSTRIAL RELATIONS:
BALANCING EFFICIENCY AND EQUITY ───────

NOAH M. MELTZ[1]

In his recent book, *The Elements of Industrial Relations,* Jack Barbash[2] highlights the key processes of industrial relations as management efficiency, work society (union) protectivism and management counter-protectivism. Within each of these processes he identifies the main components. The purpose of this paper is to suggest that Barbash's very useful identification can be used to provide an industrial relations perspective on the old dilemma of efficiency versus equity in the employment relationship. The paper argues that in industrial relations (IR) the concern is not with the two objectives as opposites, but as complements: not efficiency versus equity but efficiency and equity. The paper briefly deals with each of the objectives separately, and then looks at them as alternatives or complements. The final section suggests that industrial relations is concerned with balancing efficiency and equity.

EFFICIENCY

The notion of efficiency provides a central focus for the discipline of economics. The drive for efficiency is grounded in the fundamental assumption in economics that entrepreneurs seek to maximize profits and consumers seek to maximize satisfaction. A necessary part of the maximization of profits is the minimization of the costs for each given unit of output. Although maximization of profits is taken as the central objective, economists have long recognized that the actual behavior of individuals may temper this objective somewhat. For example, it has been observed that some firms attempt to

109

maximize sales revenue with a profit rate constraint.[3] Long-run profit maximization may not require, or in fact may only be achieved by not maximizing short-run profits. The basic assumption still remains, however, that, subject to particular constraints and multiple objectives, maximization is the ultimate goal according to economic thinking. Maximization makes the economic world go round.

Industrial relations, on the other hand, implicitly recognizes that in human society the sole pursuit of efficiency creates counter forces that can, in the end, militate against the achievement of that same goal. An employer dedicated to the purest form of short-run profit maximization without any reference to the human element in the factors of production is likely to create a negative reaction that in the long run will impede the achievement of the desired efficiency. Even in the short run, as Leibenstein observes, there can be a deviation between the optimal levels of effort from the firm's viewpoint and the actual levels that individuals are motivated to put forth.[4] Short-run efficiency can therefore arise from insufficient effort levels. This is an example of the short-run/long-run distinction previously discusses. An old adage in industrial relations spells out the cause and effect relationship: management gets the union it deserves. The pursuit of pure efficiency can be costly.

EQUITY

Equity considerations involve a recognition of the uniquely human aspects of the labor factor of production. This means the fair treatment of human beings in a work place free from arbitrary decisions, discrimination, favoritism, and free from reliance only on the narrowest measures of short-run contributions to productivity. Labor unions have long been the vehicles for introducing equity into the employment relationship as well as expanding these concepts as part of the search for more general social justice.

The pioneers in the industrial relations field, those whom Barbash[5] has termed institutional labor economists, did more than just study the institutions of the labor market. In fact they were advocates for reform of the workplace. Reform meant legislation to modify unfettered managerial control by enabling organized workers to negotiate the terms of employment.

Reform also meant legislation that ameliorated the most harmful aspects of the free operation of the market place through such laws as minimum standards of employment (minimum wages, maximum hours), anti-child labor, unemployment insurance and health and safety requirements.

EFFICIENCY AND EQUITY: ALTERNATIVES OR COMPLEMENTS?

From an industrial relations perspective the rallying cry to take labor out of the market does not mean that efficiency (productiveness, profitability) of enterprises is no longer a concern. The necessity of efficiency for the long-run viability of any organization is clearly recognized. The industrial relations view is, however, that efficiency should not be obtained solely from competition among workers that depresses the wage rate. A more constructive alternative is to increase efficiency through other factors of production in conjunction with labor. Manifestations of the complementarity of efficiency and equity considerations are the Scanlon Plan productivity sharing programs and Quality of Work Life programs.[6]

Industrial relations focuses on efficiency and equity considerations as complements for two reasons. First, the long standing identification of industrial relationists with social reform has meant an opposition to a purely Darwinian view of unrestrained labor market competition. As noted above, this is not to say that market forces in general are to be ignored, but rather that the labor market is to be tempered by more humane considerations. An unfettered competitive labor market, free from any market imperfections can attain allocative efficiency, but that process does not guarantee (and indeed may conflict with) distributive equity.

Second, the IR perspective argues that equity considerations can actually enhance efficiency. The long run decline in annual hours of work, through a combination of shorter work days and weeks and more holidays and vacations, has occurred as productivity has risen. Were the reduced hours a result of the productivity increase, a cause, or both? There is no definitive answer, but Freeman and Medoff[7] present empirical evidence indicating that unions, because of their collective voice mechanism, enhance efficiency and that this offsets some of their wage cost increases.

Similar consideration can be given to the impact on efficiency of legislation, such as unemployment insurance, employment standards and health and safety, that is designed to enhance equity. Although unemployment insurance has increased the measured rate of unemployment to some extent[8] the overall effect on efficiency of this and other social programs is at worst slightly negative, and may have in fact been positive.[9]

Another example is the positive adjustment assistance recommended for those affected by such factors as free trade or plant closings. This can be both equitable (because it compensates the losers) and efficient (because it reduces their resistance to the change).

The difficulty in disentangling the relationship between efficiency and equity considerations is the dynamic nature of the economy. In a static context the drive for increases in real wages, reduced hours and improved health and safety protection would have reduced employment far more than has occurred in a dynamic economy. It can be argued that in the long run the drive for greater equity in the workplace has not been at the expense of efficiency.

INDUSTRIAL RELATIONS: BALANCING EFFICIENCY AND EQUITY

Asserting that industrial relations is concerned with balancing efficiency and equity is not to say that other disciplines are not also concerned with efficiency and equity. The terms efficiency and equity are drawn from economic literature where both are discussed. The difference is that in economics, for example, the two tend to be viewed as competing objectives, whereas a central concept in industrial relations is that they are primarily complementary objectives. The end result is that the prescriptions which an industrial relationist would apply to a particular employment relations problem implicitly recognize that efficiency and equity considerations are primarily complementary. It is the uniqueness of this viewpoint in the context of the employment relationship that sets industrial relations apart as a separate discipline.

NOTES

1. The author would like to acknowledge the suggestion from Roberta Robb, which led to the development of this paper, and the comments received from Morley Gunderson.
2. Jack Barbash, *The Elements of Industrial Relations* (Madison: University of Wisconsin Press, 1984).
3. William J. Baumol, *Business Behavior, Value and Growth,* Revised edition, (New York: Harcourt, Brace and World, 1967).
4. Harvey Leibenstein, "X-Efficiency, Intrafirm Behavior, and Growth," in Shlomo Maital and Noah M. Meltz, eds., *Lagging Productivity Growth: Causes and Remedies* (Cambridge, Mass.: Ballinger, 1980), pp. 199–200.
5. Barbash, op. cit.
6. Bryan Downie, "Union-Management Cooperation," in J. Anderson and M. Gunderson, eds., *Union-Management Relations in Canada* (Don Mills, Ont.: Addison Wesley, 1982), pp. 316–340; see also Keith Newton, "Quality of Working Life in Canada: A Survey," in W. Craig Riddell, Research Coordinator, *Labour-Management Cooperation in Canada* (Toronto: University of Toronto Press, 1986), pp. 73–86.

7. Richard B. Freeman and James L. Medoff, *What Do Unions Do?* (New York: Basic Books, 1984).

8. Frank Reid and Noah M. Meltz, "Causes of Shifts in the Unemployment-Vacancy Relationship: An Empirical Analysis for Canada, 1953–1975," *Review of Economics and Statistics,* August 1979, pp. 470–475.

9. Morley Gunderson and Noah M. Meltz, "Labour Market Rigidities as Causes of Unemployment," in Morley Gunderson, Noah M. Meltz and Sylvia Astry, eds., *Unemployment: International Perspectives* (Toronto: University of Toronto Press, forthcoming).

8

EQUITY AS FUNCTION: ITS RISE AND ATTRITION

JACK BARBASH

THE ARGUMENT

Equity is a necessary condition of a workable industrial society. Industrial relations administers equity in the employment relationship.[1]

Industrial relations in the United States presents itself in four aspects: as a strategy in which the object is to win; as an ideology in justification of strategy; as a theory in support of a scholarly discipline of industrial relations; and as a function to administer equity in the employment relationship. This paper is mainly about this last point.

The word industrial in industrial relations no longer means only manufacturing or blue-collar factory employment. More broadly, it means any large-scale, efficiency-directed enterprise—profit or nonprofit, blue collar or white collar, public or private, capitalist or socialist. Hence, many office and other nonfactory areas of employment such as hospitals, government, insurance companies, foundations, and department stores are industrial and have to practice industrial relations.

TENSIONS OF INDUSTRIALISM

Despite their high salaries and middle-class status, employees in these areas are likely to behave like proletariats because their work has become industrialized. Industrialization means (1) an efficiency culture, which establishes a net return or bottom line as the primary success indicator; (2) the use of

114

systematic economizing techniques; (3) a complex technology of production and information; (4) a large "human capital" investment in a disciplined labor force, and a "free" labor market organized to match supply and demand; (5) complex organization (or bureaucracy) and attendant rules to administer the technology, scale, cost disciplines and labor market; (6) the accommodation of efficiency to market uncertainty; and (7) the overhead legal, police, facilitative, regulatory, procurement and planning services of a kind normally rendered by a government.

These attributes are at the same time sources of both efficiency and tension, economy and diseconomy. Efficiency in the labor input gives rise to a distributive tension between workers' wages and enterprise profits. Technology causes drudgery, monotony and alienation. The rationalization of organization creates problems of insubordination, isolation and powerlessness, or what we have come to call alienation. Uncertainty produces anxiety and maladjustments.

Tensions cannot be altogether eliminated without putting industrialism's primary efficiency function at risk. If kept within tolerable bounds tension is not deemed too high a price to pay for a decent standard of life. But at the very least, western industrialism accepts the principle that there are inevitable insecurities and that they need to be dealt with through techniques of equity.

Put another way, formal efficiency has to be mediated by equity in order to enhance real efficiency. Formal efficiency is found in the textbook disciplines or "sciences" such as economics, cost accounting, organizational behavior, finance, industrial engineering, marketing and information processing. Because broad principles can never anticipate all of the real world variables, formal efficiency needs to be modified by equity. Equity thus becomes the necessary complement to efficiency in the utilization of labor.

Operationally, industrial relations has turned out to be the staff specialization that administers and negotiates equity in the employment relationship. The pressures for equity characteristically emanate from the informal work society, the union and the state. The lesson that management learns from the encounters are then incorporated in the management's conventional wisdom. It is precisely the confrontations, as irritating as they are day-to-day, that have prodded western-style management into a superior labor performance as compared to the socialist or statist systems where legitimacy is not accorded to institutionalized countervailing power.

The industrial regime assigns the key operating role to management. Management devises the efficiency strategy, assembles the factors of production and distribution, directs the labor force and is responsible for profit and loss. The employees in the industrial scenario simply follow orders with, at the most, a modest say in their implementation. Reform movements over two centuries to diffuse management hegemony more widely have accomplished only marginal changes in management's primary role.

But as manual work has shaded into greater discretionary intellectual effort, the enlistment of employee consent becomes more significant. The consent is engineered by management, constrained always by the overshadowing imperative to earn a profit and retain independence of action.

By now modern industrial relations—whether as human relations or human resource management—takes industrial tensions as a given; that is, as necessary problems that have to be resolved. Although formal efficiency approaches the status of science, real efficiency is in good part art—or even artfulness. The art consists of finding the right blend of efficiency and industrial relations.

THE NEED FOR EQUITY

The need for equity arises from the human essence of labor as a commodity. The commodity theory of human labor appeals to the employer in his cost-minimizing and managerial roles. The employer as cost-minimizer is favorably disposed to the commodity theory because labor is cheaper that way. The employer as manager favors the commodity theory because employees are easier to control and more amenable to social dominance of the sort that Hoyt Wheeler writes about in this volume. The equity theory advanced in this paper questions both assumptions.

Labor is, of course, a commodity; it is scarce, it has use value, it is bought and sold in markets of sorts and its price is ultimately constrained by supply and demand. Labor is, nonetheless, different from other commodities—it is attached to live, infinitely differentiated human beings who tend to resist the efforts of rational management to subject them as workers to simplification, standardization and specialization. This resistance has to be bought out by measures of equity if satisfactory real efficiency is to be achieved.

The bundle of practices we call equity consists, in the main, of (1) employee participation in employment decisions including bargaining; (2) due process in resolving perceived injustice; (3) security of expectations through job rights, work rules and compensation structures; and (4) job design of a sort that is responsive to technology and organization, as well as job-holder needs. More briefly, human as distinguished from inanimate commodities require fairness, voice, security and work of consequence to make their maximum contribution to real efficiency.

The equity principle is not mechanically applied. There are equity variations based on differences in the labor market, costs, market structures, profitability, management ideologies and the distribution of power in the administration of equity.

The threats of low morale and union proneness bring management, sooner or later, to an awareness of equity. Employees will enforce equity by excessive quits, absenteeism, tardiness and indiscipline: in short, by withholding efficiency. Even a totalitarian communist management is powerless to do much about this "conscientious withdrawal of efficiency."

It is now understood, therefore, that union agitation is a result, not a cause, of the inequity tensions. The union simply calls attention to the tensions already there. As a result, the elimination of unions does not eliminate tensions. Something needs to be done to alleviate tensions or tension will overwhelm efficiency.

The fluidity of the political situation under pluralistic democracy assures that one institution or another will move in to occupy a perceived equity void. "Increasing [court and legislative] restrictions," *Business Week* remarked editorially, "on management decisionmaking could make many companies decide that collective bargaining is preferable to legislation as a means of . . . representing workers' interests."[2]

The larger implication is that the symbiosis between efficiency and equity has probably saved western capitalism from Marx's implacable scenario of "immiseration" and collapse. Marx, as it turns out, did not take into account—nor could he if the ideology of revolution's inevitability was to be maintained—the contingency that capitalism would try to remedy equity deficiencies at some point short of the revolutionary brink. Industrialisms fell prey to revolution only when they refused to heed the clamor for equity.

U.S. management's strategy of buying out the equity aspirations of the labor force has undermined the union's recruitment of white-collar membership. Human resources management (HRM) is the contemporary equity vehicle. Heath Larry, then of the National Association of Manufacturers (NAM), observed a decade ago that "a lot of companies who didn't get caught up in the wave of organizing in the 1930s have learned to beat the unions by providing the equity employees want."[3] HRM, in the view of another NAM expert carries "the same importance which the labor relations function once received."[4]

HRM is a kind of union substitution to facilitate union avoidance and union attrition. HRM does many of the things (and frequently more) that management would have had to do anyway under the compulsion of collective bargaining, including enlisting consent, paying competitive wages and "peer review" of employee grievances.[5]

EQUITY'S EVOLUTION

Equity as a concept emerged when the work-or-starve option became obsolete as a primary motivation. Full employment, the welfare state, trade unions and management paternalism have made it possible in various ways to get by without working or without working quite so hard. Employee consent, therefore, must be achieved by other means.

Human resources management may be seen as an alternative to work-or-starve. HRM gains consent by trading increments of job and employment security in return for corporate loyalty, increased labor efficiency and union avoidance. It is not clear why unions would not be equally—if not more—agreeable to a similar deal; this suggests that management buys more than increased efficiency, it also buys freedom from an active union presence.

The state augments employee equity by legislating full employment, labor standards, labor relations, equal opportunity and social welfare. The Reagan administration has slowed down the state's equity thrust somewhat. But even a Reagan administration could not let unemployment run too long, cut social security too drastically or permit its Labor Department to present only an antiunion face. At times the state may function to assert the public interest against partisan union or management interests—cases in point are incomes policies, equal employment opportunity and health and safety.

The bilateral principals alternate between collective bargaining and political bargaining to get what they want. In political bargaining the bilateral principals negotiate terms of public policy with politicians and administrators. The latter are brought to the bargaining table by the threat to withhold activists, votes and commitment from the politicians.

A democratic state cannot rely solely on coercive power to secure compliance. It, too, must depend on bargained consent. So immense and pervasive are the details of many state interventions that total compliance can only be achieved unilaterally in a police state, and even then very imperfectly. The most advanced form of gaining consent has been the "social contract between the state and trade union federations to retard inflation by restraining wage demands, in return for the state's agreement not to use unemployment to achieve this end.

The seminal conceptualizers of employee equity were Wisconsin's John R. Commons and Harvard's Elton Mayo. Commons challenged capitalism to accord equity in its own self-interest. Mayo laid the groundwork for management human relations. Human relations, in the Mayo view, was not only morally right, it was also economically efficient.[6] Arthur Okun bestowed the legitimacy of mainline economics on equity. "Equity is . . . not an extraneous constant imposed upon the market by political institutions but rather a vital lubricant of market process."[7]

EQUITY VS. FLEXIBILITY

Equity strategy has undergone two shifts in recent times. Beginning in the 1960s, if not earlier, management began to mount the union substitution strategy, alluded to earlier, which sought to displace the unions from their equity function and substitute human resources management.

In the latest shift, adverse changes in market circumstances are forcing management to retreat from equity on the ground that it costs too much and impedes flexibility. The historic investment in morale represented by equity appears to be at odds with the urgent need of the moment to make the quarterly financial report more appealing to the Wall Street analysts and less appealing to corporate raiders. Accordingly, management slashes labor costs at the same time that it transforms compensation from a fixed to a variable cost more sensitive to market movements.

Flexibility is now the ruling maxim in the management of labor.[8] Flexibility works its ways by (1) substituting profit sharing, employee stock ownership and one-time lump sum payments for wage increases that get permanently imbedded into the compensation structure, (2) substituting "disposable" part-time, temporary and home workers for full-time workers,[9] (3) substituting "outsourcing" and subcontracting for integrated production, (4) substituting two-tier wage systems for equal pay for equal work, (5) laying off career employees on an unprecedented scale,[10] (6) cutting back on pension commitments[11] and (7) reducing job classifications to achieve flexible allocation of tasks.

But flexibility comes at the cost of fragmentation in the employment relationship. Wage flexibility erodes the predictability, continuity and adequacy of wages as a living.[12] Disposable employees and "floating factories" ("replacing the monolithic factory owned by one corporation [with] a network of little plants owned by a federation of companies")[13] widen the distance between the work force and the effective employer. Job flexibility erodes job pride and job identity. Profit sharing grafts onto the wage earner elements of entrepreneurial risktaking but with few of the compensating satisfactions.

In short, the new flexibility allows for the expansion and contraction of the work force and for a volume of work free from traditional restraints of seniority, dismissal and separation allowances, fixed job responsibilities and paid nonwork—the ingredients that have advanced the equity principle in the last generation. New jobs of the 1980s are "highly tenuous with weak links between employees and employers, uncertainty about pay and length of employment, few or no benefits and little possibility for advancement. Such conditions long characterized the jobs held by women, minorities and the youngest workers and are now becoming the rule."[14]

Equity was the "humanization" of the terms of employment in return for greater employee commitment to the enterprise—corporate loyalty.[15] What was lost in flexibility was more than made up by "an experienced and reliable work force."[16] Was the old equity logic wrong? Has the object of an experienced and reliable work force become obsolete?

The view that attrition of equity is necessary to restore competitiveness is not universal. The superiority of the Japanese performance is frequently attributed to higher commitment to equity. "Honda top executives [in the U.S.] eat in the employee cafeteria, there are no private dining rooms for big shots. Everybody there wears white overalls with his or her first name sewn on them. Honda President Irimajiri has no office. He sits in the same room with a hundred other white collar workers."[17]

"Once we have hired people," Sony's Akio Morita says, "we try to make them understand our concept of a fate-sharing body and how, if a recession comes [which it has in steel, for example], the company is willing to sacrifice profit. . . . They know that management does not lavish bonuses on itself . . . , there are no 'golden parachutes' for managers except a simple lifetime parachute of guaranteed employment and life of constructive work."[18]

According to a U.S. Department of Labor study of comparative employment adjustments, "In the U.S. the costs of employment adjustment tend to be shared more heavily by the workers who are laid off from firms while in Japan these costs are shared not only by the entire workforce of a firm but also by employers, incumbent workers and secondary workers."[19] "The company is supposed to offer job security to its full-time permanent workers. A hard-hit company is loath to put its workers on the street."[20]

SOME QUESTIONS

This recital raises a basic question about whether American management's "union-free" and equity retrenchment strategy is of a piece with the short-run mentality that many observers say is responsible for the lag in research and development and the obsessive preoccupation with the quarterly financial report. "What happens three or five years from now?" a Goodyear executive asks. "Will we start losing something in the marketplace because of cutbacks in research and development, reductions in employment and postponed investment in new facilities?"[21]

Will flexibility cause unorganized employees to reexamine their union options?[22] Will flexibility bring "unwanted by-products—income inequality and inequality of opportunity," "more jobs without basic benefits," "more dead end jobs and/or segmented labor markets?" Will flexibility undermine public policy on occupational health and safety and fair labor standards?[23]

There is an even larger question: Is it in the social interest to allow unions to deteriorate considering that everywhere else unions and collective bargaining are inextricably associated with democratic pluralism? It is of some consequence that, among the advanced, market-type industrial countries, this is a relevant question only in the United States. The answer has nothing much to do with whether unions are right or mistaken in any particular case, just as management's mistakes have nothing much to do with the essentiality of the management function. To revert to our earlier allusion, it is with unionism and collective bargaining as functions, particularly with unions and collective bargaining as instrumentalities of equity in a democracy—that is the point here.

NOTES

1. The ideas in this paper owe much to my *Elements of Industrial Relations* (Madison: University of Wisconsin Press, 1984). Noah Meltz's paper in this volume has also been suggestive.
2. "Don't Fight Employee Rights," Editorial, July 8, 1985, p. 116.
3. "The New Chill in Labor Relations," *Business Week,* Oct. 24, 1977, p. 32.
4. Randolph Hale, *The New Industrial Relations in a Global Economy,* Paper presented to Industrial Relations Research Association Spring Meeting, Atlanta, 1986 (mimeo), p. 12.
5. Larry Reibstein, "More Firms Use Peer Review of Employees' Grievances," *The Wall Street Journal,* Dec. 3, 1986, p. 25.
6. See Jack Barbash, "John R. Commons and the Americanization of the Labor Problem," *Journal of Economic Issues,* Sept. 1967; see also Elton Mayo, *The Social Problems of an In-*

dustrial Civilization (Cambridge, MA: Harvard University Press, 1945) and Elton Mayo, *The Human Problems of an Industrial Civilization* (New York: Viking Press, 1960).

7. Arthur Okun, "The Invisible Handshake and Market Processes," *Brookings Report*, No. 356, 1980, p. 8.

8. Michael J. Piore, "Perspectives on Labor Market Flexibility," *Industrial Relations*, Spring 1986, pp. 146–166; see also Thomas A. Kochan and Robert B. McKersie, *U.S. Industrial Relations in Transition: Implications for the Training of Management Professionals*, Industrial Relations Center, University of Hawaii, January 1986, p. 4.

9. "The Disposable Employee Is Becoming a Fact of Corporate Life," *Business Week*, Dec. 15, 1986, pp. 52–56.

10. "Nationwide Layoff Frenzy Swamps Outplacement Firms," *Sacramento Bee* (Washington Post Service), Jan. 18, 1987, p. D2; see also Peter Behr and David Wise, "More Firms Are Shedding a Few Extra Pounds: Their Employees," *Washington Post National Weekly*, Oct. 20, 1986, p. 21.

11. "The Shrinking Nest Egg: Retirement Will Never Be the Same," *Business Week*, Dec. 8, 1986, pp. 114–116.

12. Peter Drucker, *Management* (New York: Harper & Row, 1974), p. 190.

13. Alonzo L. McDonald, quoted in Steven Prokesch, "Remaking the American CEO," *The New York Times*, Jan. 25, 1987, p. 8. See also "The Hollow Corporation," *Business Week*, Mar. 13, 1986, pp. 57–74.

14. William Serrin, "Growth in Jobs Since 1980 is Sharp but Pay and Quality Are Debated," *The New York Times*, June 8, 1986, p. 1.

15. "The End of Corporate Loyalty," *Business Week*, Aug. 4, 1986, pp. 42–45.

16. Arthur Okun, "The Invisible Handshake and Market Processes," *Brookings Report*, No. 356, Washington, D.C., 1980, p. 8. See also: Arthur Okun, "The Inflationary Process," *Challenge*, January–February 1980, p. 6.

17. "Japan, USA," *Business Week*, July 14, 1986, p. 6.

18. Hobart Rowen, "Management Made in Japan," *The Washington Post National Weekly Edition*, Nov. 10, 1986, p. 5.

19. U.S. Department of Labor, Bureau of International Labor Affairs, *United States-Japan, Comparative Study of Employment Adjustment*, Washington, D.C., 1985, p. 2.

20. Bernard J. Wysocki, Jr., "Japanese Are Suffering Unemployment Rise in a Shifting Economy," *The Wall Street Journal*, Nov. 6, 1986, p. 1.

21. McDonald, op. cit., p. 8.

22. Hank Gilman, "IBM Dissidents Hope for Increased Support as Work Force is Cut," *The Wall Street Journal*, Jan. 13, 1987, p. 1.

23. Richard S. Belous, *How Flexible Is Flexible*, paper presented to Industrial Relations Research Association, Spring Meeting, Atlanta, 1986 (mimeo), p. 7.

9

INDUSTRIAL RELATIONS THEORY, THE STATE, AND POLITICS

ANTHONY GILES

In a 1971 survey of research on public policy and labor-management relations, Aaron and Meyer commented that they had "found only one article published during [the preceding fifteen years] that sought to develop a theory that would identify variables of sufficient generality to account for the timing and character of significant developments in [U.S.] labor laws."[1] In the fifteen years that have passed since that study, this theoretical lacuna has not been plugged. Despite the fact that the role of the state in industrial relations has grown steadily more important in nearly every advanced capitalist democracy during the 1970s and 1980s in terms of both substantive intervention and the level of politicization of industrial relations issues, recent assessments of the industrial relations literature suggest that the situation remains more or less unchanged.[2] Specific types of government policy, such as incomes policy and occupational safety and health regulation, have received considerable attention; controversies bearing on the larger question have flared up (notably the debate on pluralism in Britain); and a number of scholars from outside the (conventionally defined) field of industrial relations have studied various aspects of the subject. But industrial relations researchers have not sought to develop an explicit theoretical understanding of the state. Instead, assumptions about the nature, determinants and implications of state involvement in industrial relations remain largely implicit, unexplored and undefended.

The purpose of this essay is to identify, explicate and assess these implicit assumptions. More particularly, it is suggested that four principal theories (or bundles of assumptions) pertaining to state involvement in industrial relations can be identified; that these theories offer markedly different explanatory and prescriptive perspectives; and that, although all four theories address ostensibly the same subject, in important respects they are incommensurable. This essay concludes with an argument in favor of adopting one of the theories as a conceptual starting point for research on the role of the state in industrial relations. Before embarking on this task, it will be useful to consider a significant preliminary issue—the reasons for the paucity of explicit theorizations of the state in the industrial relations literature.

THE STATE IN INDUSTRIAL RELATIONS RESEARCH

Although few attempts have been made to devise explicit theoretical frameworks within which state involvement in industrial relations can be comprehended, the field is awash in more narrowly focused and descriptive studies. The theoretical lacuna does not, therefore, derive from a lack of interest in the subject or an absence of empirical building blocks. Instead, the problem is rooted in three characteristics of the study of industrial relations: the multidisciplinary nature of the field, the tradition of "pragmatism," and the orthodox definition of industrial relations as a field of study.[3]

The failure to transform the multidisciplinary orientation of the study of industrial relations problems into an interdisciplinary approach,[4] means that researchers tend to define problems and topics in terms of their home disciplines—law, economics, politics, and sociology. Thus, research on state involvement in industrial relations is splintered into a series of specialized subtopics: individual and collective labor law, public sector industrial relations, trade union-party relationships, the role of the police and the judiciary, the administration of labor policy, and the activities of government with respect to a broad range of policy areas (health and safety, incomes policies, employment standards, labor market policy, etc.). This fracturing of the general subject is not particularly surprising, nor would it be problematic except that there have been few successful attempts at integration. Flanders' comment on the lack of a general theory of industrial relations is applicable here. "The drawback of relying on the theory of any one of the several disciplines that have impinged upon industrial relations is that it was never intended to offer an integrated view of the whole complex of institutions in the field. Theoretically speaking, these disciplines tear the subject apart by concentrating attention on some of its aspects to the exclusion and neglect of others."[5]

Fragmentation is exacerbated by another characteristic of industrial relations research on the state. On the whole, the research of labor economists, academic labor lawyers, and mainstream industrial relations specialists is usually conducted as a fault-finding exercise, the goal being to improve or revamp public policy.[6] Pragmatism (and its close cousin, relevance) is not in itself sinful; however, as Goldthorpe has pointed out, the adoption of a technocratic "problem-solving" approach usually takes for granted certain underlying premises of state action.[7] Labor economists, for example, normally examine labor market policy on the assumption that such policy is (or should be) directed towards improving allocative efficiency. Similarly, specialists in the field of labor law typically examine whether legislation and judicial interpretations are faithful to the stated aims of public policy. Similarly, much mainstream industrial relations research measures the impact of particular policies against an implicit goal or standard (such as the reduction of industrial conflict or the attainment of balance). The problem, of course, is that it is by no means self-evident that state activity is always shaped by these rationalistic goals, and, even where it is, the failure to explore the meaning of the goals obscures the role of the state.

The practical policy concerns of many industrial relations researchers fragment the study of the state in yet another way. Precisely because the object is so often to improve policy, research problems tend to be narrowly defined (how can industrial conflict be reduced?, how can legal obstacles to unionization be overcome?, how can unions be made more democratic?, how can inflation be combated?), thus discouraging reflection on the interconnections between policy areas, the broader functions of the state, or the processes by which policy is actually formulated. As Strauss and Feuille have put it: "The field's pragmatic approach has led to basic questions as to the nature of pluralistic society being ignored."[8] The need to appear neutral so as to be in a position to proffer advice further militates against a consideration of these matters.

As serious as they are, the effects of multidisciplinarianism and pragmatism pale into insignificance when compared to the third characteristic of the study of industrial relations that has blocked adequate theorization of state involvement: the way in which the boundaries of the field of study have been drawn and its objects of investigation defined. Orthodox definitions of the proper purview of industrial relations theory and research have narrowed the study of state involvement in two crucial ways—by excluding the determinants of state activity and by excluding a number of areas of public policy.

In one sense, the deepest fissure in the subject as a whole is the one running between those subtopics that are chiefly related to the shaping of state policy and those having to do primarily with the impact of state involvement in industrial relations. The scholarly population of the first camp (mostly specialists in political science and political sociology) are concerned with the "politics" of industrial relations, including the manner in which labor policy is made and administered, the nature of trade union-party relations, and the political relationships between trade union and employer confederations and the state. Those in the second camp (labor economists, specialists in labor law, and most mainstream industrial relations researchers) tend to be concerned with assessing the impact of state activity on industrial relations. As this second group constitutes the heart of the discipline, its lack of concern with the issues raised by the first group serves to exclude a range of vital questions.[9]

If the tendency to treat the state and its policies as givens was a mere oversight, the problem could be solved in short order. Unfortunately, the problem has deeper roots: "Although they may acknowledge at a theoretical level the interdependence of industrial relations with other elements of the social system, American, and to a lesser extent European researchers have tended to treat industrial relations as autonomous."[10] Indeed, in several of the analytical frameworks constructed to conceptualize industrial relations, the determinants of state policy are treated as exogenous. An early example was the "human relations school." William Foote Whyte, for instance, explicitly argued that although the influence of "outside variables" such as the economic environment should be taken into account, they should not be considered the proper subject matter of industrial relations research.[11] This demarcation was justified by the central tenet of the human relations approach: that the plant was a self-contained and tendentially harmonious (if occasionally malfunctioning) social system.

John Dunlop's concept of the industrial relations system provides another, albeit more ambiguous example of the exogenization of the state's role. Although Dunlop did not seek to exclude the state from his theory (specialized government agencies are granted status as system actors, and the power context, although apparently outside the system, is seen as a conditioning factor),[12] he drew the line at seeking to explain the role of the state. Although he argued, as opposed to the human relations school, that an "analytical framework for the study of industrial relations . . . should make the influence of the [environmental] context explicit,"[13] he later made clear what he considered to be the appropriate boundary.

> I shall regard "political systems" . . . as the power relationships in a larger society which define substantively or procedurally the status, roles and relationships of labour organizations, management and governmental agencies in any continuing industrial relations system. For the specialist in industrial relations these exterior power relations or exterior political

systems are given, not to be explained, and the intellectual task is to depict the industrial relations arrangements established by each political system and the character of the dynamic interaction between external political power and labour-management-government relations. In a sense, "political systems" set up the major players in the industrial relations game and define their major rules of play. Industrial relations provide the result of the play in a given technological and economic environment and at a given stage of economic development.[14]

Dunlop's systems approach, then, deliberately ignores the determinants of state activity. This follows from the very logic of systems theory: by delineating the boundaries of a supposedly discrete "system," and by characterizing it as relatively self-contained and inherently self-equilibrating, the determinants of state activity are excluded from the analysis and entrusted, presumably, to the care of political scientists.

There are, of course, many industrial relations researchers who adopt neither a human relations perspective nor systems theory, but most would seem to define the boundaries of industrial relations in much the same way as Dunlop. This disinclination to examine the determinants of state policy is also characteristic of most specialists in labor law and labor economics. Both tend to focus their attention on the impact of given policies and political relationships. Historians have contributed more to our understanding of the development of public policy, but with rare exception they have fought hard the temptation to develop explicit models.[15]

The obvious rejoinder to the complaint is that the existing academic division of labor is more or less acceptable, and that the overtly political dimensions of state involvement in industrial relations are best left in the hands of political scientists and political sociologists. It might be suggested, for instance, that the construction of a framework for analyzing both the making of industrial relations policy and the effects of such a policy (not to mention its "broader meaning") represents too grand a project, indeed one that borders on academic imperialism. An objection of this sort, however, flies in the face of the long-held aim of constructing a truly interdisciplinary approach.

It might also be argued that there are quasi-autonomous industrial relations structures and processes that are best analyzed in relative isolation. There are at least three reasons for rejecting such a view. First, orthodoxy encounters a paradox of its own making. If industrial relations is to have any policy relevance, it would seem to be necessary to develop an adequate conception of how policies actually are made. Second, the view that industrial relations can be studied in relative isolation rests on extremely shaky empirical grounds. In the past two decades, governments in the advanced capitalist democracies have tended to increase their involvement in industrial relations to such an extent that it is less than fruitful to ignore the causes that lie behind this trend.[16] Finally, a more theoretical case exists for doubting the autonomy of industrial relations, but as it also bears upon the last issue to be raised in this section, it is developed below.

The theoretical narrowness caused by excluding the determinants of state policy is compounded by the way in which the orthodox definition of industrial relations limits the types of policies considered to fall within the boundaries of the field. The appropriate focus of industrial relations research has been variously defined as: "the institutions of job regulation," "the individual and collective activities of labor," "the employment relationship in all its aspects," "employment relationships in an industrial economy," "the administration of the employment function," "the bargaining explicit and implicit between and among employers and employees . . . and . . . the factors that affect this bargaining," and "all aspects of job regulation—the making and administering of rules which regulate employment relationships—regardless of whether these are seen as being formal or informal, structured or unstructured."[17] The practical focus of industrial relations research, however, is much narrower than these definitions imply. Despite the claim that all aspects of the employment relationship fall within its scope, orthodoxy continues to focus on formal collective institutions and processes. As has been said of the study of industrial relations in the United States, "despite its broad claims, academic industrial relations today consists chiefly of manpower and collective bargaining."[18] As a result, the study of public policy in industrial relations is often viewed as little more than the analysis of collective labor law. For example, Archibald Cox's *Law and the National Labor Policy,* often held to be one of the seminal American overviews of the subject, is organized on the basis of four general areas of policy: "public policy toward union organization"; "the role of public policy in the negotiation of collective bargaining agreements"; "the role of the law in the administration of labor agreements"; and "the public interest in internal union affairs."[19] Canada's most influential writer on labor policy, H.D. Woods, repeatedly employed a framework based on the distinction between recognition, jurisdiction, interest, and rights disputes.[20] Similarly, Kenneth Walker suggests that there "seem to be three broad groups of industrial relations issues with which the state typically concerns itself": "the methods by which parties deal with each other," "the form and powers of the organizations of workers and managers," and "the content of substantive work rules."[21]

These conceptual schemes share a number of characteristics. First, they are hardly more than descriptive organizing frameworks with little real analytical content, except to the extent that the categories are implied to be the major elements in labor policy. Second, the three schemes are extremely parochial. Each reflects the peculiar preoccupations of state policy in the author's own nation. Third, and most important, all three reflect the narrow concentration on collective labor law so prevalent in the study of labor policy. It is true that other policies have been examined by industrial relations researchers, as well as by those in related disciplines. There is, for instance, a considerable body of literature on incomes policy, labor market policy, and occupational health and safety legislation. Where attempts have been made to analyze labor policy in general, however, these subsidiary areas are almost always left out.[22]

Simply knitting together existing studies of particular policies, or bringing subsidiary policies under the definitional umbrella of labor or industrial relations policy is not enough; it is also necessary to fill in two crucial gaps in the literature that derive from the orthodox definition of industrial relations. First, the focus on collective labor relations tends to ignore unorganized workers and their relationship to the state. Studies of the individual contract of employment, for example, are normally conducted by a specialized branch of labor law, and usually make an appearance in the industrial relations literature as a preface to the study of collective contracts; studies of welfare policies that touch upon both organized and unorganized workers are also usually treated as lying outside the mainstream of public policy and labor-management relations. This marginalization of the topic of unorganized workers is all the more surprising in view of the fact that in Great Britain, the United States and Canada the unorganized workforce outnumbers the organized. Second, the orthodox conception of the employment relationship focuses on the level of exchange and almost completely ignores production-level relations. As Richard Hyman has noted: "There is a strange irony in industrial relations scholars' ability to construct elaborate models of procedures of job regulation without the least awareness of the sphere of production which constitutes the material foundation of the bargaining arrangements that they seek to explain."[23] In consequence, research on labor policy tends to ignore the role of the state in creating and sustaining the social relations that give rise to employment in the first place. The social foundation of wage labor, industrial discipline, managerial prerogatives, and struggles over the control of work processes and rules, are to be found in the particular form of property and employment law in capitalist society; although the law cannot be said to have created these phenomena, to ignore the state's role in sanctioning the very existence of industrial relations (and its problems) is to ignore what is arguably the most crucial role it plays.

This critique of orthodoxy's conception of employment also justifies the doubts raised earlier concerning the validity of the distinction between (in Dunlop's words) "exterior power relations" and industrial relations, for it calls into question the distinction between polity and economy. More specifically, it highlights the fact that the distinction between public regulation and private industrial relationships is a specific characteristic of one type of social system—capitalism. It is on this basis that industrial relations can be said to be inevitably and thoroughly politicized.

In this section it has been suggested that there exists a conceptual lacuna in industrial relations theory with respect to state involvement in industrial relations. The persistence of a multidisciplinary approach to industrial relations, coupled with the pragmatism of many industrial relations researchers, has blocked the emergence of a broader conceptual scheme within which to study the subject. Moreover, due to the narrow definitions of industrial relations and employment, little explicit attention has been paid to the determinants of state policy, the role of the state with regard to unorganized workers, or the role of the state in underpinning the foundations of industrial relations.

It is, however, wrong to claim that there exists an absolute conceptual lacuna, for a few attempts have been made to develop explicit analytical frameworks that deal with the subject in at least partial terms. More importantly, implicit models underlie all research in the field, and it is important to examine these.

FOUR THEORIES OF STATE INVOLVEMENT IN INDUSTRIAL RELATIONS

Lurking beneath the weight of descriptive writing in the field are four theories of state involvement in industrial relations: unitary thought, pluralism, elite theory, and class theory. Each of these theories is linked to a broader paradigm of state-society relations.[24]; each has an affinity with a general explanatory model of the policy process; each tends to posit a particular role for the state in industrial relations; each is associated with a particular method of evaluating public policy; and each is predisposed to a particular prescriptive agenda (see Table 9.1).[25] In the remainder of the paper the author discusses these contending theories and argues that although each has certain shortcomings, the approach offered by class theory is the most appropriate starting point for a theory of state involvement in industrial relations.

Table 9.1. Schematic Overview of Theories of State Involvement in Industrial Relations

Description	Unitary	Pluralist	Elite	Class
Image of society	Organic whole	Overlapping groups	Stratified pyramid	Antagonistic classes
Conception of state	Active autonomous subject	Referee of group competition	Arena of resource allocation	Institutions of class domination
Explanatory models	Rational Actor Systems Theory	Group theory, public choice	Elite accommodation	Class action systemic bias
Role of state in IR	Defender of public interest	Adjudicator of union-management relations	Defend interests of elites	Defend interests of dominant class
Core policy dynamics	Public vs. private interests	Competing group interests	Competing elite interests: elite/mass control	Conflicting class interests
Analytical focus	Societal	Situational	Organization	Societal
Criteria of policy assessment	Stability	Status quo	Participation/ equality	Exploitation
Prescriptive agenda	Conservative	Liberal	Radical/ democratic	Transformative/ socialist
Associated disciplines/ traditions	Law, Economics, Human Relations	Political Science, Mainstream IR	Sociology	Political Economy Marxism

In the Public Interest: The Unitary Perspective

The unitary perspective may be said to espouse a theory of the public interest state. Unitary writers tend to portray the state as a monolithic subject endowed with an autonomous sovereign authority, possessing a will of its own that in some way manages to embody and act upon the public will (or national interest). This image of the state is linked to a concept of society as a harmonious organic whole tending toward a naturalistic equilibrium and possessing an identifiable, transcendent interest. Social subgroups (cliques, associations, classes) are seen as subsidiary, if not subversive. Conflict and dissidence are regarded in pathological terms, as unnatural, aberrant and illegitimate.[26]

The unitary perspective underlies two explanatory models of policymaking that make frequent, though often implicit, appearances in the industrial relations literature: the "rational actor" model and "systems theory".[27] In the rational actor model, policymaking is portrayed as a process of individual rational choice from among limitless options, the weighting of the benefits and costs of which are based on the state's responsibility for the national interest. Few industrial relations scholars have applied sophisticated versions of this model, but it crops up frequently in such oft-repeated formulae as "society decided to do" such and such. Three schools of industrial relations research are closely wedded to this unitary-rationalist view: human relations, economics, and technico-legal studies. This attachment results partly from the tendency of these schools to take state policy as given; but it is also the case that the core assumptions of each predispose them to the unitary-rationalist perspective.

Though the human relations school typically ignores the state and focuses exclusively on the workplace or organization, explanatory forays into the realm of public policy are conducted by transposing its organic, harmonious conception of plant society to the level of the polity. To be sure, the existence of conflict is admitted, but it is treated as an unfortunate consequence of organizational malfunction, interpersonal misunderstanding, or blindly narrow and self-interested behavior. The role of the state is simply to prevent or heal such conflict, and in so doing to fulfill its assumed function as the protector of the harmony of society. For most economists, public policies and decisions are also usually taken as given, as emanating from the authorities. Policy objectives are thought to stem either from the dictates of economic theory (as in the case of labor market policy, which is assumed to be directed toward improving the efficiency of market behavior) or from a simple community consensus. Political pressure on governments (from "narrowly self-interested pressure groups" or from a public whose expectations are "dangerously inflated") is held to foil the public interest—a line of thinking, incidentally, that quite logically leads to the over-loaded government hypothesis, rumblings about excessive democracy, and calls for the restriction of "malign influences" by locking policy into a neo-classical model of rationality.[28] The highly individual-centered approach of mainstream economics, and its theoretical abhorrence of any collective action that disturbs perfect competition or productive efficiency, underpins and reinforces this unitary conception of the state and policymaking. Finally, for analysts in the technico-legal tradition[29] state activity is treated in an even more simplistic way: statutes emanate from the sovereign authority of parliament or congress, judicial decisions from the application of self-evidently neutral principles of law and reason. As Klare points out:

Most contributions to the literature of collective bargaining law are over-whelmingly doctrinal and rule-focused in emphasis. They are written, explicitly or implicitly, from the perspective of beliefs and values about the social function of collective bargaining drawn or inferred from the stated purposes, the legislative history of and judicial glosses upon the major federal labor statutes. This literature takes as given and unques-tioned the desirability of maintaining the basic institutional contours of the liberal capitalist social order.[30]

Where a dynamic aspect of law is noticed at all, it is usually cast in terms of a response to the changing values or opinions of the community.

The other policy-making model with a close affinity to the unitary perspec-tive is systems theory.

Systems theory portrays public policy as an output of the political *system*. The concept of "system" implies an identifiable set of institutions and activities in society that function to transform demands into authoritative decisions requiring the support of the whole society. The concept of "system" also implies that elements of the system are interrelated, that the system can respond to forces in its environment, and that it will do so in order to preserve itself.[31]

It is the centrality of the notion of self equilibration in systems theory that leads it to adopt a unitary view, and to posit the existence of a national or community interest as a means of reconciling the existence of conflict with the supposed function of harmonization. This is made clear in Dunlop's claim that

The status of any one of the actors in an industrial-relations system is defined to mean the prescribed functions of that actor and the relations with the other actors in the same system. These prescribed functions and relations may be largely imposed upon an industrial-relations system from outside by the community, as in the case of legislation affecting a coun-trywide system, or they may develop within the industrial relations system and then be confirmed by community sanction or recognition.[32]

In both of its variants unitary theory assumes that public policy is for-mulated in a "rational" manner (either by an abstract rational actor or as an automatic systems output), and that the public or national interest is cen-tral to this process. This results in an analytical focus on the societal context of action, that is, unitarists seek to explain state activity by reference to society-wide values or preferences that are held to be reflected in the political process. On this view, the state's role in industrial relations is to defend the interests of the public or society as a whole, particularly where these interests conflict with the narrower or private interests of organized labor or employers. Measuring the impact of state policy in this model involves a comparison of the workings of existing policy (or the effect of a lack of policy) with a presumed notion of what constitutes the public interest. Obviously there is considerable leeway here, for definitions of the public interest can differ widely.[33] Nonetheless, unitarists normally assume that the public is interested in low levels of industrial conflict, in moderate and "responsible" behavior by trade unions, in the uninterrupted delivery of essential services, and in the absence of restrictions on efficiency. When these conditions do not obtain, societal values (such as stability, efficiency, public safety, various freedoms, etc.) are thought to be threatened, thereby requiring state intervention.

Invoking the public interest in support of a particular proposal is a convenient polemical strategy. For this reason, elements of the unitary approach are used by writers who by no means adhere to a unitary industrial relations perspective. In the case of those who adopt both a unitary view of the state and a unitary industrial relations ideology, however, it is possible to discern a certain prescriptive consistency. A hallmark of the approach is an emphasis on the use of the law to force behavioral change.[34] As for the concrete definition of the public interest, the unitary approach lays particular stress on the reduction of industrial conflict, the promotion of productive efficiency, the preservation of individual rights, and the maintenance of "orderly" relations in industry. These principles are of course shared by writers of other persuasions (notably pluralists), but the unitary-rationalists seem particularly disposed to assert the primacy of the public's interest in these matters, and are particularly enthusiastic about regulating trade unions as a means of achieving them.

How adequate is the unitary perspective?[35] The rational actor model has been the subject of a number of penetrating criticism. It has been shown that rational decisions are impossible in view of constraints on decisionmaking (information limitations, calculation problems, etc.); and it has also been demonstrated that the processes of policymaking do not function as if a single actor was formulating policy, but operate instead in a much more complicated manner.[37] Even in the field of foreign policy, where it might be supposed that rational action in the national interest might make its strongest analytical showing, it has been shown to be of very limited utility.[37] In the area of industrial politics, the approach is empty of serious theoretical content.

The notion of a concrete, identifiable national interest is also inadequate. Perhaps the most plausible case of the existence of such an interest can be made in relation to essential services disputes, which, more than any other industrial relations phenomenon, provoke calls for the respect of the public interest. Yet the very fact that the issue is one that is frequently debated reveals the impossibility of defining or measuring a concrete public interest. Moreover, studies of the actual operation of policies designed to protect the public from essential service disruptions reveal the extent to which the national interest is invoked as political justification or to mobilize public opinion.[38] Analytically, the term is used in a similar fashion: as a justification of the particular writer's own views.

One more weakness of the models associated with the unitary perspective should be noted. Because it is assumed that the state reflects the public interest or community consensus, it becomes unnecessary to demonstrate that such an interest or consensus actually existed at a particular point in time. Its existence is simply assumed. This slippage is revealed in phrases such as "society decided," "the public came to view that," and "the public consensus at the time was." The tautological character of this method is obvious.

A Congeries of Competing Groups: The Pluralist Perspective

Pluralism—often said to be the dominant philosophical, theoretical and political touchstone of industrial relations orthodoxy[39]—is in many respects radically at odds with the unitary perspective. The pluralist state, far from being an autonomous subject, is an inherently neutral set of institutions and rules with no will of its own. Far from being the embodiment of the community, it is the mechanism through which competing interests and demands within the community are arbitrated. Far from taking decisions, it is merely the vehicle through which decisions are made. This conception of the state is linked to the well-known pluralist image of society as being made up of individuals who, on the basis of a calculation of their interests, come together in a multitude of overlapping groups and associations, all vying for influence.

Pluralist explanations of state activity tend to revolve around the general propositions of group theory, in which public policy is seen as the outcome of a process wherein conflicting interest group pressures are compromised and reconciled. The nature of the outcome is chiefly shaped by the amount of influence exercised by the participating groups; and the ability to exercise influence is normally viewed as a function of the groups' organizational resources and capabilities. It is commonly assumed that the major interest groups possess roughly equal power. This general model has been used by political scientists, as well as by many mainstream industrial relations specialists.[40]

Two variants of this general explanatory model have been used in industrial relations. The purest version of the approach is public choice theory in which industrial relations policy is held to be determined by the political calculus of politicians and civil servants in the contest of competing demands and pressures from business, organized labor and other groups. Freeman and Medoff, for example, have examined national labor policy in the United States on the assumption that political decisions are chiefly shaped by the amount of resources (such as electoral support and lobbying ability) that unions and business can bring to bear on individual legislators. Most pluralists, however, tend to attribute to the state a more independent role. The reason why this is so has to do with the dilemma summarized by Hugh Clegg. "It might have been expected that a society which encourages sectionalism, squabbling and conflict would be torn apart. If societies of this kind prove relatively stable (in highly developed countries) then there must be some mechanism at work which binds the competing groups together and holds them back from rending their societies to pieces."[41] The two main solutions to this conundrum involve granting to the state a more independent role than that envisioned by public choice theorists. One has been to posit the existence of a set of widely held values or beliefs that restrain the behavior of interest groups (indeed, which are often held to define legitimate groups). In this solution, public opinion is frequently used as a major explanatory variable, as in Allan Flanders' claim that "the principles of any national system of industrial relations . . . are derived from the values by which the nation judges and legitimises the system's working and results."[42]

The other solution is to argue that the process of conflict and compromise is self-equilibrating. "Men associate together to further their common interests and desires; their associations exert pressure on each other and on the government; the concessions which follow help to bind society together; thereafter stability is maintained by further concessions and adjustments as new associations emerge and as power shifts from one group to another."[43] In principle this "invisible hand" solution does not require the postulate of a broader social consensus, but there are very few examples of this variant within the industrial relations literature. Thomas Kochan's treatment of public policy is illustrative of how pluralists rely on such solutions in their analyses of the state.[44] Although it is clear that in most respects Kochan is a pluralist, he suggests that

efforts to change laws governing unions and employers serve as a barometer of the existing social climate and of the political influence and effectiveness of these two major interest groups in society. . . . The content of the law cannot deviate too far from the norms of society without resulting in political pressure for readjustment. As the values of the larger society change the political power of unions and employers should shift correspondingly, and policy changes can then follow.[45]

The pluralist flavor of Kochan's analysis is evident in his concept of policy as the product (in part) of conflicts between interest groups; but the use of the "interests of the larger society," clearly brings in elements of the unitary framework. Public policy is seen to be determined in a dual fashion: by the pressure group process and by the state's rational and automatic refection of the public interest. It needs to be emphasized that this conflation of unitarist and pluralist principles of explanation is not a peculiarity of Kochan's analysis. For example, Jack Barbash's concept of the role of the state in industrial relations allows for two coexistent types of policy—"pressure group policy" and "positive public policy" (the latter being neutral policies formulated in the public interest).[46]

In any event, the core principles shared by all pluralists are evident enough. Public policy is formulated in the context of competing pressures and demands, and the key dynamic of the process is the pressure that can be brought to bear on the government. From this perspective the state plays an adjudicative role in industrial relations: ensuring that trade unions and employers' organizations observe the rules of the political process; reconciling and compromising their conflicting legislative demands; and enforcing the outcome of this process in the form of legislation. Accordingly, pluralists tend to focus their analysis on the situational context of action, that is, on "the conditions of mobilization of particular groups and individuals for political action and upon the strategies of influence and the outcomes of action in particular situations."[47] Thus, whereas unitarists attempt to interpret policies in terms of broad social values supposedly underlying state action, pluralists examine the processes through which pressure is exerted in and through the channels of legislative, executive and administrative decisionmaking.

The pluralist assessment of public policy revolves around the notion of balance, a criterion that stems from the pluralist image of a society that is competitive but free of fundamental conflict. Because the notion of balance (or equilibrium) is so abstract, however, pluralists usually tend to equate it to the status quo. A second normative rule of thumb is the preference for "voluntarism." The invisible hand premise and the rejection of the organic state theory lead most pluralists to argue that government interference ought to be restricted to cases where there is a plain imbalance between groups, or where the self-interested activities of collusive groups run the risk of damaging the public interest. The managerialism latent in voluntarism will be discussed later.

Pluralism is open to criticism on a number of fronts. Consider first the mechanisms to which pluralists resort as a means of explaining either social stability or the acceptance of the broad rules of the game. Although individual analysts invoke different mechanisms (ranging from the abstract social value consensus to the more concrete public opinion) all rely on one such mechanism to help explain how state policy is shaped. The existence of a broad social consensus, however, has been put in doubt on an empirical level.[48] And, on an analytical level, it may be said that the treatment of social consensus confuses positive consent with the lack of significant contestation. More seriously, the typical pluralist use of the most concrete expression of social values—public opinion—evades the critical issue of opinion formation. How is it that the public at certain points in time suddenly becomes concerned over a particular issue? How is this opinion translated into public policy? On the whole these questions have not been addressed in studies of labor policy. Here pluralist and unitary models share the same fault: in class-divided societies, the notion of public opinion is less than persuasive.

In any case, the adequacy of pluralism rests not only on the validity of the notion of consensus or opinion. The pluralist model requires the assumption that power and influence are distributed roughly evenly among individuals and groups (otherwise it becomes uncomfortably clear that true competition is negligible and that policy cannot represent anything like a balance), and that this in turn requires a roughly equal distribution of (largely economic) resources. As this is manifestly not the case in advanced capitalist societies, it follows that the pluralist model is inadequate. Although this might cause pluralists to squirm for a moment, a defense of sorts can be mounted. For instance, it might be suggested that the state actually plays a role in equalizing political influence; but just how this is to be accomplished, given that a prior inequality must be presumed, and redistribution must therefore involve acquiescence on the part of the more powerful groups, is baffling. Unless the pluralist is willing to admit that the state is sufficiently independent of interest group pressures to allow the adjustment (which would of course call into question the model itself[49]), then a rearguard action must be fought on different terrain.

In particular, it might be admitted that inequalities of influence do exist. The normal procedure for making this admission, although simultaneously salvaging some of the central notions of pluralism, is to suggest that in the past trade unions (in the case of industrial politics) were the politically disadvantaged group. The history of industrial politics is then portrayed as a long struggle to secure fairness or equality, a goal that most pluralists seem to believe was achieved sometime in the 1930s or 1940s.

The pluralist use of interest groups is wanting in a further and more fundamental respect. It is a characteristic of the pluralist model that labor and employers' organizations are essentially similar (and are similar to all other interest groups as well). This view has been cogently criticized by Offe and Wiesenthal,[50] the details of which need not be repeated here. Suffice it to say that capital (in the form of individual employers) is constituted as an interest (the enterprise) prior to the formation of an association, whereas workers must necessarily forge a collectivity before their entry into pressure group politics. The two interests are fundamentally unequal in this respect.

Higher Circles: The Elite Perspective

In contrast to the pluralist and unitary conceptions, elite theory views society as a pyramid, at the pinnacle of which reside groups of social elites (political, business, and other leaders). On this view, individuals are not equal participants in politics since access to political power is restricted by and to the elites themselves, with the majority of the people frozen out of the real, as opposed to the symbolic, political process. Classes play something of a role in elite theory, for the social pyramid can be seen as a hierarchy stratified by such variables as income, family position, occupation, status and power. Organizations, however, play a much more central part than classes. The basis of modern society is said to be the large organization, led by elites and populated by the masses.

In a sense, elite theory is a radical extension of pluralism: whereas pluralists view the state as possessing a certain number of functions—enforcing the observance of the rules of group competition, mediating between interests, and redressing power imbalances—elite theorists normally hold to a purely instrumentalist view. That is, the state is nothing other than a neutral set of institutions controlled, like private organizations, by particular groups of elites.

The dynamic of policymaking in this framework stems from two sources of tension—rivalry among groups of elites, and the relations between elites and the masses. On the one hand, elites interact in a continuous process of interorganizational bargaining and accommodation over public policy. The common values held by elites, however, as well as their shared interest in the preservation of the existing pyramid, work to narrow the range of issues over which debate takes place, thereby containing policy changes to relatively minor shifts. On the other hand, elites tend to ignore or manipulate the masses in the formulation of public policy. Control is exercised from the top in such a way as to divert pressure for real change, win acquiescence to existing policies, and mobilize support only when the need arises.

Direct applications of elite theory to labor policy are scarce, and the two subdisciplines that seem especially predisposed to the elite model—political sociology and the sociology of labor law—are not commonly regarded as being in the mainstream of industrial relations research.[51] Ironically, the most frequent use of elite theory in industrial relations research is in the area of trade union structure and government. Michels' study of the German trade unions and socialist party continues to be influential in structuring this debate: the central issue is seen as the unequal relationship between leaders and members, and the key "prescriptive" problem is how to resolve the tensions between organizational effectiveness and democracy.[52] The language of elite theory is also commonly employed in industrial relations research. For instance, Sanford Cohen's[53] analysis of labor law (the single analytical piece turned up by Aaron and Meyer's literature review) makes use of the notion of social power blocs, but closer inspection of the analysis reveals little connection with elite theory. In fact, public opinion (renamed the "prevailing ideology of property rights," but otherwise identical to the notion of a broad consensus) is held to be of key importance in labor law reform. Cohen's other major variable—the "degree of access to political power enjoyed by private power blocs"—represents simply the legislative support enjoyed by the relevant interest groups. Dunlop's use of an elite-based typology of industrial relations systems is another example of the language of elite theory being superimposed on a more orthodox conception of the state's role in industrial relations.

There are two main elite-based interpretations of industrial relations policy. For those theorists who include labor leaders as part of the elite, industrial relations policy is interpreted as the outcome of a clash of organizational interests between labor and business leaders. The divergence of interests here is narrow, however, since both groups share a broader interest in perpetuating the existing social structure that benefits them both. Dennis Olsen's analysis of the imposition of wage and price controls in Canada is an example of this stream of thought.

> The thinking and discussions on wage and price controls went on for many years, and governments could now argue, one supposes, that the whole process was "pluralistic" in that many and various groups were consulted. In fact, however, the actual leaders of the various groups (that is, those who were consulted in person) narrow down primarily to the state elites themselves—federal and provincial cabinet ministers and senior bureaucrats, corporation leaders, labour leaders, and a few prominent academics and economists, all of whom taken together would form only a tiny proportion of the Canadian population. Of course, these elite groups think of themselves as "representing" masses of people, or the "public interest," but there is little evidence to support the argument that

they actually consulted the people in question or that they actually represented the wishes of those few they did consult in the councils of state. Behind the media facade of public pluralism in a liberal society lies a frankly accepted elite practice of decision making by private negotiations among the powerful.[54]

In contrast, other elite theorists hold that labor leaders are not members of the elite, and from this point of view, state industrial relations policy is viewed as an instrument by which political and industrial elites maintain their dominance over the working class and its leaders. J. A. G. Griffith's analysis of the British judiciary, which focuses on such factors as the appointment procedures of judges and their social backgrounds, is in the elite tradition[55] and his conclusions clearly exclude labor leaders from the elite.

The judges define the public interest, inevitably, from the viewpoint of their own class. And the public interest, so defined, is by a natural, not an artificial, coincidence, the interest of others in authority, whether in government, in the City or in the church. It includes the maintenance of order, the protection of private property, the promotion of certain general economic aims, the containment of the trade union movement, and the continuance of governments which conduct their business largely in private and on the advice of other members of what I have called the governing group.[56]

Underlying both of these variants is the broader theme of social control, a theme that leads elite theorists to focus on the interorganizational channels of the elite accommodation process, and on the way in which elites take advantage of their access to resources and communication networks within organizations to control those below them. The assessment of public policy from this perspective centers, therefore, on notions of equality and democracy: policies that perpetuate the dominance of elites are held to fall short of socially desirable. As well, elite theorists draw attention to the way in which elites manage public opinion and delimit the boundaries of legitimate actions and demands. This line of thinking stems in turn from the broader prescriptive agenda of (most) elite theorists, that is, advocacy of reforms oriented toward securing true democracy. Elite theorists thus tend to decry state policies that enhance control over workers, either by their leaders (as in the case of policies that help trade union leaders maintain control over their members) or by employers (such as limits on the right to strike or protections of managerial prerogatives).

Elite theory can be criticized on several fronts. The variant most commonly used in industrial relations research—the version that views both business and labor leaders as essentially equal participants in the elite accommodation process—is really just a reformulation of pluralism. The reformulation is useful, for it draws attention to aspects of the policy-making process not readily accessible to standard pluralist methods; but it is as misleading as pluralist models in its assumption of an equality (or near equality) between elite groups. As C. Wright Mills (himself an elite theorist) once put it

> The big corporations . . . give the executives a stable basis for durable expectations; so the business member of the power elite can rely upon them in the pursuit of his short-term goals and opportunistic maneuvering. But the union, unlike the corporation, is often in a state of protest; it is on the defensive in a sometimes actually, and always potentially, hostile society. It does not provide such enduring means, which are ready-made and at the labor elite's disposal. If the labor leader wants such means, even for his little goals, he must himself build and maintain them.[57]

Moreover, although rivalry between some elite groups might be adequately portrayed as attempts to shift resources from one organization to another, the rivalry between capital and labor is of an altogether different type. Because labor is constituted as a group only in relation to the domination exercised by capital, the rivalry between them cannot adequately be expressed in terms of distributional struggles between wholly separate entities.

The Biased State: The Class Perspective

The fourth perspective that makes an occasional (although not always warmly welcomed) appearance in the industrial relations literature is class theory. In contrast to the other three paradigms, class theory portrays society as divided into classes defined by the broad divisions and antagonisms that attend the social organization of production. This focus on class relations need not imply that societies lack a certain unity, nor that non-class cleavages are imaginary, nor that it is impossible to identify elites; but it does imply that these must be related to the broader context of class divisions and capital accumulation. Associated with this view of society is the premise that the state, far from being neutral, is possessed of a bias in favor of the dominant classes.

As with the other analytical perspectives discussed in this essay, class theory has several important variants. For present purposes, two main models of the policy process can be identified—"class action theory" and the "systemic bias" model. Theorists from both of these schools agree that society is most accurately portrayed as divided into classes with opposing interests, but they disagree as to the key dynamic of policymaking (and, hence, as to the source of the state's bias).

Class action theories (of which there are both Marxist and non-Marxist versions) view state institutions as an arena not of pressure group competition or elite rivalry, but of class conflict. Public policies—or, at least those over which the interests of labor and capital differ—are therefore outcomes of class-political struggles. The key dynamic in this model is political action rooted in class interests, and, since there are marked disparities in class power (manifested in unequal control over resources and public and private institutions, including the media), state policy regularly favors the interests of capital. Moreover, unlike writers of other persuasions, class action theorists do not view the state as a neutral player: the power of the capitalist class is not simply exercised, as it were, on the state, but is entrenched within it as well (through, for example, processes of recruitment and socialization within civil service). In any case, the core of this model is that state policy is best understood as the outcome of class-political conflict. Such a perspective is central to much of the work of the self-styled "new political economy."[58] For example, researchers from this school have utilized a class action model to account for international variations in state policy on the basis of the differences in the industrial and political strategies of different labor movements.

Those who subscribe to the systemic bias variant of class theory agree that state policy regularly favors the interests of capital over labor, but identify the source of this bias in structural properties of capitalist societies. Thus, less emphasis is put on the conscious political behavior of classes and their organizations, and attention is drawn instead to a series of systemic mechanisms that cause state policymaking to favor the interests of the dominant class. Central to this approach is an analysis of the basic requirements of capital accumulation that function as constraints on state policy.

> "Economic" stability is the precondition of all the other goals which governments pursue, whatever their political complexion; yet (in the absence of mobilisation to overturn capitalist economic relations) this inevitably entails the stability of a *capitalist* economy. Hence private profit—the barometer of economic "health," and the source of new investment—has to be encouraged; and with it, intentionally or not, the associated inequalities of power and material advantage. More generally, policies must be pursued which maintain what is termed "the confidence of industry" (which means, not the majority who work in industry, but the minority who own and control industry); and this sets rigid limits to permissible radicalism. Thus political controversy focuses on issues which are marginal to the functioning and survival of capitalist relations

of production, and the privileges of the capitalist class; and in the process, the very possibility of serious political debate around the basic structure of society is obscured.[59]

Despite their differences, both of these class-based models share a more general theory of state involvement in industrial relations, which holds that capitalist society is most accurately conceived of in class terms, that the state is directly implicated in and forms a crucial part of socio-economic structure, and that in consequence the state cannot play anything like a neutral role. Industrial relations policy, then, is usually a mode of sustaining capitalist relations of production, by propping up (either through coercion or concessions) the political and industrial structures of class domination and exploitation. Thus, like unitary theory, class theory focuses upon the societal context of action (though the different conceptions of society lead to some rather obvious differences).

Class theorists tend not so much to assess public policy as to mount a critique of policy, a critique that attempts to demonstrate how state policy perpetuates exploitative relations of production to the detriment of the working class. It follows, of course, that the prescriptive agenda of class theory is transformative. Although this agenda shares some of the elements of the elite theorists' concern to extend democratic participation, it goes further by suggesting in traditional socialist fashion that nothing short of a complete restructuring of socio-economic and political institutions will suffice to end systemic inequality and exploitation.

As with the other paradigms, class models are not immune from criticism. To begin with, class theorists are often reluctant to grapple with the multiple divisions in capitalist societies, preferring instead to argue in a most unconvincing way that linguistic, sexual, regional and other divisions are misleading distractions manufactured by the bourgeoisie. In addition, not a few class theorists fall into the trap of discerning an incipient revolution in every strike or act of sabotage. More importantly, class theory falls short of a satisfactory analysis of the manner in which "bias" is constituted in the system of policymaking. It is certainly important to point out the effects of state policy in perpetuating inequality in the workplace, the enterprise, the labor market and the wider society; but class-based models are not especially well-suited to exploring the inner dynamics of state policymaking.

PRESSURE GROUPS—ELITES OR CLASSES?

If there was an acceptably neutral way to assess the adequacy of contending social theories, there would be little point in further debate. It is by now fairly well accepted, however, that (as John Niland has put it) "truly open research is rarer than might be thought: judging from their published work Marxists and non-Marxists alike seldom stumble across results in the social sciences that run counter to their preferred ideological position."[60] This is true not because social scientists are dishonest ideologues, but because theorization necessarily involves a degree of self-imposed blinkering. Indeed, the very purpose of theory—to expose, in as elegant a fashion as possible, the crucial causal mechanisms behind some phenomenon—involves an inherently selective and normative process of highlighting certain aspects of social reality while leaving other, putatively less important aspects in the shadows.

In the case at hand it is important to underline the point that the four theories of state involvement in industrial relations are incommensurate, not only ideologically, but also analytically. In the preceding discussion it was argued that, being rooted in different paradigms of state-society relations, each theory tends to be focused on a single context of action (or level of analysis). Unitarists and class theorists both tend to concentrate on the societal context of action, that is, on the broad features of society that each supposes to be integral to an understanding of the state. In contrast, elite theorists emphasize the organizational context by focusing upon "the stable coalitions of resources in organizations manned by elites and . . . the limited range of decisions within the organizational parameters."[61] In turn, pluralist models emphasize the situational context by focusing upon "the conditions of mobilization of particular groups and individuals for political action and upon the strategies of influence and the outcomes of action in particular situations."[62] The difficulty is that a focus on only one context is an inadequate means of exploring public policy. As Alford argues, "The explanatory power generated by focusing on a particular context of action is gained at the cost of neglecting certain questions. Because these definitions of state-society relations are paradigms and not merely models or theories, each tends to explain away the independence of the phenomena of central concern to the other paradigms or to subsume them under its core concepts and variables."[63]

Thus, unitary models are fundamentally incapable of treating aspects of policy that bear upon or arise from social divisions, and are less than useful in exploring the actual processes through which policy is formulated. The assumption that social values (in the rational actor model) or system needs (in the systems model) are more or less automatically reflected in policy decisions, simply assumes away the problem of how such results are produced. Research into policy then becomes an exercise in attempting to explain policy in terms of a set of social values or system needs without any reference to the manner in which the process works (or, at most, with a highly idealistic view of elected governments faithfully reflecting the will of the people). In contrast, pluralist models tend to ignore the impact of the organizational and social setting within which interest group competition takes place. Pluralists thus fail to explore the origins of particular interests, the factors that make some groups more powerful than others, and the "extent to which groups are actually created and then sustained by the actions of other groups, or by institutions at the level of society as a whole, mainly by the state."[64] Elite models, because they concentrate upon (indeed reify) large organizations, fail to explore the "concrete social and economic interests actually served by bureaucratic organizations," the manner in which those interests are related to the distribution of power among organizations, and the "origins of bureaucracies in past critical decisions and outcomes of social conflict."[65]

The main point is that an adequate understanding of the state's role in industrial relations must take into account all three contexts of action. In order to develop such an approach, however, two key choices must be made. First, it is necessary to choose between an additive and interactive mode of combining several paradigms. The former presumes that each paradigm can be preserved, and that the relationship between the levels is one of reciprocal constraint. The latter presumes that one paradigm should be taken as an analytical starting point, and that this level determines structures and outcomes at the other levels. The first method runs the risk of analytical ambiguity and internal contradiction. Although the second veers towards reductionism, it is preferable to attempting to create a "pluralist-elite-class" approach, which can only be considered absurd.

Second, it is necessary to choose between the unitary and class paradigms since each provides tools for exploring the societal context. It will by now be obvious that the key difference between the unitary and class paradigms lies in the particular image of society with which each is associated. In contrast to the unitary emphasis on social values or system needs, the class paradigm attempts to analyze policy in terms of "the basic institutions of property and the objective class relations arising from those institutions."[66] This author contends that the class paradigm is preferable on these grounds, and, as well, that in integrating elements of the class, elite and pluralist perspectives, the former ought to be taken as the analytical starting point.

It is of course impossible to cast this choice in neutral or purely scientific terms, for political convictions inexorably color analytical choices, especially at this level of analysis. Still, it may be useful to defend the choice by exploring deficiencies in the three orthodox approaches in a little more detail. To say that orthodoxy fails to construct an adequate conception of the societal context, or that it ignores key questions, is hardly the most devastating of criticisms. It is necessary therefore to show how these characteristics lead to more substantive problems.

One problem with industrial relations orthodoxy is that it tends to hive off the polity from the economy, either by conceiving of the state as a trans-historical subject (in the unitary version) or by ignoring the societal context (in the pluralist and elite versions). This profoundly ahistorical treatment of state-society relations leads orthodox writers to apply categories derived from one type of society to industrial relations in other types of societies, as in the case of attempts to employ the "three actor model"[67] to conceptualize the role of the state in non-capitalist societies. The obvious problem with such an approach is that it ignores significant differences in social structure. Although the three actor model is appropriate for capitalist societies, where economy and polity are institutionally distinct, it cannot be applied to societies where the state, management and workers' organizations are not separate in the same sense.

The separation between the economy and polity leads to a second problem—the tendency to regard the state as existing apart from the economy. That is not to say that orthodox analysis excludes economic phenomena. Because the state is seen as existing apart from the economy, however, economic phenomena are regarded as independent variables that generate problems or alter the setting of policymaking. Little attention is paid to the more fundamental role of the state in creating and sustaining the basic conditions of existence of capitalist relations of production and exchange (the institutions of private property, basic market regulations, the employment contract, and so on). Thus, state activity prompted by short-term economic problems is highlighted, and its role in perpetuating the exchange of labor and its subordination in production is overlooked.

Orthodoxy's neglect of class relations leads to a third problem—ignoring the extent to which the state's policies function to sustain the structure of social relations that put employers in a dominant position over labor. In place of class divisions, orthodoxy substitutes conflicts of interest between functionally defined stakeholders in organizations. In these terms, the enterprise is portrayed as an overarching entity within which the functional groups co-exist; and its hierarchical, authoritarian nature is assumed to be a technological or bureaucratic necessity. Thus, the broad goals of the enterprise can be presented as neutral, as transcending the sectional interests of particular groups, and the state's support of these goals can likewise be portrayed as neutral. In consequence, employers' interests are reified, first into the organization's interests, and then into the public interest, thus sanctioning as neutral the state's pursuit of such objectives as "industrial peace," "orderliness," "efficiency," and "stability." The managerial orientation buried in these goals becomes obvious when the obverse conditions are examined. Industrial disputes, disorderliness, restrictions on efficiency, and the creation of instability, are precisely the means by which workers press their claims, seek a degree of autonomy, and attempt to enlarge the scope of their influence. The usefulness of a theory that holds these to be opposed to the public interest is questionable.

This interpretational difficulty spills over into a fourth problem—the managerial biases of orthodox prescriptions. For most unitary writers there is a straightforward connection between the interests of employers and the goals that the state ought to pursue. For pluralists, the notion of voluntarism is central. As Brown has said of the pluralist perspective:

> Applied to society as a whole, or to the industrial relations "systems" within it, it [implies] that the government, or the state, becomes one party to the pluralist procedures, though perhaps one with special responsibility for asserting the "public interest," and that the state should not impose solutions to industrial relations conflicts which are best worked out autonomously by the parties involved.[68]

On the other hand, the state should intervene when an autonomous solution is not forthcoming; but even then intervention should be restricted to the establishment of procedures that will help the parties work things out for themselves. The managerial bias in this view is an indirect one, stemming from the conditions that signal that an autonomous solution is unlikely. In particular, high levels of industrial conflict, widespread challenges to managerial authority, wildcat strikes, mass picketing, and rapidly rising wage levels, are usually interpreted as signals that the parties are unable to reach an agreement. Conditions such as low wages, occupational segregation by sex and race, the persistence of hierarchical work relations, rising profits, and so on, are not seen in the same light.

CONCLUSION

The criticism of industrial relations orthodoxy advanced in this paper can be recast as guidelines for the development of a theory of state involvement in industrial relations. To begin with, it is necessary to abandon the multidisciplinary fracturing of industrial relations problems and generate a truly interdisciplinary approach, one that bridges the political and technocratic camps in particular, and one that pulls together the separate fragments of state policy into a more general framework. The scope of the subject also needs to be broadened beyond its traditional focus on formal institutions of collective distributional relations, to include state activities that shape production relations and touch upon the unorganized. In short, what is needed is a framework that meets the acknowledged definition of the discipline— the study of all aspects of the employment relationship.

A broadened, integrated, and more explicit framework would be a long step in the right direction, but it is also necessary to avoid orthodoxy's other pitfalls. In particular, the basic premises concerning the nature of society and state-society relations, which lead orthodoxy into a number of substantive interpretational difficulties, need to be abandoned. Thus, an adequate theory must include all three contexts of action, and in so doing must be able to provide an interactive analysis of the relations among those contexts. The advocacy of the class paradigm as the analytical starting point in this essay reflects a conviction that the orthodox conception is deeply flawed, especially because it treats the state as disconnected from social structures in general and social relations of production in particular.

Theoretical and methodological strictures are rarely empty of political meaning. Although the emphasis in this essay has been on the analytical weaknesses of industrial relations orthodoxy's treatment of the state, it should be remembered that orthodoxy is not bereft of political meaning.

> The philosophy of collective bargaining law, elaborated since the 1930's in doctrine, law review commentary and management literature, is an important effort to conceptualize, justify and legitimate the modern, regulatory state in the period of advanced industrial capitalism. As such it is a premier mode of elite ideological practice and an enduring contribution not just to law but to liberal political theory generally.[69]

NOTES

1. Benjamin Aaron and Paul Seth Meyer, "Public Policy and Labor-Management Relations," *A Review of Industrial Relations,* Vol. 2 (Madison: Industrial Relations Research Association, 1971), p. 4.

2. See, for example, David Winchester, "Industrial Relations Research in Britain," *British Journal of Industrial Relations,* Vol. 21, No. 1 (March 1983), pp. 111–112. As for the United States, it might be pointed out that the most recent Industrial Relations Research Association (IRRA) research review volume does not include a chapter summarizing in a general way research on public policy, but instead contains three separate assessments of different aspects of public policy, all from the perspective of labor economics; see Thomas A. Kochan, Daniel J. B. Mitchell and

Lee Dyer, eds., *Industrial Relations Research in the 1970s: Review and Appraisal* (Madison: Industrial Relations Research Association, 1982).

3. There is, of course, no single industrial relations orthodoxy in the sense of a unified and coherent theory to which the vast majority of specialists in the field adhere. Indeed, in the next section considerable attention will be devoted to a number of variants found within the field. The term orthodoxy is therefore meant to suggest only a loose understanding of the major elements of industrial relations and its conceptual referents. Note also that no reference is made to the "discipline" of industrial relations in this paper; the term "field of study," though less elegant, is more accurate.

4. Kingsley Laffer, "Is Industrial Relations an Academic Discipline?" *Journal of Industrial Relations,* Vol. 16 (March 1974).

5. Allan Flanders, *Management and Unions: The Theory and Reform of Industrial Relations* (London: Faber & Faber, 1970), p. 85.

6. See, for example, John T. Dunlop, "Policy Decisions and Research in Industrial Relations and Economics," *Industrial and Labor Relations Review,* Vol. 30, No. 3 (April 1977), pp. 275–276; and Thomas A. Kochan, "Theory, Policy Evaluation and Methodology in Collective Bargaining Research," *Proceedings,* Industrial Relations Research Association, 1976.

7. John H. Goldthorpe, "Industrial Relations in Great Britain: A Critique of Reformism," *Politics and Society,* Vol. 4, No. 4 (1974), p. 426.

8. George Strauss and Peter Feuille, "Industrial Relations Research: A Critical Analysis," *Industrial Relations,* Vol. 17, No. 3 (October 1978), p. 274. They go on to note that "One reason for this complacency is the fact that a fair amount of industrial peace has been purchased in America. Probably the price for this has not been excessive, so far, but the framework for analyzing these questions does not exist. Indeed, the questions have hardly been raised at all." In light of their own criticisms of U.S. industrial relations research, one might take issue with the costing of the tradeoff.

9. Political scientists and political sociologists are often guilty of the reverse fault, that is, ignoring the impact of the policies they study. Because the focus of this paper is on industrial relations theory, this point cannot be developed further.

10. Peter Gourevitch, Peter Lange and Andrew Martin, "Industrial Relations and Politics: Some Reflections," *Industrial Relations in International Perspective: Essays on Research and Policy,* ed. by Peter Doeringer (New York: Holmes & Meier, 1981), p. 401.

11. John T. Dunlop and William Foote Whyte, "Framework for the Analysis of Industrial Relations: Two Views," *Industrial and Labor Relations Review,* Vol. 3, No. 3 (April 1950), pp. 399–401.

12. See John T. Dunlop, *Industrial Relations Systems* (New York: Henry Holt, 1958), Ch. 1.

13. Dunlop and Whyte, op. cit., p. 390.

14. John T. Dunlop, "Political Systems and Industrial Relations," *International Institute for Labour Studies Bulletin,* No. 9 (1972), pp. 103–104.

15. Two exceptions worthy of note: Keith Middlemas, *Politics in Industrial Society: The Experience of the British System Since 1911* (London: André Deutsch, 1979); and Paul Craven, *"An Impartial Umpire": Industrial Relations and the Canadian State, 1900–1911* (Toronto: University of Toronto Press, 1980).

16. Even where there has been an apparent reversal of this trend, the withdrawal or inactivity of the state highlights the importance of its role in industrial relations. The lack of action by the American government in the area of union certification, and the withdrawal of the British government from its role in minimum wage-setting, are cases in point. As policy theorists have

argued, policy must be understood to include decisions not taken as well as decisions that are taken; therefore, the absence of state action cannot be taken to imply an autonomy from politics.

17. Respectively: Dunlop, *Industrial Relations Systems,* Ch. 1; Flanders, op. cit., p. 86; V. L. Allen, *The Sociology of Industrial Relations* (London: Longman, 1971), p. 21; H. G. Heneman, "Towards a General Conceptual System of Industrial Relations: How Do We Get There?" *Essays in Industrial Relations Theory,* ed. by Gerald Somers (Ames: Iowa State University Press, 1969), p. 4; Jack Barbash, "The Elements of Industrial Relations," *British Journal of Industrial Relations,* Vol 2, No. 1 (March 1964), p. 66; Laffer, op. cit., p. 72; George Sayers Bain and H. A. Clegg, "A Strategy of Industrial Relations Research in Britain," *British Journal of Industrial Relations,* Vol. 12, No. 1 (March 1974), p. 95.

18. Strauss and Feuille, op. cit., p. 275.

19. Archibald Cox, *Law and the National Labor Policy* (Los Angeles: Institute of Industrial Relations, University of California, 1960), p. ix.

20. See, for example, H. D. Woods, "Canadian Collective Bargaining and Dispute Settlement Policy: An Appraisal," *Canadian Journal of Economics and Political Science,* Vol. 21, No. 4 (November 1955), pp. 447-449; and *Labour Policy in Canada* (2nd ed.) (Toronto: Macmillan, 1973).

21. Kenneth F. Walker, "The Role of the Government in Industrial Relations (with Special Reference to Australia)," *Labour Relations in the Asian Countries,* Monograph (Tokyo: The Japan Institute of Labour, 1967), p. 196.

22. A recent partial exception is Jack Barbash's discussion of the components of the state's role in industrial relations, which includes welfare policy and labor market intervention (but which ignores some other necessary elements to be discussed below). Jack Barbash, *The Elements of Industrial Relations* (Madison: University of Wisconsin Press, 1984), Ch. 8.

23. Richard Hyman, review of *Collective Bargaining and Industrial Relations* by Thomas A. Kochan, *Industrial Relations,* Vol. 21, No. 1 (Winter 1982), pp. 109-110.

24. See Robert R. Alford, "Paradigms of Relations Between State and Society," *Stress and Contradiction in Modern Capitalism,* ed. by Leon N. Lindberg et al. (Lexington: D. C. Heath, 1975), for a general discussion of the pluralist, elite and class paradigms. The discussion of the unitary paradigm here represents an extension of Alford's discussion.

25. An exercise of this type unavoidably does considerable violence to the analyses and positions of individual writers. In particular, to link specific explanatory models with sharply defined prescriptive agendas (and, by implication, with the terrain of political ideologies that industrial relations specialists so often prefer to wish away) risks offending those who do not fit wholly into one or another of the perspectives. A pertinent example is Alan Fox, who, when taken to task by Stephen Wood and Ruth Elliott, in their article "A Critical Evaluation of Fox's Radicalisation of Industrial Relations Theory," *Sociology,* Vol. 13, No. 1 (January 1979) for a seeming inconsistency between his critique of pluralism and his reluctance to advocate rapid and wholesale change, argued that he was a victim of "tramline" or "package-deal" thinking. See Alan Fox, "A Note on Industrial Relations Pluralism," *Sociology,* Vol. 13, No. 1 (January 1979). If an objection of this sort comes to mind, the reader might want to read "theoretical syndrome" in place of "theory" in the discussion.

26. The distinction between the "unitary" and "pluralist" perspectives is an extension and adaptation of Alan Fox's discussion of industrial relations ideologies; see his *Industrial Sociology and Industrial Relations,* Royal Commission on Trade Unions and Employers' Associations, research paper No. 3 (London: HMSO, 1966) and "Industrial Relations: A Social Critique of Pluralist Ideology," *Man and Organization,* ed. by J. Child (London: Allen & Unwin, 1973).

For a recent discussion using categories similar to those developed in this paper, see Bill Rees, "Frames of Reference and the 'Public Interest,' " *Labour Law and the Community: Perspectives for the 1980s,* Lord Wedderburn of Charlton and W. T. Murphy, eds., (London: Institute of Advanced Legal Studies, 1982).

27. The discussion of explanatory models of policymaking in this and later sections draws on the following sources: Thomas R. Dye, *Understanding Public Policy* (5th ed.; Englewood Cliffs, NJ: Prentice-Hall, 1984), Ch. 2; Peter Aucoin, "Public-Policy Theory and Analysis," *Public Policy in Canada,* ed. by G. Bruce Doern and Peter Aucoin (Toronto: Macmillan, 1979); Graham T. Allison, *Essence of Decision: Explaining the Cuban Missile Crisis* (Boston: Little, Brown, 1971).

28. See, for example, Samuel Brittan, *The Economic Consequences of Democracy* (London: Temple Smith, 1977). For a critique of this school, see Claus Offe, *Contradictions of the Welfare State,* ed. by John Keane (Cambridge, MA: MIT Press, 1984).

29. In contrast to "socio-legal studies." See Lord Wedderburn of Charlton, Roy Lewis and John Clark, eds., *Labour Law and Industrial Relations: Building on Kahn-Freund* (Oxford: Clarendon, 1983).

30. Karl E. Klare, "Labor Law as Ideology: Toward a New Historiography of Collective Bargaining Law," *Industrial Relations Law Journal,* Vol. 4 (1984), p. 451.

31. Thomas Dye, *Understanding Public Policy* (Englewood Cliffs, NJ: Prentice-Hall, 1971), p. 36 (emphasis in original).

32. Dunlop, *Industrial Relations Systems,* p. 99.

33. See John Niland, "Research and Reform in Industrial Relations," *Journal of Industrial Relations,* Vol. 23, no. 4 (December 1981), pp., 486–487. Although Niland seems to accept that the public interest can be used as an objective standard by which to assess public policy; he also discusses briefly some of the problems inherent in its definition.

34. See Fox, "Industrial Relations: A Social Critique of Pluralist Ideology."

35. The criticisms that follow, as well as those directed at the other theories canvassed in this section, concentrate on specific attributes of the relevant explanatory models. Later in the paper a more general critique of orthodox theories will be put forward.

36. The classic critique of rationalism is Charles E. Lindblom, "The Science of 'Muddling Though,' " *Public Administration Review,* Vol. 19 (Spring 1959).

37. See Allison, op. cit.

38. See Christopher Whelan, "State Intervention, Major Disputes and the Role of the Law," in *Labour Law and the Community: Perspectives for the 1980s,* Lord Wedderburn of Charlton and W. T. Murphy, eds., (London: Institute of Advanced Legal Studies, 1982).

39. Two classic manifestos are: W. Milne-Bailey, *Trade Unions and the State* (London: Allen & Unwin, 1934); and Clark Kerr, "Industrial Relations and the Liberal Pluralist," *Proceedings,* Industrial Relations Research Association, 1955.

40. Pluralism has been put to several other purposes in the field of industrial relations: as an analogy to understand the internal processes of trade unions and, thereby, to legitimate U.S. state policies imposing "democratic" principles on the internal affairs of trade unions (see Richard Hyman, "Pluralism, Procedural Consensus and Collective Bargaining," *British Journal of Industrial Relations,* Vol. 16, No. 1 [March 1978], p. 20); to support the conception of the collective bargaining process as a mini-democracy and in this way to justify the grievance-arbitration process as analogous to the function of the judiciary (see Katherine Van Wezel Stone, "The Post-War Paradigm in American Labor Law," *Yale Law Review,* Vol. 90, No. 7 [June 1981], p. 5); and to conceptualize the industrial enterprise (see Fox, *Industrial Sociology and Industrial Relations).*

41. H. A. Clegg, "Pluralism in Industrial Relations," *British Journal of Industrial Relations,* Vol. 13, No. 3 (November 1975), p. 309.

42. Flanders, "Industrial Relations: What Is Wrong with the System?," p. 93.

43. Clegg, "Pluralism in Industrial Relations," p. 310.

44. Thomas A. Kochan, *Collective Bargaining and Industrial Relations: From Theory to Practice to Policy* (Homewood: Irwin, 1980).

45. Ibid., p. 59.

46. Barbash, *The Elements of Industrial Relations.*

47. Alford, "Paradigms of Relations Between State and Society."

48. See, for instance, Michael Mann, "The Social Cohesion of Liberal Democracy," *American Sociological Review,* Vol. 25, No. 3 (June 1970); Michael Best and William E. Connolly, *The Politicized Economy* (Lexington: D. C. Heath, 1976), pp. 127–129.

49. For an example of the confusion that this introduces, see Kerr, "Industrial Relations and the Liberal Pluralist," pp. 9–10.

50. Claus Offe and Helmut Wiesenthal, "Two Logics of Collective Action: Theoretical Notes on Social Class and Organizational Form," *Political Power and Social Theory,* Vol. 1 (1980).

51. Some examples are cited below. See also Middlemas, *Politics in Industrial Society;* and Wedderburn, Lewis and Clark, *Labour Law and Industrial Relations.*

52. Robert Michels, *Political Parties: A Sociological Study of the Oligarchical Tendencies of Modern Democracy,* trans. by Eden and Cedar Paul (New York: The Free Press, 1968). For the modern debate see: George Strauss, "Union Government in the United States: Research Past and Future," *Industrial Relations,* Vol. 16, No. 2 (May 1977); and the brief comments in Richard Hyman, *Industrial Relations: A Marxist Introduction* (London: Macmillan, 1975), pp. 61–65.

53. Sanford Cohen, "An Analytical Framework for Labor Relations Law," *Industrial and Labor Relations Review,* Vol. 14, No. 3 (April 1961).

54. Dennis Olsen, *The State Elite* (Toronto: McClelland and Stewart, 1980), p. 117.

55. J. A. G. Griffith, *The Politics of the Judiciary* (2nd ed.; Douglas, Isle of Man: Fontana, 1981), especially Chs. 3, 7, and 9.

56. Ibid., p. 240.

57. C. Wright Mills, "The Labor Leaders and the Power Elite," *Power, Politics and People: The Collected Essays of C. Wright Mills,* ed. by Irving Louis Horowitz (Oxford: Oxford University Press, 1967), p. 103.

58. See, for example: Gourevitch, Lange and Martin, op. cit.; Douglas Hibbs, "On the Political Economy of Long-run Trends in Strike Activity," *British Journal of Political Science,* Vol. 8 (1978); Michael Shalev and Walter Korpi, "Strikes, Industrial Relations and Class Conflict in Capitalist Societies," *British Journal of Sociology,* Vol. 30, No. 2 (June 1979).

59. Richard Hyman, *Industrial Relations: A Marxist Introduction* (London: Macmillan, 1975), p. 125.

60. Niland, op. cit., p. 484.

61. Alford, op. cit., p. 150.

62. Ibid.

63. Ibid., pp. 150–151.

64. Ibid., p. 151.

65. Ibid.

66. Ibid., p. 150.

67. See for example, Bruce Herrick, "Research Needs in Labor and Economic Development," *Industrial Relations,* Vol. 8, No. 3 (May 1969), pp. 218–219.

68. Richard K. Brown, "From Donovan to Where? Interpretations of Industrial Relations in Britain Since 1960," *British Journal of Sociology,* Vol. 29, No. 4 (December 1978), p. 442.

69. Klare, op. cit., p. 456.

10

A Survey of Theories
of Industrial Relations

Braham Dabscheck

This paper compares and contrasts five established theoretical approaches to the study of industrial relations. They are Dunlop's systems model, pluralism, Marxism, corporatism, and theories of regulation. In addition we examine a new generation of theorizing. In examining these competing theories attention is directed to the notion of the public interest, the role of the state, and the level of analysis. The paper concludes that the concept of the public interest has no useful analytical role in a theory of industrial relations, that the state should be viewed as an independent variable, and that a disaggregated societal-based model should be employed. Finally, the role of any institution or part of the system needs to be viewed in terms of its interaction with the total system, or other institutions or parts of the system.

Industrial relations scholars periodically indulge in the soul searching and heartrending exercise of questioning the legitimacy of their discipline. Industrial relations is a relatively young discipline and, apparently, lacks the respectability of older, so-called more established disciplines. Accompanying such feelings of disquiet, industrial relations scholars usually make a plea for the development of theory or theories. The development of theories and debates not only adds to the discipline's academic respectability, but also has the important function of assuaging feelings of guilt that there must be more to life than the case study and the discovery of new mountains of facts.

In May 1982, R. Marsden pointed to what he believed to be "the apparent absence of a theory of industrial relations."[1] Several comments concerning this claim will be offered. First, the observation comes from a dilettante who has made a quick excursion into industrial relations on vacation from another discipline—a perennial occupational hazard for academic industrial relations.

155

On a superficial and limited reading of the literature he presents what are meant to be profound insights. Interestingly, most of Marsden's article tenders criticisms of competing theories within industrial relations, in particular Dunlop's systems model and Marxism. Although Marsden may regard these attempts as being inadequate, they nonetheless provide a focus for theoretical debate.

Second, why should there be a theory of industrial relations? There is not *a* theory of sociology, *a* theory of economics, *a* theory of politics, or *a* theory of history. Other disciplines are characterized by the existence of a number of competing theoretical stances. The diversity and clash of competing theories in other disciplines provides them with their richness and interest, and simultaneously enhances their academic respectability. Why should industrial relations travel down a route that other disciplines have refused to follow?

Third, and most importantly, Marsden is seemingly unaware of the important theoretical developments in industrial relations of the last two decades. The 1968 Donovan report on British industrial relations[2] and the use of wages and incomes policies in both Britain and Western Europe have spawned an increasingly vociferous debate that has witnessed the development of new and competing paradigms with industrial relations. Strauss and Feuille, in observing the British scene, have commented that "current British industrial relations research is now enjoying a Golden Age."[3]

Developments among North American and Australian scholars, on the other hand, have been somewhat desultory. American researchers appear to be divided into three separate camps: the labor (usually neo-classical) economists, the institutionalists, and the behavioral scientists. For more than a decade, reviewers of the American scene have referred, somewhat unsuccessfully, to the need for the "integration of the three approaches."[4] It may be that Australian and American debate has lagged because the two countries' institutional forms—Australia's usage of industrial tribunals and the American reliance on collective bargaining—have, for want of a better term, remained relatively stable over time. The study of relative stability may be less interesting and challenging, and less likely to lead to innovation than the study of change and discontinuity.[5] And it might be easier to conduct research into industry X, or union Y, or arbitration case Z than to encounter the frustrations associated with the amorphous world of theory.

The object of this paper is to compare and contrast five theoretical approaches to the study of industrial relations. They are Dunlop's systems model, pluralism, Marxism, corporatism, and theories of regulation. In examining these approaches, attention will be directed to three key issues. First the notion of the public interest, whether the respective theories incorporate such a notion or use an alternative analytical device to explain the nature of the interaction(s) that characterizes industrial relations; second, the nature and role of the state and, in particular, whether the state is viewed as an independent or dependent variable; and third, whether the theory is aggregated or disaggregated or societal- or firm-based.

DUNLOP'S SYSTEMS APPROACH

J. T. Dunlop's systems approach and the criticisms it has generated are well known and will only be briefly examined.[6] Dunlop defined an industrial relations system as consisting

> of three groups of actors—workers and their organizations, managers and their organizations, and governmental agencies concerned with the work community. These groups interact within a specified environment comprised of three interrelated contexts: the technology, the market or budgetary constraints, and the power relations in the larger community and the derived status of the actors. An industrial relations system creates an ideology or a commonly shared body of ideas and beliefs regarding the interaction and roles of the actors which helps to bind the system together.[7]

He also argued that: "The establishment of . . . procedures and rules . . . is the center of attention of an industrial relations system . . . the establishment and administration of these rules is the major concern or output of the industrial relations subsystem of industrial society."[8]

An initial criticism directed at this approach is that, although strong on structure, it tells us little about process and the motivation of the actors. To breathe some life into the theory, it is necessary to assume that the actors want to achieve their respective goals. Second, as Margerison has pointed out, Dunlop's definition of industrial relations, with its concentration on rules and rule making, raises the charge that he "tends to ignore the essential element of all industrial relations, that of the nature and development of conflict itself . . . industrial relations [according to Dunlop] . . . is more concerned with studying the resolution of industrial conflict than with its generation."[9] This also opens Dunlop to the charge that the systems model is a conservative tool designed to ensure the maintenance of the status quo. Finally, criticisms have been directed at his treatment of actors—more than three distinct actors can interact within an industrial relations system.

Dunlop is silent, or at best ambiguous, with respect to the notion of the public interest. His notion of a common ideology shared by the actors and his focus on rules and rule making may imply that the absence of either would not enhance the attainment of the public interest. He does, however, contemplate the possibility of an industrial relations system without a common ideology. "In a community in which the managers hold a highly paternalistic view toward workers and the workers hold there is no function for managers, there would be no common ideology in which each actor provided a legitimate role for the other; the relationship within such a work community would be regarded as volatile, and no stability would likely to be achieved in the industrial relations system."[10] The role of the state is poorly developed in Dunlop's model. He employs the term governmental agencies to incorporate the role of the state into his model. The state's involvement within an industrial relations system is more complex than this. Dunlop's analysis excludes the role of government(s) and the various superior courts that supervise the operation of industrial relations governmental agencies. Dunlop could avoid this criticism by claiming that the various organs of the state pursue a common and unified objective. It is equally, if not more likely, however, that they could be pulling and pushing in different directions. In Australia, for example, state and federal governments need to be distinguished; industrial tribunals assert their independence from government; and superior courts make decisions that both define and restrict the powers available to unions and employers as well as the various organs of the state.

Dunlop is also ambiguous as to whether or not governmental agencies should be regarded as dependent or independent institutions. Presumably, in Dunlop's hands, such agencies aid the other two actors as they interact with each other. It is unclear, however, whether these agencies follow the bidding of the parties, the direction of an external body (such as government), or are allowed to develop their own approach to the issues confronting them.

Dunlop focuses his analysis on the internal operation of a representative industrial relations system. Implicit in his approach is the notion that each system is unique; its form and evolution are determined by its own set of external constraints. Dunlop, then, implicitly assumes that there are no interconnections between respective industrial relations systems; to do otherwise would complicate his model and open up the possibility of having to analyze the actions and strategies of numerous actors. It is conceivable, however, that in seeking to arrive at an adequate understanding of industrial relations within a particular nation state that the interdependency, or the nature of the relationship, that exists between different industrial relations (sub)systems may be equally, if not more, crucial than that which occurs within respective industrial relations (sub)systems.

PLURALISM

Many disciplines within the social sciences, other than industrial relations, such as philosophy, anthropology, sociology and political science, have developed theoretical approaches to analyze different phenomena that they have respectively described as pluralism. So varied and diverse are notions of pluralism within the social sciences, that it might be more appropriate to refer to what Hyman describes as "pluralism's pluralism."[11] This section will not attempt the daunting task of surveying the intellectual roots, evolution and nuances of pluralism within different disciplines.[12] It will examine, however, the North American political science model of pluralism, as developed in the 1950s, to provide a reference point for the subsequent examination of industrial relations pluralism.

North American political science pluralism of the 1950s represents a model of political decisionmaking depicting the interaction that occurs between and among private interest groups and the various organs of the state. The political process is viewed as being open and fluid, "essentially a twofold process involving competition among political elites and bargaining among interest groups."[13] In this model, power is dispersed among a large number of varied and diverse interest groups. No single interest group or elite is able to become dominant because of the countervailing power of other interest groups and elites. Or, as Connolly says, "Pluralism . . . portrays the system as a balance of power among overlapping economic, religious, ethnic, and geographical groupings. Each group has some voice in shaping socially binding decisions; each constrains and is constrained through the process of mutual group adjustments; and all major groups share a broad system of beliefs and values which encourages conflict to proceed within established channels and allows initial disagreement to dissolve into compromise solutions."[14] The political system, then, is regarded as one of checks and balances, a self-regulating mechanism in which interest groups, in pursuing self-interest, restrain each other. It is akin to the economists' marketplace, in which political entrepreneurs compete with each other for political favors in furthering the objectives of their respective organizations.

The concept of the public interest within this model operates at two distinct levels. The first is where it is seen to be important that the system should continue to operate. At a superficial level, political science pluralism may appear to be a static model designed to ensure the maintenance of the status quo. The model, however, is concerned with understanding the process of political change—of explaining how the system moves from one position of balance or equilibrium to another. Change is viewed as occurring incrementally or discretely, rather than in big chunks or in a revolutionary manner, and results from the incessant interaction of numerous and varied interest groups. Furthermore, to talk of balance or equilibrium is not to imply that there is an equality of power between interest groups. There will be differences in the distribution of power at different times; no single interest group, however, will be able to dominate all other interest groups.

Second, when references are made to the public interest it should simply be viewed as a tactical device employed by interest groups to enhance the respectability of naked self-interest. As Barkin argues,

> Absolutely no public has its own static interest any more than an absolute reality with unvarying truth exists. Publics are ways of conceiving activities, and interests are means of indicating the value assigned to them by their participants and others. No such thing as *the* public activity, *the* society, or *the* public interest exists. The public interest as such, the claim of a specific group that its interests should be recognized and shared by all other groups, is a myth.[15]

Political science pluralism is ambiguous with respect to the role of the state. The arena model views the state as the locus in which interest groups jockey with each other for their respective places in the political sun. The state is dependent in the sense that interest groups capture the state, or rather that appropriate part of the state, to enhance the pursuit of their organizational goals. The umpire model, on the other hand, regards the state as independent. It not only establishes the rules of interaction and adjudicates disputes, but also initiates action to ensure that any interest group that becomes too powerful is brought back to the field. (Presumably if the state becomes too powerful private interest groups initiate action that will restrain its activities.) Alternatively, the umpire model can be watered down to include the various organs of the state as an additional set of interest groups involved in the exchanges that occur within a plural society.

Political science pluralism employs a disaggregated, societal-based model that views the political system as consisting of a multitude of small disconnected parts or subsectors. Interest groups organize themselves and marshal resources at those parts of the system of relevance to them and, by definition, ignore those parts seen as being irrelevant. The model assumes that the nature of the links between the various parts or subsectors of the system are limited and weak.

The major criticism of political science pluralism is that, although it may usefully analyze the nature of the interaction that occurs between established groups, it ignores or downplays the existence of new groups who find it difficult to gain access to the mainstream of political life. It is also criticized as being a distortion of social reality and for being essentially conservative. Wolff, for example, argues that "pluralist theory functions ideologically by tending to deny new groups or interests access to the political plateau. It does this by ignoring their existence in practice, not by denying their claim in theory. The result is that pluralism has a braking effect on social change; it slows down transformation in the system of group adjustment but does not set up an absolute barrier to change."[16]

It might be interesting to speculate on how this political science model of pluralism could have been adapted to the study of industrial relations. This model, with its focus on a large number of groups pursuing self-interest in a disaggregated manner (i.e., at that part of the system where concessions are forthcoming), would appear to have a natural affinity with the world of industrial relations, in which interactions between different unions, employers, and organs of the state also occur in a disaggregated manner. In industrial relations, of course, the parties do not confine the pursuit of self-interest to the polity, but also have access to what might be called the economists' marketplace. The advantage of explicitly incorporating the market into the analysis is that it helps to overcome the problem of the denial of access to new groups, which is a weakness of political science pluralism. Changes in the market have the potential of providing new interest groups with increased benefits and concomitant prestige, notwithstanding their inability to gain access to the cartel that dominates the political process. As new industries or sectors rise (and old ones fall), as respective organizations increase (or decrease) their effectiveness in the marketplace, they simultaneously bring about a new balance that enshrines their enhanced (or reduced) position. The market then would become an additional variable that would reflect changes in the relative positions of the various interest groups regarded as constituting a pluralistic industrial relations system.

A major problem, however, with applying political science pluralism to industrial relations is its ambivalence concerning the role of the state. This might be rectified by assuming that the various organs of the state are independent organizations pursuing their own unique objectives. The various organs of the state could simply be viewed as just another set of institutions operating within the framework of a pluralistic industrial relations system. With a few modifications, then, it is conceivable that political science pluralism could have been adapted to the world of industrial relations. However, the model that was subsequently developed had little connection with the North American political science model.[17]

Industrial relations pluralism[18] is essentially a British phenomenon and is generally linked to the ferment of ideas associated with the Donovan inquiry into British industrial relations in the second half of the 1960s. Possibly the clearest exposition is provided by Alan Fox,[19] although in his hands its ultimate function was that of a straw man[20] Fox argues that the firm should be viewed in plural terms. "The enterprise is a coalition of individuals and groups with their own aspirations and perceptions which they naturally see as valid and which they seek to express in action if such is required . . . individuals and groups with widely varying priorities agree to collaborate in social structures which enable all participants to get something of what they want; the terms of collaboration being settled by bargaining."[21] Fox also assumes that there is "something approximating a balance of power" between the parties and that they pursue a policy of mutual survival.[22] He is uncertain, however, about how to regard the role of conflict.

> A certain amount of overt conflict and disputation is welcomed as evidence that not all aspirations are being either sapped by hopelessness or suppressed by power. On the other hand, conflict above a certain level is felt to be evidence that the ground rules need changing; that marginal adjustments in rewards or work rules are required; that management is failing in some way to find the appropriate compromise or synthesis.[23]

And he is wary of the possibility that the parties may pursue claims that could lead to the breakdown of plural consensus.

> It would obviously be possible for one party to make claims which the other found totally unacceptable and on which compromise or synthesis proved impossible. The pluralist presumption would be that in such a case the consensual ethic governing joint regulation would be ruptured, and a forced collaboration would emerge when one party succeeded in coercing the other. The operation of a pluralistic system requires that such situations should be the exception rather than the rule, and that in the main the claims of each party fall within the range found bearable by the other.[24]

Some comparisons can be drawn between Fox's model of industrial relations pluralism and that of North American political science. Fox's analysis is couched at the level of the firm, whereas the political science model is societal. Hence, Fox's analysis is restricted to a small number of interest groups, whereas political science pluralism incorporates hordes of interest groups. Directing attention to this difference in numbers may appear to be carping, but it does expose several problems in Fox's analysis. Political science pluralism does not require an equality of power to exist between the numerous interest groups. It is recognized that, at any time, inequalities in the balance of power can exist. The model maintains, however, that no single interest group will be able to dominate all other interest groups. An interest group that increases its power will be dragged back to the field by the actions of other interest groups—the notion of checks and balances. With Fox's model, on the other hand, there are only a small number of interest groups—basically workers/unions and employers/capital—and it is necessary to postulate an equality of power; to not do so would imply that one interest group dominates the other, which, by definition, destroys the assumption of a plural firm.

Fox's firm-based model eschews interest groups going outside the firm, for example making use of politics, in seeking to achieve their goals. The political science model, on the other hand, is explicitly concerned with the interaction of interest groups as political animals. The problem of Fox adopting a narrow firm-based approach is that, not only does he ignore the reality and, it could be argued, much of the richness of real world industrial relations, but also, and most significantly, he has no way of incorporating the role of the state into his analysis. Given Fox's concern with the continuation of bargaining, tolerable levels of industrial conflict and mutual survival it might be implicitly assumed that the state can intervene under the rubric of the public interest. Dunlop's systems model is stronger on the role of the state than is Fox's model of industrial relations pluralism.

Interestingly enough, Fox himself is one of the strongest critics of industrial relations pluralism and has mounted attacks on two flanks.[25] His first line of attack is to argue

> that industrial society, while manifestly on one level a congeries of small special interest groups vying for scarce goods, status, or influence, is more fundamentally characterized in terms of the overarching exploitation of one class by another, of the propertyless by the propertied, of the less by the more powerful. From this view, any talk of "checks and balances," however apt for describing certain subsidiary phenomena, simply confuses our understanding of the primary dynamics which shape and move society—a useful confusion indeed for the major power holders since it obscures the domination of society by its ruling strata through institutions and assumptions which operate to exclude anything approaching a genuine power balance.[26]

The industrial relations pluralist model, then, is seen as a distortion of reality, a confidence trick designed to maintain and legitimize the status quo. There is a degree of confusion, however, associated with his analysis. First, in criticizing industrial relations pluralism he has switched the level of analysis away from the firm to society as a whole, away from special interest groups to classes (or are they strata?). Some explanation of the reasons for the implications of such switching should have been provided. Second, and notwithstanding the above point, he appears to be generalizing his firm-based model across society as a whole, which introduces a new set of theoretical problems.

We will follow Fox and assume the existence of a large number of firms of the type he has described. An additional assumption will, however, be incorporated into the analysis, namely, that the firms compete with each other. All that has been done here is to broaden Fox's model to incorporate the external world in which the firm operates (and to move away from concentrating on the internal machinations of the firm). A number of interesting implications result from employing this approach. First, although there may be inequalities of power within firms, it needs to be established that all firms will be characterized by the same distribution of power between interest groups or classes within the firm. It is conceivable, if not highly likely, that the relative distribution of subservience and domination will vary between firms. Second, there could be disparities in the distribution of power or dominance between, as distinct from within, firms. Strong or prosperous firms, and the interest groups or classes contained therein, may enjoy an abundance of economic and social rewards vis-à-vis weaker firms, and the respective interest groups or classes therein contained[27] (as well as those who are unemployed). Third, there is the possibility that different firms will form coalitions with each other to restrain the activities of other firms. And fourth, coalitions may be formed by different interest groups or classes within firms to restrain the activities of other (coalitions of) interest groups or classes. Two subtypes could be distinguished. The first could be where interest groups or classes from the same authority position within firms combine, and in the second, interest groups or classes from different authority positions within the respective firms could combine to counter the activities of other firms or coalitions of interest groups or classes.

Fox's second line of attack was to argue, in an influential article coauthored with Allan Flanders, that British industrial relations was subject to, what Durkheim would describe as, a condition of anomie. They interpreted this to be "a state of normlessness resulting from a breakdown in social regulation."[28] They went on to identify the following four sources of disorder in British industrial relations:

1. "Situations in which one group, against the resistance of another seeks to change the procedural norms and nature of the system."

2. "A similar situation with respect to the system's substantive norms; the degree of tension between the prevailing norms and aspirations of one or more relevant groups has become so great that it provokes challenge and conflict."

3. "An absence of regulation about certain issues on which one group at

least has normative aspirations . . . problem situations come under ad hoc, piecemeal solutions, often arrived at only after conflict between opposing groups who have brought their divergent interest and values to bear upon the particular case. Until agreement has been reached on the need for regulation, however, the prospect of recurrent disorder persists."

4. "When these second and third sources of disorder multiply, their very frequency and extent may, in appropriate circumstances, create . . . a progressive fragmentation and breakdown of existing regulative systems."[29]

Two criticisms of this analysis will be offered. First, side-stepping the questions of whether they have interpreted Durkheim's notion of anomie[30] appropriately (of course, if they have used it differently it becomes their notion of anomie), they appear to have confused change with anomie. It is extremely difficult to believe that they could be surprised that the interest groups/classes/actors in industrial relations will make substantive claims that either side will not regard as being unreasonable (factor two), that they will differ over the procedural ways in which conflict should be regulated (factors one and four), or that they will bring new items to the bargaining table (factor three). All would be regarded as being an integral part of the operation of industrial relations systems in the so-called western capitalist part of the world. Furthermore, given their sociological backgrounds, it is difficult to comprehend why they eschew and denigrate the role of conflict. Political science pluralism, for example, would have little difficulty in accommodating itself to the issues raised by Fox and Flanders. It would predict that the various interest groups operating in industrial relations would make both substantive and procedural bids, bring new issues to the bargaining table, and that through such interactions a new balance or equilibrium would be achieved. Second, Fox and Flanders fail to appreciate that those who have benefited from the changes that have occurred—Goldthorpe, for example, identified the gains achieved by workers at the shop floor in the 1960s[31]—would experience some difficulty in being convinced by wise men from universities that the system was, in fact, anomic.

MARXISM

A number of problems are associated with examining the role of Marxist theory within industrial relations. First, Marxism in the social sciences, as distinct from industrial relations, is a dynamic and fluid area characterized by major, and at times bitter, debates. Taylor, in a paper delivered at the 1982

Australia and New Zealand Association for the Advancement of Science (ANZAAS) Congress, pointed to the existence of numerous variations within Marxist and radical sociology. Significantly, he found it easier to urge others to adopt an avowedly Marxist approach to the study of industrial relations than to develop or apply his own Marxist approach.[32] Second, Marxists regard it as inappropriate to abstract the study of industrial relations from the totality of social phenomena; industrial relations is too narrow a focus to be worthy of separate study. Third, and as a result of the above two factors, Marxism is relatively underdeveloped within industrial relations.

Richard Hyman has probably devoted more time than any other writer in an attempt to develop a distinctly Marxist approach to industrial relations.[33] He has identified two key assumptions in such an approach.

The first is that capitalist social relations of production reflect and produce a structured antagonism of interests between capital and labor. The second is that capitalism simultaneously organizes workers collectively (since the capitalist labor process is essentially collective in character), and hence generates the material basis for effective resistance to capital and the priorities of the capitalist mode of production. What is conventionally studied as industrial relations may then be conceived as a fetishized presentation of the class struggle and the various forms in which it is (at least temporarily) constrained, fragmented and routinized.[34]

Whereas the systems approach refers to actors, and pluralism to interest groups, Marxists are concerned with classes. Hyman argues that between the capitalist class and the working class "there exists a radical conflict of interests, which underlies everything that occurs in industrial relations."[35]

Although classes may spring from their positions as determined by the capitalist mode of production it is unclear whether Marxist analysis is firm- or society-based. One approach has been to focus analysis on the labor process at the firm level.[36] Furthermore, attention is directed at the process of technological change and the concomitant division of labor that separates and divides the working class; reducing and weakening their ability to combine as a class and usher in revolutionary change.[37] Alternatively, the analysis of class relations is generalized from the firm to society as a whole. All sections of the working class are seen to have interests in common, which unite them in a total and all-encompassing struggle with all sections of (united) capital.

In generalizing from the firm to society, however, Marxism runs into the same problems as Fox's model of pluralism (and Dunlop's systems model). The distribution of power between classes or interest groups in different firms will manifest itself in different ways, and conflict between firms, rather than within firms, may be more significant for gaining an understanding of the workings of capitalism.[38] This generalized society-based Marxist model, in postulating the existence of class conflict, is built on the assumption of coalition formation. It is very specific with respect to the formation of coalitions. Coalitions will only be formed by classes or interest groups from the same authority position within respective firms, that is, workers form coalitions with workers, capital with capital. It ignores the possibility of coalition formation by firms, or by classes or interest groups across authority positions, that is, workers and capital in firm A combine with capital in firm B to restrain the activities of workers in firm B and vice versa, or combine against workers and capital in firm C.

Criticisms can also be directed at the proposition that class conflict is essentially revolutionary. It needs to be established that the conflict that separates classes is of an explosive type that will bring about revolutionary change.[39] It is conceivable that classes will be able to regulate the conflict that divides them and, through negotiation, slowly and less dramatically bring about change.[40]

Furthermore, unions, in pursuing the interests of workers, have, generally speaking, sought economic improvements in the here and now rather than embark on a course of revolutionary change. Marxists could respond to this by maintaining that unions and their members are subject to false consciousness and advocate the need to replace the leadership of unions by intellectuals from the revolutionary party who will lead unions to their appointed (Leninist) destiny. This, in turn, raises the vexed issue of what is true consciousness (the knowing of something that may not exist in the real world), and the possibility that both the membership and the homegrown leaders of unions might reject the social mysticism of intellectuals who emerge from outside the economic struggle.[41] Additionally, as Crouch has argued, "As soon as workers acquire some power, capital makes concessions to them; and given workers' incremental approach, they take the concessions, with the result that the pattern of demands and gains follows the contours of the concessions which capital is able and willing to make not that of the points which might overthrow capitalism."[42] Our earlier examination of the systems approach and pluralism reveals that the role of the state was inadequately developed. Marxism, in comparison, has a well developed stance with respect to the state.[43] As Engels asserted "the executive of the modern State is but a committee for managing the common affairs of the whole bourgeoisie."[44]

Two problems can be identified in this approach. First, the state can and does make concessions to workers and unions. The usual response of Marxists, including Hyman, is to describe this as a policy of incorporation that has the intention "of integrating the working class into capitalist society, thus serving as a mechanism of social control."[45] The state (or rather capital) is prepared to grant short-term concessions to unions and workers as a means of ensuring long-term dominance and control. This response runs into some serious problems. First, how long is the long term and what is the use of such a notion if the long term is defined as consisting of a stream of short terms? Second, is social change something that occurs in a grand and spectacular fashion at certain times, or is it a gradual process occurring on an incremental basis? The answer is that social reality is more consistent with the predictions of political science pluralism than it is with Marxism.

The second problem is that capital is not homogeneous; it consists of competing factions and fractions.[46] The implication of this is that a concession gained from the state by one fraction of capital may or will impose additional costs and burdens on, or have been at the expense of, other fractions of capital. For example, increased tariffs may provide aid to that fraction of capital (and the workers employed therein) that competes with overseas producers and could simultaneously increase the cost of inputs to other fractions of capital (and impose costs on other workers who are forced to purchase the commodity or commodities concerned at a higher price). What determines the distribution of state largesse between different fractions of capital? One answer could be that the most powerful fractions of capital are most successful in acquiring concessions from the state. The problem with this answer, however, is why the state, as in Australia, for example, provides aid and protection to struggling and declining industries with old and outdated capital or machinery, to the chagrin of the high-productivity, resource-based industries. Furthermore, is it conceivable that the state may play an important part in determining which competing claims of the fractions of capital or interest groups receive aid and protection?

CORPORATISM

The use of wages and incomes policies in Britain and Western Europe during the 1960s and 1970s was accompanied by the development of a theoretical literature described as corporatism. Its major theoretical innovation is that it regards the state, in its relationship with the other institutions that constitute society, as being autonomous and independent. In the words of Anderson, "the state is no longer the passive recipient of group pressures, but an autonomous force in the political equation."[47]

There is debate within the literature as to whether corporatism should be viewed as "a political structure,"[48] "an economic system,"[49] "a system of interest representation,"[50] or "an institutional pattern of policy formation."[51] Crouch defines corporatism as "a system of politico-economic organization. . . . The economy remains capitalist in the sense of being privately owned, but the stability of the system is ensured through the close integration of political, economic and moral forces, rather than through their separation. And workers (and others) are subordinated, not through individualism, but through the very fact of belonging to collectivities, organizations; the organizations which represent them also regulate them."[52] In a corporatist world the state directly intervenes in the operation of the political or economic system under the banner of the public interest.[53] Society, so it is argued, cannot afford the luxury of competition and conflict between the various organizations that constitute society. Conflict and competition must be replaced by cooperation and consensus in pursuit of the common good. The state directly intervenes to bring about an end to conflict and to lead the way down the path of national progress. Corporatism requires organizations to put aside sectional interests and concentrate on the so-called needs of the nation as a whole. The state interprets and defines these needs and incorporates and harnesses the activities of organizations in pursuing the common good. The state and representatives of capital and labor interact and make decisions for the good of all. The responsibility of the representatives of labor and capital is to not only educate their respective constituents as to the wisdom of the decisions reached, but also to act as agents of control to ensure that the decisions reached are observed and enforced.

The literature defines three models of corporatism. Schmitter, for example, contrasts a societal and state corporatism.[54] The difference between the two centers on whether control comes from above or below. In societal corporatism, control is exercised from below and reduces the independence of the state in that "the legitimacy and functioning of the state . . . [is] primarily or exclusively dependent on the ability of singular, noncompetitive, hierarchically ordered representative 'corporations.' " In state corporatism, on the other hand, the state is seen as being dominant in that "similarly structured 'corporations' were created by and kept as auxiliary and dependent organs of the state which founded its legitimacy and effective functioning on other bases."[55] The third model, developed by Crouch, is defined as bargained corporatism. The state bargains and negotiates with the various organizations or interest groups that are constituent sections of society.[56] The advantage of this model is that, although it treats the state as an independent variable, it simultaneously acknowledges that the state cannot pursue its objectives in isolation from the actions and desires of the various institutions that constitute society. If the state is to achieve its goals, it will need to bargain, negotiate, and enter into compromises. In a sense, Crouch's notion of bargained corporatism can be viewed as a special case of political science pluralism, that is, an aggregated, societal-based model that explicitly incorporates the state as a separate and independent entity.[57]

Two major criticisms have been directed at corporatism. The first concerns the assumption that there can be an end to conflict and that cooperation and consensus can be brought into being by an omnipotent state. It is conceivable that the various organizations that make up society may reject the interpretation of the public interest defined for them by the state. If they continue to assert self-interest, and if there are no constraints on their activities, the corporate consensus desired by the state will quickly disintegrate. More fundamentally, conflict, notwithstanding attempts by the state to assume its existence away, is an ever-present feature of social life. Furthermore, the supposition that the state can enforce consensus is a contradiction in terms. If the state has to resort to force to induce recalcitrant organizations to observe consensus, it will become an agent of repression and control (as in fascist Germany and Italy) and simultaneously destroy a key assumption upon which corporatism is based.

The second criticism concerns the level of analysis at which corporatism proceeds. Corporatism analyzes society in terms of lumps of aggregates; it refers to the state, capital and labor. It implies that all three are monolithic and that peak representative bodies can control and regulate their respective constituent parts. The relationship, however, between central union bodies and affiliates, and of individual unions and their rank and file members, is dynamic and complex. Central union bodies are not in a position to dictate to affiliates, and rank and file members will pursue claims directly with employers at the shop floor level.[58] Similarly, the relationship between the various fractions of capital is dynamic and complex. The various fractions of capital are in continual competition with each other; what is income to one is a cost to another. Furthermore, as mentioned earlier, the state is not a single uniform entity. Distinctions can be drawn between the government—or in a federal system such as Australia's, governments—and the various courts, tribunals, and statutory bodies that regulate the affairs of the numerous institutions within society.

THEORIES OF REGULATIONS

Crouch, with the characteristic modesty of the (British-trained) sociologist, claims that "It is remarkable to what extent the recent spread of interest in the state has led to the elaboration of social theory solely within the Marxist tradition. . . . It is particularly strange that so little has emerged from the American pluralist tradition of political science, which has for so long dominated the subject and prided itself on the superiority over Marxism of its ability to conceptualise the political."[59] What is even more remarkable, however, is that someone as perceptive and diligent as Crouch has ignored the development of corporatism, an area in which he himself has made major contributions (or is it that anyone who writes about the state is by definition a Marxist?), and can be so blind to perhaps the major intellectual innovation that has occurred in North American social science during the 1970s, namely, the development of theories of regulation. Theories of regulation are concerned with analyzing the relationship between regulatory bodies and the economic agents or interest groups they regulate. They combine contributions from political science, law, administration, and economics, and critically examine institutions that have been brought into being to regulate, among other things, airlines, railways, television, airwaves, utilities, occupational safety, health and protection of the environment. Such theories can also be applied to institutions that regulate the various interest groups involved in industrial relations. For Australian students, the activities of industrial tribunals would seem to be an obvious area of interest.[60]

Two competing models of regulation can be contrasted. The first is referred to as capture theory, in which government and regulatory bodies are viewed as passive instruments that are simply used and manipulated by private interest groups. Although the rhetoric of regulation is to protect the public from so-called breakdowns in the economic system, the reality is "that, as a rule, regulation is acquired by the industry and is designed and operated primarily for its benefit."[61] In short, interest groups make use of the coercive power of the state to protect and advance self-interest.

Capture theory employs the conventional supply and demand framework of the economist to explain the phenomenon of law making. Laws are not made in a vacuum; they result from the interaction of politicians and interest groups. Politicians are viewed as being similar to entrepreneurs seeking to enhance their electoral success. They supply programs and support legislation that enhance their ability to win votes and to raise finance to support their electoral campaigns. Interest groups demand programs and legislation that protect and promote their interests. They are more aware of the costs and benefits of regulation and are better informed and more able to lobby politicians than the public at large. The benefits of regulation are concentrated, whereas the costs, which the general public incur, are diffused. Capture theory maintains that the superior organization and political effectiveness of interest groups ensures that regulation will serve their interests, rather than those of the general public.

Two major criticism can be leveled at capture theory. The first concerns the assumption that regulators meekly do the bidding of interest groups. Capture theory may provide useful insights into the nature of the interaction between interest groups and the politician, but it fails to explain why regulators should be equally hapless and passive. Second, capture theory assumes that the interests of the regulated are uniform. What happens in situations where regulators are confronted by a number of well-organized interest groups whose interests are opposed? How do regulators arrive at a decision, in a situation like this? Is it conceivable that regulators attempt to apply their own ideas to the problems associated with regulation?

The second model of regulation can be loosely described as a bargaining theory.[62] It assumes that the individuals who preside over regulatory bodies are independent and have their own notions of how the various problems associated with regulation can be resolved. Regulators interact with interest groups and seek to lead them down a desired path of regulation. The personnel of regulatory bodies are involved in a balancing act; an act, however, that is more complex than simply balancing the competing claims of interest groups. They balance the expectations of the parties with their interpretation of what the problems of regulation require.[63]

Both models of regulation are disaggregated and societal-based. Various interest groups focus attention and devote resources to the part of the body politic that is relevant to them and interact with their own unique fraction of the state. Capture theory views the notion of the public interest as a smokescreen behind which interest groups seek to justify and rationalize the pursuit of self-interest. The bargaining theory is silent on the role of the public interest. It would acknowledge that regulators would be ever hopeful that interest groups, government(s), review courts, and the general public would regard their decisions as being consistent with the attainment of the public interest. It is more concerned, however, with noting the independence of regulators and analyzing their interactions with the regulated. Both models explicitly examine the role of the state. Whereas capture theory regards the state as a passive victim of interest groups, bargaining theory views regulators as being independent entities, whose desires and interest cannot be ignored in developing an understanding of the processes of social change.

CONCLUSIONS ON ESTABLISHED APPROACHES

This paper has examined five theoretical approaches to the study of industrial relations. Dunlop's systems model provides a shell within which industrial relations phenomena can be analyzed. The model is poorly developed with respect to processes, the motivation of actors, and the role of the state, and it downplays the importance of conflict.

Fox's straw-man model of industrial relations pluralism is also poorly developed. His firm-based model encounters problems when it is generalized to society as a whole, and it is even more inadequate than Dunlop's model with respect to the role of the state. Furthermore, Fox (and Flanders) finds it difficult to distinguish change from anomie. It was suggested that the North American political science model of the 1950s could be adapted to the study of industrial relations.

There are a number of difficulties associated with Marxist approaches to the study of industrial relations. The first and major difficulty concerns the amorphous breadth of Marxism and the associated view that industrial relations is too narrow an area for Marxist scholarship. It also encounters difficulties with respect to the level of analysis—whether it should be firm-based or societal-based, the nature of conflict within capitalism, and unions pursuing short-term economic goals rather than revolutionary change. Marxism explicitly tackles the role of the state; it is a dependent variable acting as an agent of capital to enhance capitalist reproduction or incorporate and tame trade unions.

Corporatism, unlike Marxism, views the state as an independent variable that seeks to replace conflict and competition with consensus and cooperation in furtherance of the common good. The state incorporates representatives of capital and labor, who in turn discipline their constituent parts to ensure the attainment of the common good. The major criticisms of corporatism are the (contradictory) possibility that force may be necessary to ensure consensus, the aggregated societal-based level of analysis, and the assumption that representative bodies have the power and authority to control affiliates.

Theories of regulation are concerned with examining the relationship between economic agents and the various state entities that regulate their activities. Regulation theories employ a disaggregated societal-based level of analysis. Two basic models of regulation were distinguished. Capture theory postulates that the regulatory agency will be captured by the regulated and will serve their interests rather than those of society as a whole. Bargaining theory, on the other hand, views the regulatory agency as an independent variable that enters into bargains with the regulated in seeking to lead them down an ideal path of regulation.

In examining the respective approaches, attention has been directed to three key issues: the notion of the public interest, the nature and role of the state and the level of analysis. In conclusion, this author offers some thoughts on these issues.

It should be acknowledged that the public interest will be part of the rhetoric associated with industrial relations in the sense that various organizations will seek to gain support for themselves under the guise of the public interest. Notwithstanding this, however, the public interest has no analytical use because of the problems associated with defining what, in fact, is public interest. As the discussion of political science pluralism revealed, there are many publics each with its own interest. Furthermore, and in distinction from political science pluralism, the continuation of the operation of the system should not be viewed as being in the public interest. The problem for a model that makes such an assumption is that it cuts itself off from inquiring into the interesting analytical questions of why a particular system changes or disintegrates, and is replaced by a new or different system. Social scientists should never disqualify themselves from studying what is because of a firmly held ideological position, or because changed events or circumstances no longer fit into an "established" theory.

Following both corporatism and the bargaining model of regulation, the state should be viewed as an independent variable. The state has its own objectives, which are analytically unique and distinct from those of other institutions. The state, like other institutions in society, does not exist in a vacuum and interacts, or is involved in a conflict struggle, with the other institutions that constitute society. Furthermore, it is inappropriate to view the state in an aggregated, monolithic form. It consists of many different parts, all of which have their own objectives. In the context of Australian industrial relations, distinctions need to be drawn between the government (or rather governments), the industrial tribunals that regulate industrial relations, the superior courts that supervise the operation of the system, and other state institutions that may be found to be relevant.

A disaggregated societal-based model of industrial relations should be employed. The problem with representative (Dunlop) or firm-based (Fox) models is that they break down when applied to society as a whole. And the weakness of corporatism and Marxism in seeking to aggregate and combine organizations into large lumps is that they ignore the differences and diversity of interests that exist among so-called similar organizations.

An industrial relations system consists of all the organizations that operate within the system: the various unions with their different levels of operation, the owners of capital and their various representative bodies, and the numerous and diverse organs of the state.[64] The study of industrial relations is concerned with the totality of the interactions among these organizations. These organizations all have their own goals and objectives, and in seeking to realize them, they become embroiled in conflict. And it is this conflict that is the cause of change within the system. The role of any institution, or part of the system, needs to be seen in terms of its interaction with the total system, or other institutions or parts of the system.

COMMENTS ON NEWER THEORIES

A new, if not major, problem that apparently confronts those who dabble in industrial relations theory is to incorporate, or respond to, what might loosely be called the emergence and rise of (new?) militant management or aggressive anti-unionism. At the risk of making a broad generalization that sweeps away the nuances of history, legislative changes and judicial decision-making it might not be unfair to say that in the thirty year period after World War II management/employers/capitalists were apparently prepared (in English-speaking OECD-type countries at least) to seek the realization of their industrial relations goals within existing systems of industrial relations regulation.

More recently, however, we have witnessed among certain factions or fractions of management/employers/capitalists a more militant, aggressive or pro-active approach to industrial relations with the pursuit of policies designed to weaken if not eliminate and destroy trade unions. In addition, in Australia, aggressive anti-unionists also wish to eliminate or abolish Australia's system of industrial tribunals and escape what they believe to be the rigors of having their relationship with their respective workforces regulated or subject to the involvement of governmental agencies.[65] More generally, such fractions of management/employers/capitalists wish to conduct their relationships with their workforces free of the encumbrance of having to negotiate with collective organizations such as trade unions and the external regulation or supervision of state-sponsored third party neutrals. Furthermore, it should be noted that the Reagan and Thatcher administrations have pursued policies that have been antipathetic to unions. The question that needs to be answered is: How can industrial relations theory respond to these facts?

Before attempting to answer this question it might be useful to point out that it should not be surprising that certain fractions of management/employers/capitalists and governments (or for that matter other organs of the state) have adopted aggressive anti-union stances. As students of labor history are aware, industrial relations is littered with countless examples of major (recognition) struggles between unions, on the one hand, and management/employers/capitalists and the state, on the other hand. In a sense, all that the emergence of this recent aggressive anti-unionism has demonstrated or reaffirmed is the essential conflictual or contestable nature of industrial relations.

A first theoretical implication of this realization is that industrial relations models based on notions of stability, harmony and shared ideologies are rendered somewhat impotent. In terms of the approaches examined in this paper Dunlop's systems model, Fox's firm-based pluralist model and corporatist theories would appear to be particularly moribund. Aggressive anti-unionism by certain fractions of management/employers/capitalists would be viewed as a logical extension of the analysis developed by labor process writers in the Marxist tradition. It is also consistent with the disaggregated societal-based model developed in this paper—our aggressive anti-unionists are simply a new element whose activities need to be analyzed and considered in examining the real world of industrial relations.

Kochan, McKersie and Cappelli have sought to develop what they regard as a new industrial relations theory that accommodates or incorporates the aggressive anti-unionism of militant management and the state. What is surprising, however, is that they have attempted this by resurrecting or introducing modifications to Dunlop's systems model. They have suggested that two major modification should be made to systems theory. The first, borrowing from the literature of organizational behavior, is to introduce the notion of strategic choice to decisionmaking; and the second, to identify different locations at which strategic choices, or more correctly industrial relations, may occur. Kochan, McKersie and Cappelli distinguish between three different locations. They are, first, "those associated with workers as individuals or work groups and their relations with the immediate work environment"; second, "the familiar ones associated with the practice of collective bargaining and the implementation of personal policy"; and third, the "global level" that may involve tripartite (corporatist?) national level negotiations between government, unions and employer associations, and also "where unions are pressing for a more meaningful role in decisions regarding investment, union recognition, introduction of new technology, controls over outsourcing or subcontracting and the design of work organization systems in new plants . . . government policies toward union organizing . . . [and] business decisions . . . [concerning] which markets to pursue, where to locate plants, and whether to make or buy components."[66]

In a sense Kochan, McKersie and Cappelli's use of the term"location" is similar to the level-of-analysis concept developed in this paper. If industrial relations phenomena can occur at different locations (in the sense that they use the term) then it is important to consider the level of analysis (in my terms) that would be most useful and relevant for analysis.

Several comments will be offered concerning their new theoretical approach. First, it is interesting that in seeking to accommodate themselves (theoretically) to the rise of aggressive anti-unionism Kochan, McKersie and Cappelli decided to employ an organizational behavior term or concept. Although it is undoubtedly tautologically correct that the various independent organizations involved in industrial relations (let alone other areas of social activity) make strategic choices, the very idea of strategic choices nonetheless begs the question of why or for what reasons strategic choices are made. Kochan, McKersie and Cappelli have focused on the means of decisionmaking rather than the ends or goals of such decisions. The question they need to address themselves to is what goals or objectives are those involved in industrial relations desirous of achieving as they make their respective strategic choices?

Those involved in industrial relations are embroiled in a never-ending struggle for domination and control, where different and various organizations seek to assert authority over those with which they interact. The nature of this struggle is such, and the recent emergence of aggressive anti-unionism provides stark or dramatic empirical proof "that one of the actors, or a combination of actors, will seek to destroy another actor."[67] Rather than delving into the literature of organizational behavior Kochan, McKersie and Cappelli would have been better advised to examine social science-based literatures, such as economics, politics and sociology, which have well-developed models based on conflict and competition. Dimmock and Sethi, in reviewing Kochan, McKersie and Cappelli's work, have suggested that labor movement theories developed by the founding fathers of intellectual academic industrial relations would provide a more useful basis for understanding the emergence of militant management and aggressive anti-unionism because of their explicit recognition of the role of power and conflict that pervades industrial relations.[68]

Second, it is unclear why Kochan, McKersie and Cappelli have attempted to develop their new or alternative model within the tradition of Dunlop's systems theory. Systems theory is based on the assumption of a shared ideology between industrial relations actors. They are attempting to develop a model based on aggressive anti-unionism, a situation of explicit conflict that is the antithesis of shared ideology—a situation of which, to be fair, they are aware.[69] To the extent that there is such a divorce between Dunlop's systems model and the real world would it not be more advisable to experiment with the development of completely different or alternative models?

Third, and this is a continuation of the comments in the above paragraph, Kochan, McKersie and Cappelli's usage of the concept of location poses additional theoretical problems for Dunlop's systems model. It should be remembered that Dunlop defined an industrial relations system as consisting of three actors. In fact he was very explicit, if not dogmatic, on this point, stating that "every industrial relations system involves three groups of actors."[70] Kochan, McKersie and Cappelli, in developing the idea of locations at which industrial relations can occur, implicitly increase the potential numbers of actors who participate in industrial relations. In examining the interactions that occur between different actors at different locations it is conceivable that we would need to identify, if only for empirical reasons, increasing numbers of actors. This paper has maintained that the number of actors who participate in industrial relations has important theoretical considerations. As the number of actors increases the various ways in which they may combine and interact also increases. As has already been argued in this paper it is conceivable that different sets of actors will enter into coalitions with each other (either within or across their respective positions in the authority structure) to achieve their goals and objectives at the expense of other (coalitions of?) actors.

It should also be remembered that their third location—the global level—incorporates the role of government (and potentially other organs of the state) and finance capital. To the extent that government (or the state) becomes a key actor in its own right it would follow that for both theoretical and empirical reasons it would be necessary to conceive of industrial relations in (global) societal terms. Or to state this proposition in an alternative form: If the implication of Kochan, McKersie and Cappelli's idea concerning location is that we need to relate the whole (the global nature of industrial relations) to any particular part (locations one or two) to be able to comprehend and understand what is occurring in that part, it necessarily follows that there is a need to develop models of industrial relations based on the whole. Or in other words, in terms of the arguments developed in this paper, to be able to understand, or approach an understanding of what is happening in real world industrial relations we need to develop a societal-based model.

So far this section has argued, in exploring the theoretical problems posed by management militancy and aggressive anti-unionism, that there is a need to develop or make use of models based on conflict and competition; and, given the involvement of the state and finance capital and the various locations where industrial relations phenomena occur that such a model should be societal-based. The final problem considered is whether or not such societal-based models should be aggregated or disaggregated. The weakness of aggregated models, whether they be corporatist or Marxist, is, as has already been argued in this paper, that they ignore the diversity that exists among apparently similar organizations. Not all management/employers/capitalists are aggressively anti-unionist. There is much diversity in their approaches to industrial relations. Similarly, different organs of the state have different industrial relations goals and objectives. And different unions vary in their ability to achieve their organizational goals or resist the pressures placed on them by their respective fractions or factions of management/employers/capitalists and the state.

A disaggregated societal-based model recognizes the diversity of the various and numerous ways in which industrial relations phenomena occur, and is able to accommodate different and numerous interconnections or interrelationships that may evolve within and between the various organizations and subsystems that constitute the totality of real world industrial relations.

NOTES

1. R. Marsden, "Industrial Relations: A Critique of Empiricism," *Sociology*, May 1982, p. 232.

2. *Royal Commission on Trade Unions and Employers Association*, Chairman Lord Donovan (London: HMSO, 1968).

3. George Strauss and Peter Feuille, "Industrial Relations Research: A Critical Analysis," *Industrial Relations*, October 1978, p. 271.

4. Thomas A. Kochan, "Theory, Policy Evaluation, and Methodology in Collective Bargaining Research," *Proceedings of the Industrial Relations Research Association*, 1976, pp. 238–248; see also Gerald G. Somers, ed., *Essays in Industrial Relations Theory* (Ames: Iowa State University Press, 1969); George Strauss, "The Study of Conflict: Hope for a New Synthesis Between Industrial Relations and Organizational Behaviour"? Industrial Relations Research Association, 1977; Clark Kerr, "Industrial Relations Research: A Personal Retrospective," *Industrial Relations*, May 1978; and Peter B. Doeringer, ed., *Industrial Relations in International Perspective: Essays on Research and Policy* (New York: Holmes and Meier, 1981). For commentaries on the Australian scene, see M. A. Gurdon, "Patterns of Industrial Relations Research in Australia," *Journal of Industrial Relations*, December 1978; and V. Taylor, *Australian Industrial Relations Research and the Need for Heretics* (mimeo), Paper presented at 52nd ANZAAS Congress, Macquarie University, May 10–14, 1982.

5. Australian industrial relations has been characterized by a debate over the relative merits of compulsory arbitration and collective bargaining. For a recent contribution see John Niland, *Collective Bargaining and Compulsory Arbitration in Australia* (Kensington: University of New South Wales Press, 1978).

6. For a recent restatement of Dunlop that incorporates the use of econometric/statistical techniques (a Dunlop with muscles) see Thomas A. Kochan, *Collective Bargaining and Industrial Relations* (Homewood, IL: Irwin, 1980). See the Review Symposium in *Industrial Relations*, Winter 1982, especially the comments of Richard Hyman, pp. 100–113.

7. John T. Dunlop, *Industrial Relations Systems* (New York: Henry Holt, 1958), p. 383.

8. Ibid., p. 13.

9. C. J. Margerison, "What Do We Mean by Industrial Relations? A Behavioural Sciences Approach," *British Journal of Industrial Relations*, July 1969, p. 273.

10. Dunlop, op. cit., p. 17.

11. Richard Hyman, "Pluralism, Procedural Consensus and Collective Bargaining," *British Journal of Industrial Relations*, March 1978, p. 17.

12. For literature in this area see S. Ehrlick and G. Wooton, eds., *Three Faces of Pluralism: Political, Ethnic and Religious* (Westmead: Gower, 1980); D. Nicholls, *Three Varieties of Pluralism* (London: Macmillan, 1974); A. S. McFarland, *Power and Leadership in Pluralist Systems* (Stanford, CA: Stanford University Press, 1969); W. E. Connolly, ed., *The Bias of Pluralism* (New York: Atherton Press, 1969); D. Barkin, *American Pluralist Democracy: A Critique* (New York: Van Nostrand Reinhold Co., 1971); W. A. Kelso, *American Democratic Theory: Pluralism and Its Critics* (Westport: Greenwood Press, 1978); and Hyman, op. cit., pp. 17–22.

13. Kelso, op. cit., p. 13.

14. Connolly, op. cit., p. 3.

15. Barkin, op. cit., p. 96.

16. R. P. Wolff, "Beyond Tolerance," in R. P. Wolff, B. Moore, Jr. and H. Marcuse, eds., *A Critique of Pure Tolerance* (London: Jonathan Cape, 1969), p. 54.

17. Some limited attempts were made by American writers. See Clark Kerr, "Industrial Relations and the Liberal Pluralist," in Clark Kerr, *Labor and Management in Industrial Society* (New York: Anchor Books Doubleday, 1964); and Clark Kerr, John T. Dunlop, Frederick Harbison, Charles Myers, *Industrialism and Industrial Man* (Ringwood: Penguin, 1973), pp. 270–277.

18. In the literature it is alternatively referred to as the theory of job regulation or the Oxford approach.

19. Alan Fox, *Industrial Sociology and Industrial Relations*, Research Paper 3, Royal Commission on Trade Unions and Employers' Association (London: HMSO, 1966); Alan Fox, "Industrial Relations: A Social Critique of Pluralist Ideology," in J. Child, ed., *Man and Organization: The Search for Explanation and Social Relevance* (London: George Allen & Unwin, 1973); Alan Fox, *Beyond Contract: Work, Power and Trust Relations* (London: Faber and Faber, 1974), Ch. 6; and Alan Fox, "A Note on Industrial Relations Pluralism," *Sociology*, January 1979.

20. Flanders and Clegg are also important writers in this tradition. See for example Allan Flanders, *Industrial Relations: What is Wrong with the System?* (London: Faber and Faber and Institute of Personnel Management, 1965); and Hugh A. Clegg, "Pluralism in Industrial Relations," *British Journal of Industrial Relations*, November 1975. For reviews of developments within British industrial relations pluralism see Hyman, op. cit., pp. 22–36; and S. Wood and R. Elliot, "A Critical Evaluation of Fox's Radicalisation of Industrial Relations Theory," *Sociology*, January 1979.

21. Fox, *Beyond Contract*, pp. 260–261. Hyman and Fryer describe pluralism as "a process of antagonistic cooperation." R. Hyman and B. Fryer, "Trade Unions—Sociology and Political Economy," in J. B. McKinlay, *Processing People: Cases in Organizational Behaviour* (London: Holt, Rinehart and Winston, 1975).

22. Fox, *Beyond Contract*, pp. 263 and 265.

23. Ibid., p. 262.

24. Ibid., pp. 264–265.

25. The literature refers to this as the radical perspective. For a review see Colin Crouch, *Trade Unions: The Logic of Collective Action* (Glasgow: Fontana/Collins, 1982), pp. 24–28. For other critiques see Hyman, op. cit.; Hyman and Fryer, op. cit., pp. 167–170; R. Hyman and I. Brough, *Social Values and Industrial Relations: A Study of Fairness and Inequality* (Oxford: Basil Blackwell, 1975), pp. 157–183; and J. H. Goldthorpe, "Industrial Relations in Great Britain: A Critique of Reformism" in T. Clarke and L. Clements, eds., *Trade Unions Under Capitalism* (Glasgow: Fontana/Collins, 1977).

26. Fox, *Beyond Contract*, p. 274.

27. This, of course, is the message of dual and segmented labor market theories.

28. Alan Fox and Allan Flanders, "The Reform of Collective Bargaining: From Donovan to Durkheim," *British Journal of Industrial Relations*, June 1969, p. 156.

29. Ibid., p. 161.

30. See Hyman and Brough, op. cit., pp. 173-178; Goldthorpe, op. cit.; J. H. Goldthorpe, "Social Inequality and Social Integration in Modern Britain," *The Advancement of Science*, December 1969; and J.E.T. Eldridge, *Sociology and Industrial Life* (London: Nelson, 1971), pp. 73-119.

31. Goldthorpe, "Industrial Relations," especially pp. 191-202.

32. Taylor, op. cit. Although Taylor ushers a call for heretics, he simultaneously advocates a Marxist approach. He is seemingly unaware that he is worshipping at an alternative orthodox church.

33. In addition to other Hyman references, see Richard Hyman, *Marxism and the Sociology of Trade Unions* (London: Pluto, 1971); Richard Hyman, *Industrial Relations: A Marxist Introduction* (London: Macmillan, 1973); and Richard Hyman, "Theory in Industrial Relations: Towards a Materialist Analysis" in P. Boreham and G. Dow, eds., *Work and Inequality: Ideology and Control in the Capitalist Labour Process*, Vol. 2. (South Melbourne: Macmillan, 1980). Also see V. L. Allen, *The Sociology of Industrial Relations* (London: Longman, 1971), esp. Ch. 2. For a critique of Hyman see I. Oostermeyer, "Richard Hyman and Industrial Relations Theory: A Radical Alternative or a Radical Dilemma?" (mimeo), Working Paper, Dept. of Industrial Relations, University of New South Wales, October 1978.

34. Hyman, "Theory in Industrial Relations," p. 42.

35. Hyman, *Industrial Relations*, p. 23.

36. For some Australian work in this area see M. Bray, "The Labour Process: A New Approach to the Study of Industrial Relations?" (mimeo), Working Paper, Department of Industrial Relations, University of New South Wales, May 1981; and M. Bray, "Contract Labour and the Choice of Productive Techniques within a Firm: Towards an Analytical Framework," (mimeo), Paper delivered at the 52nd ANZAAS Congress, Macquarie University, May 10-14, 1982.

37. See J. Collins, "Fragmentation of the Working Class," in E. L. Wheelwright and K. Buckley, eds., *Essays in the Political Economy of Australian Capitalism*, Vol. 3, (Sydney: Australia and New Zealand Book Co., 1978).

38. In a geographically large nation regional differences may also be important (city versus country, large states versus small states). It may also be appropriate to examine conflict between indigenous members of the population and immigrants, religious and ethnic groups, and male domination in a patriarchal society.

39. In his volume, *Marxism*, Hyman tackles the issue of whether or not unions are capable of achieving revolutionary change. Also see the discussion in Crouch, op. cit., pp. 127-138.

40. For further discussion see Rolf Dahrendorf, *Class and Class Conflict in an Industrial Society*, (London: Routledge and Kegan Paul, 1959), pp. 124-136.

41. For a debate concerning the role of labor movements see V. I. Lenin, "What Is to Be Done?," in *Lenin on Trade Unions* (Moscow: Progress Publishers, 1970); and Selig Perlman, *A Theory of the Labour Movement* (New York: Augustus Kelly, 1949).

42. Crouch, op. cit., p. 131. Also see the discussion in Colin Crouch, "The State, Capital and Liberal Democracy" in Colin Crouch, ed., *State and Economy in Contemporary Capitalism* (London: Croom Helm, 1979), pp. 24-36.

43. See for example R. Miliband, *The State in Capitalist Society: The Analysis of the Western*

System of Power (London: Quartet, 1973); B. Jessop, "Recent Theories of the Capitalist State," *Cambridge Journal of Economics,* December 1977; and A. Stepan, *The State and Society: Peru in Comparative Perspective* (Princeton, NJ: Princeton University Press, 1978), pp. 17–26.

44. Quoted in Hyman, *Industrial Relations,* p. 121.

45. Ibid., p. 143.

46 For further discussion see D. Strinati, *Capitalism, The State and Industrial Relations* (London: Croom Helm, 1982), especially Chap. 5.

47. C. W. Anderson, "Political Design and the Representation of Interests," *Comparative Political Studies,* April 1977, p. 129. Also see Stepan, op. cit., pp. 26–45.

48. L. Panitch, "The Development of Corporatism in Liberal Democracies," *Comparative Political Studies,* April 1977, p. 66.

49. J. T. Winkler, "Corporatism," *European Journal of Sociology,* January 1976, p. 103.

50. P. C. Schmitter, "Still the Century of Corporatism" in P. C. Schmitter and G. Lehmbruch, eds. *Trends Toward Corporatist Intermediation* (Beverly Hills: Sage Publications, 1974), p. 13.

51. G. Lehmbruch, "Liberal Corporatism and Party Government," *Comparative Political Studies,* April 1977, p. 94.

52. Colin Crouch, *The Politics of Industrial Relations* (Glasgow: Fontana/Collins, 1979), pp. 123–124 (emphasis in original).

53. Marxists interpret these to be synonymous with the needs of capital. See Panitch, op. cit.; L. Panitch, "Recent Theorization of Corporatism: Reflections on a Growth Industry," *British Journal of Sociology,* June 1980; and L. Panitch, "Trade Unions and the Capitalist State," *New Left Review,* January–February 1981. For a critique of Panitch's work on corporatism see A. Booth, "Corporatism, Capitalism and Depression in Twentieth-century Britain," *British Journal of Sociology,* June 1982.

54. Lehmbruch distinguishes between liberal and authoritarian corporatism.

55. Schmitter, op. cit., p. 20.

56. Crouch's definition concentrates on the bargaining between the state and unions, and ignores capital/employers. He is apparently uninterested in examining the concessions gained by capital from the state outside the labor market. See Crouch, *Politics of Industrial Relations,* pp. 188–196; and Colin Crouch, *Class Conflict and the Industrial Relations Crisis: Compromise and Corporatism in the Policies of the British State* (London: Humanities Press, 1977), pp. 262–269.

57. For further discussion of the similarities between corporatism and pluralism, see the excellent discussion in R. M. Martin, "Pluralism and the New Corporatism," *Political Studies,* March 1983.

58. For a discussion of the nature of the relationship between the Australian Congress of Trade Unions (ACTU) and its affiliates see Braham Dabscheck, "The Internal Authority of the ACTU," *Journal of Industrial Relations,* December 1977. Panitch maintains that British attempts at incomes policies floundered because of the response of the shop floor. See Panitch, "The Development of Corporatism," pp. 81–83.

59. Crouch, "The State, Capital," op. cit., p. 13.

60. See Braham Dabscheck, "Theories of Regulation and Australian Industrial Relations," *Journal of Industrial Relations,* December 1981. This section draws heavily from this article.

61. G. J. Stigler, "The Theory of Economic Regulation," *Bell Journal of Economic and Management Science,* Spring 1971. Also see Marver H. Bernstein, *Regulating Business by Independent Commission* (Princeton, NJ: Princeton University Press, 1955); A. Posner, "Theories of Economic Regulation," *Bell Journal of Economics and Management Science,* Autumn 1974; and V. P.

Goldberg, "Regulation and Administered Contracts," *Bell Journal of Economics,* Autumn 1976.

62. See J. Q. Wilson, "The Dead Hand of Regulation," *Public Interest,* Fall 1971; J. Q. Wilson, "The Politics of Regulation" in J. W. McKie, ed., *Social Responsibility and the Business Predicament* (Washington, DC: Brookings Institution, 1974); J. Q. Wilson, *The Investigators: Managing FBI and Narcotics Agents* (New York: Basic Books, 1978); J. Q. Wilson, ed. *The Politics of Regulation* (New York: Basic Books, 1980); P. L. Joskow, "Inflation and Environmental Concern: Structural Change in the Process of Public Utility Price Regulation," *Journal of Law and Economics,* October 1974; J. R. Baldwin, *The Regulatory Agency and the Public Corporation: The Canadian Air Transport Industry* (Cambridge, MA: Ballinger, 1975); and M. E. Porter and J. F. Sagansky, "Information, Politics and Economic Analysis: The Regulatory Decision Process in Air Freight Cases," *Public Policy,* Spring 1976.

63. For a study of an Australian industrial relations regulator see Braham Dabscheck, *Arbitrator at Work: Sir William Raymond Kelly and the Regulation of Australian Industrial Relations* (Sydney: George Allen & Unwin, forthcoming).

64. For further elaboration of these ideas see Braham Dabscheck, "The Australian System of Industrial Relations: An Analytical Model," *Journal of Industrial Relations,* June 1980, esp. pp. 196–204.

65. See Braham Dabscheck, "New Right or Old Wrong? Ideology and Industrial Relations," *Journal of Industrial Relations,* forthcoming.

66. Thomas A. Kochan, Robert B. McKersie and Peter Cappelli, "Strategic Choice and Industrial Relations Theory," *Industrial Relations,* Winter 1984, pp. 22–23.

67. Dabscheck, "The Australian System," p. 199.

68. S. J. Dimmock and A. S. Sethi, "The Role of Ideology and Power in Systems Theory: Some Fundamental Shortcomings," *Relations Industrielles,* 1986, no. 4.

69. Kochan, McKersie and Cappelli, op. cit., p. 20.

70. J. Dunlop, op. cit., p. viii.

11

SOCIAL DOMINANCE ——————————
AND INDUSTRIAL RELATIONS ——————————

HOYT N. WHEELER

Changing times often call for changed understandings. It is not surprising, therefore, that the rapidly shifting field of industrial relations finds itself in deep need of new ideas. The study of the fundamentals of human nature is one promising, and yet neglected, basis for new thinking. It is proposed here that one particular aspect of what it means to be human, the predisposition to seek social dominance, has the potential to be especially helpful in improving our understanding of human behavior in the employment relationship. It is the thesis of this paper that a predisposition to pursue social dominance is innate, has certain characteristic patterns of operation, and has important and interesting implications for public policy, practice, and research in industrial relations.

THE PREDISPOSITION FOR SOCIAL DOMINANCE

Innate Predispositions

Do innate predispositions exist? This question has been the subject of hot debate among biologists, psychologists, theologians, and others for many years.[1] The main arguments in favor of innate predispositions involve (1) the universality of certain behaviors, including social dominance, both among humans and our closest animal relations; and (2) the observed functionality of these behaviors for natural selection purposes. The main argument to the contrary is the behaviorist contention that human beings have no instincts and behave as they have learned to behave, chiefly through reinforcement or anticipated reinforcement of certain behaviors.

184

To begin with, we know from the Darwinian theory of natural selection that some behaviors are passed on from generation to generation because they aid in survival. This proposition is the very foundation stone of modern biology. In addition, persuasive evidence of innateness has been discovered by ethologists. Among the most impressive of the ethological studies are those of Irenaus Eibl-Eibesfeldt. His work clearly documents the existence of many common behaviors across an extraordinarily wide variety of cultures. Also of considerable weight are the findings of Nobel prize-winning biologist Konrad Lorenz and Niko Tinbergen. The admittedly controversial work of the sociobiologist, Edward O. Wilson, contains a sound core of scientific support for the proposition that there is such a thing as human nature.[2]

On the other side of this debate are distinguished scholars such as Steven Jay Gould, James Chowning Davies, and Ashley Montagu. Montagu, for example, accuses the ethologists and sociobiologists of "biologism," the erroneous notion that human behavior is explicable in the same way as that of animals who do not share our genius for culture.[3]

As close as one can come to a definitive solution of this debate has been furnished by the British moral philosopher, Mary Midgley.[4] Midgley agrees with the ethologists that there is such a thing as human nature, but maintains, as do the ethologists, that this does not mean that human behavior is biologically determined. Instead, she argues that it consists of open instincts that, although often conflicting with one another, influence behavior. There is, as Lorenz describes it, a "parliament of instincts."[5] In addition to conflict with other instincts, the sway of an instinct is modified by culture, learning, and circumstances. This is the human condition, to be torn by often competing inclinations that must somehow be sorted out.

Social Dominance

Those who believe in innate predispositions agree that social dominance is among them. Ethologists and sociobiologists have studied this phenomenon intensively. Psychologists, sociologists, and industrial relations scholars have often considered social dominance and its effects, although they have not often called it that.[6]

With respect to the existence of dominance orders among higher animals in general, Lorenz has written that the "so-called ranking order" is a principle necessary for the development of advanced social life.[7] Desmond Morris observes that there is always a "struggle for social dominance" in any organized group of mammals, which gives rise to the establishment of a hierarchy.[8] According to Morris, this is the "basic way of primate life."[9]

Human beings in particular are believed by the ethologists to be "loaded" with the hierarchy system.[10] Ethologists, along with some anthropologists, see man as a "born status-seeker"[11] and "rank-maker."[12] Hierarchies are, according to the ethologists, instinctual and not merely the invention of man's rationality.[13] It must be emphasized, however, that they are talking about "open" instincts, in Midgley's terminology, instincts that are modifiable and compete with other instincts for the control of behavior.

It has long been recognized that the Freudian school of thought in psychology is heavily biological. It should not, therefore, be surprising to find that Freud and his apostate disciple Alfred Adler believed in the existence of an innate tendency toward social dominance. Freud saw human beings as being influenced by both a "desire for freedom" and a "thirst for obedience,"[14] Adler's break with Freud was in part engendered by his view that it is a "tendency toward domination and superiority," rather than sex, which is the fundamental drive wheel of human behavior.[15] More modern psychologists such as Abraham Maslow, Stanley Milgram and Jack Brehm, have convincingly documented dominant and subordinate behaviors as fundamental human actions.[16]

The ubiquity of social dominance in human organizations has been much discussed by sociologists. Hierarchy and compliance with hierarchical authority have been described by such sociologists as Amitai Etzioni, and Daniel Katz and Robert L. Kahn as "universal" and a "pervasive law of organization."[17] This confirms at least part of the ethological argument for dominance orders as an innate aspect of human behavior. In addition, Rolf Dahrendorf has brilliantly argued regarding the effects of social dominance hierarchies in organizations.[18]

A number of scholars have made use of social dominance or related notions in writing about industrial relations. Jack Barbash has ascribed to authority relations the capacity for generating tensions that lead to industrial conflict. William F. Whyte sees the tendency of workers to build self-defense organizations as being rooted in their need to resist dominance. Such diverse writers as P. K. Edwards, Charles Perrow and Erich Fromm have linked the struggle for control and status to conflict in the work relationship that leads to strikes and worker organization.[19]

It can be seen from the above discussion that the conclusion that social dominance is an important force in human social relations does not depend solely upon acceptance of a biological framework of analysis. Although this writer is convinced that a biological basis for this phenomenon exists, one might reach the same general conclusions on the basis of the psychological, sociological and industrial relations literatures, without regard to the biological studies.

The Operation of Social Dominance

Social dominance operates in certain characteristic ways in both human and animal social groups. There is always the construction of a hierarchy, a struggle for position, the acceptance of subordinate status by lower level members, behavior by the dominants to signal their status, and the constant existence of some degree of "status tension."

Status tension is an important aspect of social dominance systems. According to Konrad Lorenz, the fact that all social animals are status seekers leads them constantly to enter into situations of high tension. This is especially true between individuals who occupy immediately adjoining positions in the hierarchy. Although the establishment of a dominance hierarchy constrains the overall occurrence of aggression, there is always some potential for conflict.[20]

Social dominance systems are maintained by a common set of signals. These signals are used by baboons and our other close relatives, as well as by man. Desmond Morris and George Maclay and Humphrey Knipe have systematically described these dominance signals.[21] Morris calls these the "golden rules" of dominance. According to him, as a baboon signals dominance with a beautiful, luxurious, coat of hair, a human dominant signals dominance with rich clothing. There is a body language associated with dominance. This has been described as the dominant assuming a calm, relaxed, posture, having "high dominance bearing," a high dominance "strut," or relaxed and deliberate body movements. Preservation of face is necessary for the maintenance of dominant status. Size is also a dominance signal. To be a "big man" is a sign of dominance. A human being may attempt to magnify his or her size by wearing a crown or a large cloak, sitting on a throne, being carried aloft or requiring bowing or prostrating by subordinates. The threat of physical contact, and the actual inflicting of punishment, are sometimes used. It is this "primeval canine tooth" that may form the ultimate underpinning for status.

Dominants receive the lion's share of the group's physical resources. They are addressed with deferential movements and language. This may range from calling a human superior "your highness" to a male baboon presenting himself to another male in a female sexual position.

The Connection with Industrial Relations

The employment relationship is one of social dominance. It consists, in essence, of the exchange of an employee's promise to obey for an employer's promise to pay.[22] In nearly all work organizations, an employee becomes nested in a position in a hierarchy. We would expect, therefore, to see signs of social dominance in operation in these social groups.

The social dominance signal of more attractive appearance for higher-ups is present in work organizations. The superior's more luxurious clothing even included at one time a white shirt, which would be soiled by manual work, in contrast to the typical garb of the blue-collar worker. Relaxed posture, high dominance swagger (a deliberate and purposeful gait) and the absence of signs of anxiety all fit what Vance Packard has described as "executive bearing."[23]

Although large body size may not be a requirement for high position in a work organization, the language used to describe high executives often uses this imagery. Being described as a "big man," or being "looked up to," is common parlance. The preservation of supervisory face and dignity is an essential dynamic of the industrial relationship. The seriousness of insubordination as an industrial offence may be based in part upon this concern for face. The use of deferential language is well established in work organizations. Addressing supervisors and managers as Mr. or Ms. while calling subordinates by their first names is rather common practice.

Tensions between occupants of adjoining rungs of an organizational hierarchy may partially explain the existence of multistep grievance procedures. Managers several rungs above the rank-and-file employee may be better able to act cooly on the merits of a problem, because they are relatively free of status pressures.

Persons at the higher levels of organizations do enjoy the sort of benefits that one would expect for dominants. They are more highly paid, park their cars in reserved spaces, have luxurious surroundings and receive various other executive "perks." Does this simply mean that their labor market worth produces such results? It seems more plausible to argue that we are instead seeing a dominance hierarchy in operation.

IMPLICATIONS FOR INDUSTRIAL RELATIONS

Does it serve any purpose to know about the operation of social dominance in work organizations? That is, does it produce any conclusions, or even useful avenues of inquiry, for public policy, practice, or research in industrial relations?

In regard to public policy, several suggestions seem warranted. First, the U.S. National Labor Relations Board rules with respect to communications by employers to employees during union representation campaigns might be reconsidered. Under Section 8(c) of the National Labor Relations Act, employers have the right of "free speech" to express their opinions to employees. This may permit the exercise of social dominance by managers—a real interference with the ability of employees to make uncoerced decisions regarding unionization. A dominant speaking to a subordinate eye-to-eye is not engaged in a simple act of rational persuasion. Instead, intimidation is necessarily involved because of the social dominance relationship. This might lead one to believe that employer "captive audience" speeches and apparently innocuous interrogations should be prohibited. On the other hand, written communications might be allowed, at least those that do not assert the dependency of the employee on the employer.

Second, the inevitability of status tension within work organizations argues in favor of the basic assumptions underlying the National Labor Relations Act. The act assumes the existence of such tensions and provides mechanisms for resolving them. The expected universality of such tensions logically leads one to the further step of proposing universal tension resolving mechanisms such as works' councils or grievance procedures.

A third suggestion lies in the area of the doctrine of employment-at-will. On the surface it appears fair to permit either party in the employment relationship to terminate employment when he or she wishes. However, if it is ordinarily the case that holding the job is a matter of extreme importance for the employee and of only moderate importance to the employer, and the employee is in a socially subordinate position, a different picture emerges. This circumstance would lend itself to especially oppressive social dominance pressures, because it leaves the employee subject to arbitrary treatment at the hands of the dominant. Indeed, this is one of the extreme signals of social dominance—that the subordinate is subject to harm (loss of job in this case) at the caprice of the dominant. If the parties are seen as equals making a sales transaction employment-at-will makes sense. If, instead, the heart of the matter is a dominance-subordinance relationship, the potential for painful oppression of the subordinate is very high. It may be that the gain in efficiency produced by this situation makes it worth the pain inflicted on the subordinate, but we should at least clearly understand what is occurring.

A final area in which some public policy suggestions might be made is with respect to penalties against employers for violating legal rights of employees. If it is deemed in the public interest for employees to assert the right to organize into unions, report health and safety problems, or file workers' compensation claims, it should be recognized that it is necessary to provide very strong protections for employees who engage in these actions. This is because such challenges to occupants of higher rungs in the organizational hierarchy have such a strong likelihood of bringing down retribution against the subordinates involved. A dominant who is challenged by having a subordinate call in a higher authority very naturally responds punitively. Decent, law-abiding, persons in dominant positions will have a strong inclination to behave as typical dominants and punish the uppity subordinate, even if this violates the law. It is important to recognize that where a subordinate challenges a dominant we are dealing with something more than a rational decision maker acting in a calculated fashion. We are also dealing with a human animal whose dominance is under attack.

In regard to practice, there are also a number of implications of the recognition and understanding of social dominance in work organizations. For example, we might expect to encounter considerable difficulties in constructing non-hierarchical organizations. The "brother society" is possible, and natural, but the "father society," has very powerful roots in human nature. Furthermore, simply understanding the origins of our own feelings may help us operate more successfully in the work setting.

For union practitioners, a sensitivity to social dominance phenomena helps in several ways. First, it can make union officials more aware of managerial social dominance games such as staring down, insisting on respect language, and the like. Second, it may argue for union officers avoiding the appearance of direct confrontations with managers, as this may stir up the usual response of a challenged dominant, that is, aggressive action. Third, union officials should be very much aware of the "face" needs of managers. Fourth, unions should recognize that social dominance may be one of the root causes of employee willingness to form unions.[24]

One of the most interesting areas where a sensitivity to the dynamics of social dominance can inform union practice relates to the usefulness and dangers of the assumption of the trappings of social dominance by the union leaders. The common justification of expensive clothes, fancy automobiles, and impressive offices is that they are necessary in order to put union officers on the same level as high management officials. This makes sense as a method of signaling managers that they are dealing with someone of equal status, and thereby perhaps prompting managerial behaviors that are more desirable from a union viewpoint. Furthermore, identification of the rank-and-file member with the union leaders, to the extent that it exists, may make it possible for the rank and file to enjoy vicariously the joys of being of equal status with the boss. The danger is that the trapping of dominance that are assumed for the purpose of being used against employers can be turned against the union's members. Leaders become accustomed to the pleasures of dominance and do not readily abandon them. They thereby interfere with democracy, which they exist to forward.

From the standpoint of managers, awareness of social dominance concerns might lead to alertness to the potential of narrowing social dominance differentials as a means of reducing tensions between workers and managers. This would argue for Japanese-style practices such as eliminating executive dining rooms, differences in dress and reserved parking places for managers. To the contrary, the training of managers as leaders might be structured to include training in the use of social dominance techniques such as executive bearing, eye power, and the like.

Managers should consider whether the common practice of controlling employee behavior through systems of punishment is based upon its effectiveness, or upon its being unthinkingly utilized as a natural concomitant of a pecking order. They should expect some tensions to exist in work organizations by virtue of their hierarchical nature, and should not naively expect these to disappear when rational systems and communications are established. Managers should be especially sensitive to tensions between occupants of immediately adjoining levels of the hierarchy. Last, they should not be surprised if the establishment of egalitarian forms encounters resistance or results in the formation of informal hierarchies. They might even utilize appeals to nurturing and other forms of mutual aid to deal with the aggression generated when persons struggle for position.

There are a number of interesting research questions that can be pursued when one recognizes the possibility of the existence of social dominance behaviors in organizations. The most obvious one is whether, or to what extent, identifiable social dominance behaviors in fact exist in various industrial relations processes. A second is whether social dominance is at the root of instances of striking and organizing.

One might wish to inquire about the effectiveness of social dominance techniques in bargaining and grievance handling. Similarly, an investigation of the effects of employer speeches and interrogations would be of considerable interest for public policy purposes.

One might explore whether employees feel more oppressive social dominance pressures where they are subject to being terminated at the pleasure of the employer. Perhaps experimentally, a researcher could test the intensity of the reaction of the occupant of a higher rung of the organizational hierarchy to a subordinate's appeal to outside forces. The effects of union officer use of dominance signals such as elaborate offices or expensive clothing, both on management and on the rank and file, could be studied. The experience with quality circles and other egalitarian work groups might usefully be examined from an ethological perspective.

CONCLUSIONS

Social dominance does exist as an innate human behavioral predisposition. it has a number of recognizable features and dynamics. Understanding these has the potential for informing both policy and practice in industrial relations. It also raises a number of interesting research questions. Clearly, it is a subject that could do with some demystifying and examination. If nothing else, this should help us approach with a fresh eye the "whyness" question with respect to industrial relations phenomena.

NOTES

1. Arthur C. Caplan, ed., *The Sociobiology Debate* (New York: Harper & Row, 1978).

2. Charles Darwin, *The Origin of Species* (Baltimore: Penguin Books, 1979). Ethology is the "naturalistic study of whole patterns of animal behavior"; see Edward D. Wilson, *Sociobiology* (abridged edition: Cambridge, MA: Belknap Press, 1980), p. 5, also pp. 274–275. Irenaus Eibl-Eibesfeldt, *Love and Hate,* trans. by Geoffrey Strachan (New York: Holt, Rinehart & Winston, 1972). Konrad Lorenz, *On Aggression,* trans. by Marjorie Kerr Wilson (New York: Harcourt, Brace & World, 1966). Niko Tinbergen, "On War and Peace in Animals and Man," in *The Sociology Debate,* ed. by Arthur C. Caplan, p. 86.

3. Stephen Jay Gould, "Biological Potential vs. Biological Determinism," in *The Sociology Debate,* ed. by Arthur C. Caplan, pp. 343–351. James Chowning Davies, "Review of the Biology of Peace and War: Men, Animals and Aggression, by Irenaus Eibl-Eibesfeldt," *American Political Science Review,* Vol. 74, No. 3 (September 1980), p. 796. Ashley Montagu, *The Nature of Human Aggression* (Oxford: Oxford University Press, 1976).

4. Mary Midgley, *Beast and Man* (New York: The New American Library, 1978).

5. Lorenz, *On Aggression,* pp. 81–82.

6. See Hoyt N. Wheeler, *Industrial Conflict: An Integrative Theory* (Columbia: University of South Carolina Press, 1985) pp. 114–139 for a more detailed discussion.

7. Lorenz, *On Aggression,* p. 40.

8. Desmond Morris, *The Human Zoo* (New York: McGraw-Hill, 1969), p. 41.

9. Desmond Morris, *The Naked Ape* (New York: Dell Publishing, 1967), p. 120.

10. Ibid.

11. George Maclay and Humphrey Knipe, *The Dominant Man* (New York: Dell Publishing, 1972), p. 4.

12. Lionel Tiger and Robin Fox, *The Imperial Animal* (New York: Holt, Rinehart & Winston, 1971), p. 33.

13. Maclay and Knipe, *The Dominant Man,* p. 16.

14. Sigmund Freud, *Civilization and Its Discontents,* trans. and ed. by James Strachey (New York: W. W. Norton Co., 1961), p. 43. Sigmund Freud, *Group Psychology and the Analysis of the Ego,* trans. and ed. by James Strachey (New York: W. W. Norton & Co., 1959), pp. 13, 59.

15. Alfred Adler, *The Practice and Theory of Individual Psychology* (New York: Harcourt, Brace & Co., 1927), p. 7.

16. A. H. Maslow, "Dominance-Feeling, Behavior, and Status," *Psychological Review,* 44 (1937), pp. 404–429. Stanley Milgram, "Some Conditions of Obedience and Disobedience to Authority," *Human Relations,* 18 (1965), p. 74. Jack W. Brehm, *A Theory of Psychological Reactance* (New York: Academic Press, 1966).

17. Amitai Etzioni, *A Comparative Analysis of Complex Organizations,* rev. and enl. ed. (New York: The Free Press, 1975), p. 3. Daniel Katz and Robert L. Kahn, *The Social Psychology of Organizations* (New York: John Wiley & Sons, 1966), p. 204.

18. Rolf Dahrendorf, *Class and Class Conflict in Industrial Society* (Stanford, CA: Stanford University Press, 1959).

19. Jack Barbash, *The Elements of Industrial Relations* (Madison: University of Wisconsin Press, 1984), p. 35. William F. Whyte, *Money and Motivation* (New York: Harper & Row, 1955), p. 234. P. K. Edwards, *Strikes in the United States, 1881–1974* (New York: St. Martin's Press, 1981), pp. 243–244. Charles Perrow, "The Sixties Observed," in *The Dynamics of Social Movements,* ed. by Mayer N. Zald and John D. McCarthy (Cambridge: Winthrop Publishers, 1979), p. 36. Erich Fromm, *Escape from Freedom* (New York: Holt, Rinehart & Winston, 1941), p. 126.

20 Lorenz, *On Aggression,* p. 41. See also R. A. Hinde, *Biological Bases of Human Social Behavior* (New York: McGraw-Hill, 1974), p. 343.

21. Morris, *The Human Zoo,* pp. 42–45; Maclay and Knipe, *The Dominant Man,* pp. 46–64, 67, 70, 75–97, 103, 116, 122–127.

22. John R. Commons, *Legal Foundations of Capitalism* (Madison: University of Wisconsin Press, 1968), p. 284; 56 *CJS, Master and Servant,* 1 (1948).

23. Vance Packard, *The Pyramid Climbers* (New York: McGraw-Hill, 1962), p. 96.

24. Wheeler, *Industrial Conflict: An Integrative Theory,* pp. 102–140.

III

THEORY AND PRACTICE IN COMPARATIVE INDUSTRIAL RELATIONS

12

Industrial Relations Theory and Practice: A Note

R. Oliver Clarke

The thirst for knowledge and understanding is generally considered one of the more admirable characteristics of mankind. It is by no means evenly distributed. Those who possess it most strongly—or who are possessed by it—tend to seek jobs in research, to write or to teach. The great majority of people in industry—since we are speaking here of industrial relations—spend their working lives in management, production, maintenance work, administration, or the provision of day-to-day services.

Commonly, a chasm of mutual incomprehension, and often mistrust, separates those primarily concerned with thinking from those primarily concerned with action. The thinkers lament the tendencies of the doers to ignore the results of research and to take quick short-term decisions on matters of importance, instead of applying rigorous analysis in solving their problems. The doers frequently regret the failure of the thinkers to address themselves to major real-life problems in a policy-oriented way and criticize shortcoming and naivities in the thinkers' understanding of real situations, as revealed in their writings. And when a policymaker speaks of a research report as being "academic" he does not mean it as a compliment.

For the present purpose, somewhat arbitrarily, I have classed thinkers as those concerned with the evolution of theory and with research, and doers as public or private decisionmakers. The distinction is not, of course, as clear as this statement suggests. A good number of people who could be classed as thinkers are also high-level decisionmakers. The case of the decisionmaker who has a passion for theory is much rarer—successful industrial relations practitioners commonly have little spare time for fundamental thinking or even for reading the results of research. Theoreticians and researchers concerned with industrial relations may be independent, working in universities or research institutes, or they may be employed by a government department or trade union, for instance, to carry out specified projects.

The main purpose of pure theory is to provide a conceptual framework for research and teaching. The value of research and analysis is to enrich understanding and to provide a sound basis for decisionmaking. If theory gives us a perspective for viewing a subject, research typically shows how and why a particular situation has arisen, what lessons can be drawn from comparable experience and what the implications are for the future.

But how useful are theory and research to industrial relations practitioners? Kurt Lewin once wrote that "there is nothing so practical as a good theory."[1] And near the end of his "General Theory" J. M. Keynes (both an outstanding theoretician and a policymaker) asserted that "the ideas of economists and political philosophers, both when they are right and when they are wrong, are more powerful than is commonly understood. Practical men, who believe themselves to be quite exempt from any intellectual influences, are usually slaves of some defunct economist. Madmen in authority, who hear voices in the air, are distilling their frenzy from some academic scribbler of a few years back."[2]

John Dunlop, for one, at least for more recent times, specifically disagrees with Keynes' statement. Dunlop, another who has made an outstanding contribution to theory and achieved distinction as a practitioner, stated that "academic scribblers are the slaves to politicians; they seek to bring elegance and rationalisation and sometimes a modicum of respectability, to direction already chosen by practical leaders confronted by hard and immediate problems. Decisions largely flow from relative short-term necessity and interest conflict, not from the ideas of intellectuals, their voices in the air or from their memoranda. And interest groups are far too pragmatic to be the puppets of intellectuals."[3]

I do not find these two statements inconsistent. Though "slaves" is too strong a word, few policymakers are immune from ideas that are "in the air," whether they stem from a defunct economist or from the media of the day. Kenneth F. Walker has cited examples of the influence of theory on practice dating back to Ricardo's "iron law of wages" and Nassau Senior's proof that the last two hours of work alone produced profit.[4] But this is not to deny that most decisions are taken under the pressure of events and the need to reconcile conflicting interests rather than on the basis of research findings. In major collective negotiations the lengthy analysis prepared by the respective research departments count for little compared with the threat of a strike, the balance of bargaining power, and the state of the employer's order book.

At least the statements cited serve to put the value of theory into perspective. The key issue, however, is how to secure the best fit between thought and action, so that both theoretical and practical approaches can be brought to bear on the problems of the day.

Of course, many decisionmakers have something to learn about the uses of what is loosely called research. Certainly there are research projects sloppily prescribed, inadequately supervised, and for which the results are finally filed with no action taken—even though all concerned, each having a stake in the project, combine to describe it as useful and important. It is probably true that the most critical component of a research project is deciding what questions are to be asked. But by and large practitioners will pay attention if they see the theoretician's contribution as balanced, thoroughly worked out, well presented and useful.

The problem of fit raises two issues. First, what are the most constructive relationships between researcher and user, and second, how is the subject of research to be decided upon?

The desirability of clear specification of the project, its objective, and the nature of the report to be made need not be stressed here, though it is useful to draw attention to the importance of ensuring that so far as possible there is direct contact between the researcher and the user.

There is another aspect of the relationship of theory and practice that needs to be taken into account, namely the differing interests of the various groups concerned, including the economic and power interests. An example of the interplay of such interests has been well described by Barbash in an analysis of the quality of working life (QWL) movement.[5] Managements have tended to view QWL as a means of increasing efficiency and improving working conditions (and in some cases as a way of reducing interest in trade unions among their workers). Within management there may be differences, for instance, junior management and supervisors feel their authority diminished by new work organization in different areas. Trade unions, at least in countries where industrial relations are traditionally adversarial, may see the worker-management cooperation involved in developing new forms of work organization as leading to a weakening of workforce solidarity. The role of QWL researchers and consultants is not simple. Apart from the job in hand they have occupational interests to consider; a need to show an impact on the world of work. They want to be impartial but they are usually paid by management to secure a prescribed result and may be seen by workers as allies of management.

Turning to the more general case of industrial relations research, a great deal of it is commissioned with a view to underpinning particular claims or responses, or to support policy positions taken by employers or trade unions.

In such circumstances, researchers cannot but be influenced by the needs of those for whom the work is conducted. And, at least those who need to earn their living by research, even if they are not directly employed by one side or the other, are likely to pay some regard to the interests of those who commission research when selecting subjects and the aspects to be examined.

Returning to the more general case where the researcher has freedom of choice of subject: It is, of course, perfectly right and proper for a researcher to choose a subject simply because it is interesting, or to work on purely conceptual problems associated with the field, but such work is not necessarily useful to policymakers. Indeed, in his presidential address of 1976 to the International Industrial Relations Association, Dunlop referred somewhat scathingly to the utility of industrial relations research in the United States, to the "vast distances—as if it were in millions of light years—that in my experience separate academic analysis from effective policy decisions and performance."[6]

According to Walker, industrial relations theory might be useful to practitioners if it could help them to do one or more of the following three things: "a) to understand the present industrial relations situation, b) to forecast trends, [and] c) to bring about desired changes in the present or the future (and avoid undesired events)."[7]

As to specific areas in which research would seem useful, leaving aside the many subjects of sectional and local importance (obviously one could not list all of the subjects on which theoreticians could contribute usefully to policy making) and allowing for the differences between countries, I suggest the following. The list makes no pretense at being complete, it is merely indicative. It is mainly concerned with deepening understanding on the wider industrial relations issues confronting the advanced industrialized market economies today.

1. Trade Unions and Employers' Associations. Trade unions and to a lesser extent employers' associations are confronting new challenges to an extent unprecedented since the Second World War. How they evolve is manifestly of the greatest importance for the future of industrial relations. Yet relatively little work is being done on these bodies' membership, structure, and policies, or even on such currently important issues as how unions are to face the changing structure of employment. Also, more work needs to be done on the statistical problems of union membership and membership density.

2. The Role of the State. After half a century of steadily increasing involvement in industrial relations, the state—at least in several countries—is limiting its activity and in some cases decreasing the extent of regulation. The relationship between the state and trade unions has been changing. The state has recently been taking a somewhat harder line in its relations with its own employees. We need to have a picture of what is involved and to know where these trends are leading.

3. Conflict Between Decisions Taken in Industry and Public Policy. In several countries there is still a tendency, despite heavy unemployment and low levels of industrial activity, for wages and non-wage labor costs to rise more rapidly than is consistent with price stability. In some cases they result in more unemployment. If lower unemployment and higher business activity were achieved that tendency would almost certainly become more marked, probably leading governments to strengthen monetary and fiscal policies, with adverse effects on growth and unemployment. We are still not clear what it is in industrial relations systems that afflicts some countries with this problem while others escape it.

4. Wages and Collective Bargaining. There is still much to be done on charting the evolution of wages and wage differentials. The changes taking place in collective bargaining generally are still not fully appreciated, notably the significant trend towards decentralization in several of the countries where bargaining has traditionally been highly centralized. More work would also be useful on how collective bargaining is facing the problems of structural and technological change.

5. The Changing Pattern of Employment. The old division between blue- and white-collar work, and workers' expectations of entering the labor market in a specific and continuing full-time job, are breaking up. Largely unstandardized forms of work, such as part-time and temporary employment, are proliferating. Clandestine employment has become more important in several countries. Working hours and the working lifetime are becoming shorter and more flexible. The industrial relations implications of all these changes have not been fully worked out.

6. Industrial Relations Aspects of Unemployment and Labor Market Flexibility. Unemployment is presently the most serious social problem that many industrial countries face. Some people, notably in Europe, argue that if wages were more flexible, labor mobility increased, protective regulations eased, and barriers to efficient deployment of labor removed, many more jobs could be created. A substantial and varied range of new public policy measures to help the unemployed have been introduced. Clearly, many industrial relations questions are involved.

7. Structural and Technological Change. Several major industries in advanced industrialized countries have been undergoing severe contraction. They, and many other industries, are also affected by the current wave of technological change, notably as a result of advances in micro-electronics.

Job security, notably in relation to the case where large numbers of workers lose their jobs at the same time, has become a major issue. It is important that the introduction of technological change should not face unnecessary obstacles and, which is partly a corollary, that it should be introduced in a manner that generally improves the position of workers. Consequences for employment and skills need to be worked out. In all these cases quite a lot of work on the industrial relations aspects has been done. But there is room for more.

8. Labor-Management Relations in the Enterprise. Management's labor policies and labor-management relations in the enterprise have been changing under pressure from the economic environment. In some countries where adversarial relationships have been traditional there is new interest in labor-management cooperation to ensure competitiveness. Several European countries have been innovative, notably during the 1960s and early 1970s, in institutional forms of worker participation: now the focus of interest, albeit on a modest scale, is on workers' involvement in workplace decisions that affect them most directly. Then too, there is interest in several countries in giving workers individual (and in some cases collective) rights to shares in profits and ownership, even to making the share in profit a substantial part of remuneration. On all of these subjects there are quite a lot of studies but few that provide a perspective on the whole subject area.

NOTES

1. Kurt Lewin, "Field Theory in Social Science," monograph, Tavistock Institute, London, 1952, p. 169.

2. J. M. Keynes, *The General Theory of Employment, Interest and Money* (London: Macmillan, 1936), p. 383.

3. John Dunlop, Presidential Address to the 4th World Congress of the International Industrial Relations Association, September 1976 (mimeo), p. 3.

4. K. F. Walker, "Towards Useful Theorising about Industrial Relations," *British Journal of Industrial Relations,* November 1977.

5. See Jack Barbash, "New Perceptions of Work: Industrial Relations Implications," paper for International Institute for Labour Studies, *Seminar on New Perceptions of Work,* Vienna, April 1982 (mimeo), on which the present essay has drawn freely, The QWL movement is notable as one where theoreticians have had a marked influence on doers.

6. Dunlop, op. cit., p. 2.

7. Walker, op. cit., p. 308.

13

Industrial Relations: The Minnesota Model

Brian G. Bemmels and Mahmood A. Zaidi

For several decades industrial relations scholars have been trying to establish as precisely as possible a definition for "industrial relations." These efforts have resulted in a variety of definitions, systems models and prescriptions for teaching industrial relations. Some view industrial relations as being relatively narrow in focus, concentrating on the labor movement and collective bargaining, while others have taken a broader view of industrial relations. Universities around the world with industrial relations programs have each developed their own model of industrial relations largely reflecting the interests and views of their faculties. These models typically symbolize how industrial relations is taught at each of these universities, what subjects are included in their curriculums, the background education and work experience of their students, and the methodology of research endeavors.

The purpose of this paper is to describe one of these industrial relations models—the Minnesota Model. The evolution of this model spans a little over forty years, during which time certain basic elements discussed below remained relatively constant, and emerging issues such as public sector disputes, structural unemployment and comparable worth required topical emphasis. The first part of this paper is a description of the prevailing industrial relations model, as we see it at the Industrial Relations Center of the University of Minnesota. The second part is a description of how industrial relations is taught under this model.

THE MINNESOTA MODEL

An important component of the Minnesota model of industrial relations is its focus upon the systems framework of analysis. Consequently, we develop our description of the Minnesota model within the general systems theory framework (see Berrien, 1968; Boulding, 1956; and Miller, 1965). An open system consists of five basic components, each of which will be described more fully below: (1) the environment; (2) inputs; (3) transformation mechanisms; (4) outputs; and (5) feedback. Our model is patterned after Dunlop's (1958) seminal work on industrial relations systems, and is formulated in general terms to permit international and comparative applications to industrial relations in other industrial societies (see Scoville, 1982).

Minnesota takes a comprehensive and integrative view of industrial relations. Perhaps the Minnesota definition of industrial relations is best described as the study of *all* employment relationships in industrial society. As noted by Barbash (1985), "industrial" in industrial relations no longer applies solely to manufacturing industries, but more broadly to any large-scale, efficiency-oriented enterprise that employs workers, including government, foundations, and other nonprofit organizations. Furthermore, industrial relations in the Minnesota view applies to all dimensions of employment: nonunion as well as unionized employees, employees at all levels of the organization including managers and executives, the operation of labor markets, the role of government policy in employment relations and support systems and preparation for employment.

Environment

The environment of the industrial relations system consists primarily of other social systems. In a modern society, the industrial relations system is but one of many systems within society. It is this collection of other systems that makes up the environment within which the industrial relations system operates. One of the more salient systems in the environment of the Minnesota model is the economic system. The operation of the economic system (including product markets, money markets, central planning, capital and technology) and its outputs (such as business cycles, the product mix, inflation and interest rates) have a profound impact on industrial relations.

Other important systems in the environment include the political system, the actors in which have the power to influence the structure and regulate the operation of the industrial relations system and the legal system that is responsible for the interpretation, administration and enforcement of those regulations. The final system in the environment is the social and cultural system, or what Dunlop (1958) called the "ideology" of the industrial relations system. This includes the values, beliefs, and expectations of society as well as workers and managers. Prominent among these in industrial relations are the work ethics, views on the role of government intervention, and in most Western societies a steadfast belief in the capitalist, free enterprise system.

Inputs

The inputs to the industrial relations systems are the goals, values, and interests of the actors in the system. The actors consist of four groups: (1) the employing organizations and their representatives, (2) the employees and, if organized, their unions or other organizations, (3) the various levels of governments, including administrative agencies, boards and the courts, and (4) other private agencies including consultants, arbitrators and lawyers. All of these actors play a role in the establishment and maintenance of employment relations. The goals and interests of the actors, especially those of the employing organizations and the employees, are inherently in conflict, which brings us to the central input to the industrial relations system—the conflicts of interest in employment relationships. Cost discipline and efficiency are crucial to any employing organization, while employees' interests are centered around fair wages, job security, and a healthy and comfortable work environment (see Heneman and Yoder, 1965, pp. 98–100).

Conflict in industrial relations is generally associated with union-management conflict in collective bargaining. Minnesota takes a broader view of the conflict of interests in industrial relations, and in addition to the traditional collective bargaining issues includes the employer-employee conflicts of interest resolved through job analysis and job evaluation, promotion systems, job design, the interaction of supply and demand in the labor markets or government decree. Although we view conflicts of interest as the central inputs to the industrial relations system, we recognize that for some industrial relations problems (such as increasing labor productivity or improving occupational health and safety) the actors have common interests. These non-conflictual problems and exchange relations (see March and Simon, 1958, and Blau, 1964) are included as inputs to the system as well.

Transformation Mechanisms

Since the central inputs to the industrial relations system are the conflicts of interest and other problems regarding employment relationships, the transformation mechanisms (the heart of the system) are essentially mechanisms for conflict resolution and problem solving. In the Minnesota model there are four such mechanisms. The first is labor markets. Labor markets refers to the interaction of the supply and demand for labor services.

Through the actors' pursuit of self interest, labor markets play a key role in the establishment of wages, hours and other terms of employment. Some may argue that labor markets are a part of the economic system and therefore should be included in the environment of the industrial relations system rather than as one of the transformation mechanisms. We feel that the close interaction of labor markets with the other mechanisms in the industrial relations system suggests that they should be included as a central part of the system, although the linkages between capital, product, and labor markets are considered.

A second transformation mechanism is professional human resource management (HRM). This includes all of the activities generally associated with human resource management, such as recruitment, selection, compensation and employee development. HRM is essentially the resolution of problems and conflicts of interest through unilateral action by the employer based on rational calculations or through individual bargaining between the employer and employee. A key aspect of the Minnesota approach to human resource management is the emphasis on prevention of undesired outcomes as opposed to "reaction management."

The inclusion of HRM as one of the transformation mechanisms is what distinguishes the Minnesota model of industrial relations from many of the others that focus primarily or exclusively on union-management relations (Dunlop, 1958, Kerr et al., 1960, Hameed, 1967, Flanders, 1968, Blain and Gennard, 1970, Wood et al., 1975, Craig, 1975, and Singh, 1976). HRM activities are the primary mechanism for resolving conflicts of interest and other problems regarding the employment relationship for the unorganized employees in an industrial economy. Since in most modern industrial economies a vast majority of employees are unorganized (for example, over 80 percent in the United States and over 60 percent in Canada), the Minnesota view that industrial relations includes the employment relationships of all employees necessitates the inclusion of HRM as one of the core transformation mechanisms in the industrial relations system.

The third transformation mechanism in our model is collective bargaining, including the organization of employee and employer organizations, the negotiation of collective agreements, procedures for resolving disputes in the negotiation of collective agreements and contract administration. This is the core of most industrial relations system models, and is included as one of the transformation mechanisms in our model.

The fourth transformation mechanism is government regulation. In most modern industrial societies there remain few if any aspects of industrial relations that are not under government regulation. This is a result of conflict between the interests of the general public and the outputs of the other three transformation mechanisms. When such conflicts occur, the government often intervenes to protect the public's interest. Thus, minimum wage legislation, unemployment insurance programs, incomes policies, equal employment opportunity legislation, and regulations on collective bargaining are common. Regulation of collective bargaining, at least in the North American systems, has been restricted to regulation of the procedures and not the outcomes of collective bargaining, although there is evidence that this principle is waning in the Canadian industrial relations system (Bemmels, Fisher, and Nyland, 1986).

Each of these four mechanisms plays an important role in problem solving and the resolution of conflict in employment relationships. Which will predominate in the resolution of any single problem or conflict depends upon the nature of the problem, the employer, and whether the employees are organized. For a given problem and set of circumstances, one mechanism may be very slow and ineffective while another can deal with the problem in a satisfactory manner relatively quickly. The mechanisms interact with each other very closely as well as with the other systems of the environment.

Outputs

The outputs of the industrial relations system are the solutions to the conflicts of interest and other nonconflictual problems that are worked out by the actors in the industrial relations system through the four transformation mechanisms. Thus, the outputs include wages, hours, fringe benefits, and other terms and conditions of employment, The outputs also include strikes, lockouts, turnover, unemployment, and other manifestations of conflict and unsolved problems when the transformation mechanisms fail. Indirectly the outputs determine organizational effectiveness (such as profitability and growth) and employee effectiveness (such as job satisfaction, attendance, motivation and productivity).

Feedback

The final basic component of the industrial relations system is the feedback of the outputs to the other systems in the environment, and eventually back into the industrial relations system. A system that is functioning properly will resolve the conflict (or at least most of it) and other problems that are brought into the system by the actors. If such is the case, the system will generally stabilize. However, if the problems are not resolved to the satisfaction of the actors of the industrial relations or other systems in the environment, the outputs of the industrial relations system will feedback to produce changes in the inputs. This in turn will lead to changes in the outputs until they achieve (or at least approach) a solution that is satisfactory or provides a workable accommodation to the actors of the industrial relations and other systems. Thus, feedback produces an open and dynamic industrial relations system that is ultimately capable of resolving new conflicts and problems as the environment and inputs change with the progression of industrial society.

TEACHING THE MINNESOTA MODEL OF INDUSTRIAL RELATIONS

Teaching industrial relations at Minnesota[1] parallels the prominent role of human resource management in the Minnesota model. In addition to industrial relations systems and research methodology courses, Minnesota focuses on five subject areas: (1) labor market analysis, (2) collective bargaining, (3) compensation, (4) staffing, training and development, and (5) organization theory and administration. Thus, two of the four transformation mechanisms in the Minnesota model (labor markets and collective bargaining) are each covered in one of the required subject areas, while two of the subject areas are devoted to human resource management. Organization theory is included as a subject area under the premise that understanding employment relationships between employing organizations and individuals or their organizations necessitates a thorough understanding of the organizations themselves. Eleven of the twenty-nine graduate level industrial relations courses and Ph.D. seminars offered at Minnesota under these five subject areas are courses in human resource management, five are in organization theory, seven are in labor market analysis, and six are in collective bargaining. Government regulation in industrial relations is not singled out for exclusive attention as a separate subject area (except in selected ad hoc courses). Generally, the relevant statutes, court decisions, administrative guidelines, and arbitral jurisprudence that influence the other three mechanisms are covered, where appropriate, in each of the courses.

All students are required to take courses in two supporting disciplines. Generally, these are economics, psychology, sociology, history or law. This provides students with a thorough knowledge of the environment of industrial relations and supports the comprehensive and integrative nature of the program. The industrial relations courses (especially the systems seminar) focus on the integration of the knowledge from the "mother disciplines" into a unified industrial relations framework.

Research methodology is, of course, of primary importance in the Ph.D. program. The methodology is varied reflecting the varied perspectives of the respective behavioral sciences. Continuing Minnesota's tradition of "dustbowl empiricism," the emphasis is on model building and testing. However, due to the nature of many industrial relations problems, this also requires an emphasis on measurement for both descriptive and analytical purposes. Although the methodology of the study of collective bargaining and labor markets draws heavily from economics, the prominent role of human resource management in the program necessitates an emphasis on measurement theory, factor analysis and survey techniques as well. Although a student's emphasis in research methodology corresponds with the selected subject areas of specialization, all Ph.D. students receive a solid grounding in psychometrics, as well as the philosophy of science, econometrics, statistics, and legal research.

Minnesota teaches industrial relations at many levels of education. In addition to the Ph.D. and masters degree programs[2] are the Employer Education Service, Labor Education Service, and Extension courses. This, of course, requires a large staff of specialists with varied work experience and educational backgrounds.

In sum, Minnesota maintains a strong program in collective bargaining and labor market analysis, with an integrated emphasis and specialization on human resource management.

NOTES

1. The actual projected number of students enrolled in the program are as follows:

Program	Fall, 1968	1988–89 Goals
M.A.I.R. Day	105	100
M.A.I.R. Evening	73	140
Ph.D.	17	22

2. Over the forty-year history of the Industrial Relations Center, the placement (and continuing employment) of the Master's and Ph.D. program graduates has been very successful. This success is a reflection of the adaptability of the programs to meet the demands of the relevant markets.

REFERENCES

Barbash, Jack, "What Is Industrial Relations and Where Does It Seem to be Going." Paper presented at a meeting of the IIRA Working Group on Industrial Relations as a Field and Industrial Relations Theory, Maastricht, Holland, October 10–12, 1985.

Bemmels, Brian, Fisher, E. G., and Nyland, Barbara, "Canadian-American Jurisprudence on 'Good Faith' Bargaining." *Relations Industrielles/Industrial Relations,* (forthcoming).

Berrien, F. K., *General Social Systems.* New Brunswick, NJ: Rutgers University Press, 1968.

Blain, A. N. J., and Gennard, J., "Industrial Relations Theory: A Critical Review." *British Journal of Industrial Relations,* Vol. 8, No. 3, November 1970, pp. 389-407.

Blau, Peter M., *Exchange and Power in Social Life.* New York: John Wiley & Sons, 1964.

Boulding, Kenneth, "General Systems Theory: The Skeleton of Science." *Management Science,* Vol. 2, 1956, pp. 197-208.

Craig, Alton W. J., "A Framework for the Analysis of Industrial Relations Systems." In B. Barrett, E. Rhodes, and J. Beishon, editors, *Industrial Relations in the Wider Society: Aspects of Interaction.* London: Collier/Macmillan, 1975. pp. 8-20.

Dunlop, John T., *Industrial Relations Systems.* New York: Henry Holt and Co. 1958.

Flanders, Allan, "Collective Bargaining: A Theoretical Analysis." *British Journal of Industrial Relations,* Vol. 6, No. 1, March 1968, pp. 1-24.

Hameed. Syeed M. A., "Theory and Research in the Field of Industrial Relations." *British Journal of Industrial Relations,* Vol. 5, No. 2, July 1967, pp. 222-236.

Heneman, Herbert G., Jr., and Yoder, Dale, *Labor Economics,* second edition. Cincinnati: South-Western Publishing Co., 1965, pp. 93-116.

Kerr, Clark, Dunlop, John T., Harbison, Frederick, and Myers, Charles A., *Industrialism and Industrial Man.* Cambridge, MA: Harvard University Press, 1960.

March, J. G. and Simon, H. A., *Organizations.* New York: John Wiley & Sons, 1958.

Miller, J. G., "Living Systems: Basic Concepts." *Behavioral Science,* Vol. 10, No. 3, 1965, pp. 193-237.

Scoville, James G., "A Review of International and Comparative Industrial Relations in the 1970s." In Thomas A. Kochan, Daniel J. B. Mitchell, and Lee Dyers eds., *Industrial Relations Research in the 1970s: Review and Appraisal.* Madison, WI: Industrial Relations Research Association, 1982, pp. 1-43.

Singh, R., "Systems Theory in the Study of Industrial Relations: Time for a Reappraisal?" *Industrial Relations Journal,* Vol. 7, No. 3, Autumn 1976, pp. 59-71.

Wood, S. J., Wagner, A., Armstrong, E. G. A., Goodman, J. F. B., and Davis, J. E., "The 'Industrial Relations Systems' Concept as a Basis for Theory in Industrial Relations." *British Journal of Industrial Relations,* Vol. 13, No. 3, November 1975, pp. 291-308.

14

The Underlying Philosophy of the Industrial Relations Theory Course at the University of Western Australia

This paper attempts to explain briefly the underlying philosophy of the Industrial Relations Theory (IRT) course at the University of Western Australia. (A copy of the 1986 course outline is included in Appendix.) The paper is not intended to be a scholarly contribution; rather, it sets out the approach of one teacher in one course in one institution. The writer has taught IRT, a semester-length course, for ten of the thirteen years it has been offered. The paper is an outcome of this hands-on teaching experience from 1976 to the present. It commences by outlining the historical and educational background within which IRT has evolved. Then it discusses four basic, underlying principles of the course: the importance of clear and rigorous definition of key terms and concepts, the need for students to be introduced to IRT in its historical context, exposure to a variety of contrasting theoretical perspectives, and emphasis on the development of an ability to apply theory usefully when analyzing practical issues and problems.

Historical and Educational Context

Like all courses, the IRT course is partly a product of the historical and educational context within which it was conceived and developed. The teaching of Industrial Relations (IR) at the University of Western Australia commenced in 1954. The first course, a full-year undergraduate unit, was a joint venture between three Departments: Economics, which dealt with five areas—collective relations, industrial conflict, wages and hours of work, social control of industrial relations, and industrial arbitration in Australia; Psychology, which taught a segment on relations at the work place; and Philosophy, which provided a philosophical analysis of IR.

In 1962, the first postgraduate course in Industrial Relations was introduced as an option in the Honors degree in Economics. In 1973, additional IR offerings, which included IRT, were introduced and it became possible for a student in the Honors year to undertake a course of study comprising six half-units in IR, graduating with Honors in Economics (Industrial Relations). In 1978, the university introduced a Master of Industrial Relations (MIR) degree, the first and only degree titled as such in Australia.IRT became a compulsory course in a full-time MIR Preliminary year of six subjects. Pursuant to a restructuring of the MIR in 1984, IRT became a compulsory first year half-unit in a two year degree (full-time) comprising a total of twelve half-units. The six first-year subjects were labor history, industrial relations systems, industrial relations theory, industrial relations law, economics of labor, and industrial and organizational behavior. In the second year, six courses were to be chosen from the following seven: industrial relations issues, personnel management and administration, union organization, industrial disputes, industrial advocacy, research methodology, and research project. In 1986, approximately 60 students were enrolled in the MIR, the great majority of whom were mature-aged and engaged in part-time studies.

DEFINITIONS AND CONCEPTS

In a typical year, a substantial number of students entering the MIR have not undertaken any previous studies in IR. IRT begins by addressing the question: "What is IR?" In the first session, students are asked to write down their own definition of the subject and comments on these are then provided by the lecturer and discussed by the group as a whole. Part of the underlying rationale for this exercise is that students gain worthwhile insight into the nature, scope and focus of the subject by having to articulate their own view of IR and to become more acutely aware of the diversity of perceptions of others.

This process leads to a consideration of a number of well-known definitions of IR in the literature, such as those of Kenneth F. Walker, Jack Barbash, George Bain and Hugh A. Clegg, and Richard Hyman. Students new to academic IR are usually unaware of the size of the body of literature on IRT and consideration of such definitions is a useful entry point to the literature. The lecturer's own definition is also given—that IR is "the study of the interactions between and among employees and employer, their respective organizations, and intermediaries, focusing on the regulation of jobs." The underlying rationale for this definition is then given. For example, specific reference is made to "intermediaries" because of the importance of conciliation and arbitration in the country context in which the course is taught.

Students are next introduced to basic concepts such as partial theories, general theories, and models, both within the broad context of the social sciences and in IR in particular. In so doing reference is made to the work of writers such as Ackoff (1962) and Barrett and Beishon (1975). The purpose is to cement in the students' minds the notion that although theories and concepts are used loosely by the man-in-the-street, members of a course in IRT should strive constantly to achieve and maintain a degree of analytical rigor in their written and verbal work.

HISTORICAL EVOLUTION OF THEORY

Part of the underlying philosophy of the IRT course is that students can achieve a better understanding of theory if they have a broad appreciation of its origins and subsequent development. This view is consistent with the philosophy of the MIR degree, which contains a separate course on labor history. There is minimal duplication between the two courses, however, because IRT deals with the historical development of theory in much less depth and within a broader theoretical perspective than is attempted in labor history. IRT assesses the contributions of theorists such as Karl Marx, Sidney and Beatrice Webb, John R. Commons and Selig Perlman. It also seeks to identify general trends in the evolution of theory, such as the broadening out of the subject in the 1950s away from the preoccupation with trade unionism in favor of theories of collective bargaining and industrial relations in a wider sense.

SPECIFIC THEORISTS AND THEORETICAL APPROACHES

A crucial strand of the underlying philosophy of IRT is that IR is both a multi-disciplinary and interdisciplinary field of study. Thus, the course covers a wide variety of theoretical approaches, giving particular attention to those that seek to develop an integrating theoretical focus for the subject. Some attention is given to John Dunlop's systems theory, followed by a consideration of the work of others that have sought to test and refine hypotheses derived from it. Allan Flanders' institutional approach is also covered, including C. J. Margerison's "behavioral science" critique of that approach. Clegg's institutional view of IR theory is also examined. A number of sociological and social psychological perspectives are covered, including those of Alan Fox and George Strauss. Gerald Somers' bargaining power and exchange model is another approach that is discussed. Finally, Richard Hyman's neo-Marxist approach is considered, including his critique of orthodox theory and his contribution to the pluralist debate.

Students are made aware that a basic knowledge of the work of these various theorists is a fundamental course requirement. But they are encouraged to specialize in particular areas that are of special interest to them so that they can gain a deeper understanding and feel more confident about them. They are also permitted to develop an interest in theoretical approaches other than those specifically listed in the course outline. Although there is this element of choice in the course structure, members usually adhere fairly closely to the theorists covered in classes. On occasion, they have selected other theorists for special study, for example, Colin Crouch's framework on the politics of industrial conflict has been chosen. In recent years, the exam paper has contained a compulsory question asking students to describe and appraise the contributions of six IR theorists to be selected from a list of a dozen or so.

Application of Theory to Practice

By and large, students who enroll in the MIR degree have an expectation that their degree will provide them with a qualification that will help equip them for full-time employment as IR practitioners, whether with employers, employers' associations, unions, government, or conciliation and arbitration tribunals. On the other hand, part of the basic rationale for the existence of the IRT course is that theory is necessary and important in any serious academic study of the subject. Thus, for a combination of reasons, the development of an ability to apply theory usefully to practice has become central to the course philosophy. Bain and Clegg's view that a "definition cannot by its very nature be 'right' or 'wrong'; it can only be more or less useful for purposes of analysis," is relevant in this regard. Similarly, Lewin's dictum that "there is nothing so practical as a good theory" is adopted as a guiding principle in the course.

Experience has shown that many students do not quickly and easily comprehend how they can use theory to help analyze a practical problem or issue in IR. Therefore, the process of educating them in how to use theory commences early in the course. At the outset, they are encouraged to select a seminar topic (see course outline) dealing with a theoretical approach that has special appeal to them, with an eye towards using it in their project to guide the analysis of an IR issue or problem of their choice. It is a course requirement that each member conceives and formulates an essay topic, in consultation with the lecturer, and they are encouraged to do this as early as possible. Students undertaking the MIR by coursework are not accustomed to being required to take such an initiative and often need guidance during the early stages as how best to marry a theory and a practical problem. For example, there is the problem of whether to choose a theory first and then pin-point an empirical area or whether to find a theory after having settled on an area. Challenges such as these are a valuable part of the learning process. They help the student to gain a deeper understanding of the theory or theories to be applied and to realize that not all theoretical approaches are equally appropriate as frameworks of analysis for a given real-world IR problem. The achievement of an appropriate fit sometimes tends to be a matter of trial and error, but to prevent students from embarking on a wild-goose chase, topics are not finally approved until the lecturer judges them to be viable. Occasionally, a student is unable to think up a suitable topic. In such circumstances, the lecturer offers suggestions; in so doing, the theorist suggested is likely to be from a broad disciplinary field with which the student concerned is familiar.

Another aspect of course philosophy is that the value of theory as an analytical tool is dependent not only on the intrinsic worth of the theory itself, but also on the skill of the user. Feedback and advice to students is, therefore, important in their development of such skills. Some feedback is given formally, within a group setting in classes. Towards the end of the course students are required to give a progress report of work on their projects prior to submission. The course also emphasizes the importance of student participation in discussion and debate in this process; in fact, 15 percent of a student's marks are based on such participation in the course. After projects are assessed, they are returned with written comments so that students have an opportunity to consider this extra feedback before the final examination and to demonstrate any additional knowledge or understanding in the exam. This provides a further indicator of students' theoretical development and gives them additional reinforcement concerning the nature of the theoretical concepts and techniques they have been dealing with.

In the past ten years, about one hundred IRT students have responded, in some cases very successfully, to the challenge of relating theory and practice in their projects. The most frequently applied theorists have been Dunlop, Craig, Perlman, Fox, and Hyman, but numerous other theoretical approaches have also been adopted. One of the most interesting developments has occurred when students have created composite models, drawing upon two or more theoretical perspectives to form a new combined framework. This has involved adapting and modifying the original theoretical perspectives in order to enhance the usefulness of such composite models as research frameworks. Single-theorist and composite models have been used to assist in the analysis of a wide variety of problems or issues both overseas and in Australia; in some cases, students have analyzed their own work experiences as practitioners. The topics that have been covered are much too numerous to list in detail, but some of the more interesting include the British coal miners' strike, trade unionism in communist societies, the development of trade unions in Malaysia, IR on Christmas Island, the role of management in Barrow Island oil industry IR, wage determination in Australia, the Prices and Incomes Accord and IR in Australia, the Western Australian Industrial Relations System, and the Halal slaughtermen's dispute in Western Australia.

Although the IRT course is relatively new and small in comparison with many other programs, in my view it has made an interesting and promising start. IRT encourages students to choose projects that are both practical and of special interest to them, a feature that has generally been well received by students. The course philosophy has been considerably adapted and refined in the past ten years, but there is still much scope for improvement and further development.

APPENDIX

Course Guide

Purpose of Course Guide

The purpose of this guide is to give course members essential information concerning the organization of the subject, its aims and objectives, reading material, lecture topics, seminar and essay topics and other relevant course information. Please read it very carefully.

Contents

1. Aims and Objectives
2. Main References
3. Guidelines for Seminar Presentation

4. Seminar Topics
5. Essay
6. Assessment (Preliminary Information)

1. AIMS AND OBJECTIVES

(a) Aims:
The broad aims of this course are:
(1) To enhance course members' knowledge and understanding of industrial relations theory;
(2) To strengthen their appreciation of the importance, relevance and usefulness of industrial relations theory.

(b) Objectives:
More specifically the course seeks to encourage and motivate course members to:
(1) Improve their ability to express ideas on industrial relations theory coherently and concisely in written form. This will be achieved through the seminar, essay and final examination requirements;
(2) Improve their capacity to express ideas on theory verbally in a clear and precise way. This will be achieved through presenting seminar papers and "around-the-table" discussion of these papers;
(3) Read perceptively and widely on its subject matter; and
(4) Specialise in those areas of the course that are of particular interest insofar as this is consistent with mastering the course as a whole.

(c) Overall Implementation:
For these aims and objectives to be achieved, students will undergo a broad programme which includes: reading, lectures, seminar presentations and discussions, an essay and a final written examination.

2. MAIN REFERENCES

(a) General
There is no suitable text-book for this course. However, John Dunlop's *Industrial Relations Systems* is essential reading for those who have not undertaken any previous study of Industrial Relations Theory. The Open University booklet *Approaches to Industrial Relations* and Michael Poole's *Theories of Trade-Unionism: A Sociology of Industrial Relations* are further introductory studies. Specific references for topics will be given during the course. These references will be mainly drawn from the list below but additional sources will also be prescribed from time to time.

The following list contains books and articles either directly or indirectly relevant to the course. Read widely but perceptively—you are not expected to read all titles.

(b) Reserve Collection
A request has been made for the titles asterisked and also marked (RC) to be placed in the Reserve Collection. If you are not familiar with the rules governing this section of the Library, you will find the relevant information booklet, available from the Library, to be a helpful guide.

Books

Ackoff, Russell L. *Scientific Method: Optimising Applied Research Decisions.* John Wiley & Sons, 1962, Ch. 4.

Ackoff, Russell L. *Redesigning the Future: A Systems Approach to Societal Problems.* John Wiley & Sons, 1974, esp. pp. 11–19.

Barbash, Jack. *The Elements of Industrial Relations.* University of Wisconsin Press, Madison, 1984.

*Barrett, B., Rhodes, E., and Beishon, J. (Eds.). *Industrial Relations and the Wider Society.* Collier-Macmillan & Open University, 1975, esp. Ch. 1-4 (RC).

Blain, A. N. J. *Pilots and Managements.* George Allen & Unwin, 1972, Ch. II & XIII.

Blain, A. N. J. *Industrial Relations in the Air.* University of Queensland Press, St. Lucia, 1984, Ch. 6.

Boulding, Kenneth E. *Conflict and Defense: A General Theory.* New York, Harper & Row, 1962, Ch. 11.

Craig, A. W. J. *The System of Industrial Relations in Canada.* Prentice-Hall, Canada, Scarborough, Ontario, 1983, Chs. 1, 3, 11, 12.

Dabscheck, B. and Niland, J. *Industrial Relations in Australia.* George Allen & Unwin, Sydney, 1981, Chs. 1, 2, 4.

Dewey, John. *How We Think.* D. C. Heath, Lexington, 1933, Ch. 15.

Dufty, N. F. *Changes in Labour-Management Relations in the Enterprise.* OECD, 1975, Ch. 11.

Dufty, N. F. *Industrial Relations in the Public Sector: The Firemen.* Brisbane: University of Queensland Press, 1979.

*Dunlop, J. T. *Industrial Relations Systems.* Henry Holt, New York, 1958 (RC).

*Dunlop, J. T. *Dispute Resolution: Negotiation and Consensus Building.* Auburn House, Dover, Mass., 1984 (RC).

Eldridge, J. E. T. *Industrial Disputes.* Routledge and Kegan Paul, London, 1968, pp. 19-23.

Emery, F. E. *Systems Thinking.* Penguin Modern Management Readings, 1969, esp. Ch. 14.

*Flanders, Allan. *Managements and Unions: The Theory and Reform of Industrial Relations.* Faber Paperbacks, 1975 (RC).

Flanders, Allan. *Industrial Relations: What Is Wrong with the System?: An Essay on its Theory and Future.* Inst. of Personnel Management, London, 1965.

Fogarty, Michael. *The Rules of Work.* Chapman, London, 1963.

Ford, G. W. et al. *Australian Labour Relations: Readings,* 3rd edition. Melbourne, Macmillan, 1980. Ch. 1 by Ford, G. W. and Hearn, June M.

Fox, Alan. *A Sociology of Work in Industry.* London, Collier-Macmillan, 1971, pp. v-vi, 182-91.

*Fox, Alan. *Beyond Contract: Work, Power and Trust Relations.* Faber & Faber, London, 1974, esp. Chs. 1, 5, 6, 7, 9. (RC).

*Goodman, J. F. B., Armstrong, E. G. A., Davis, J. E. and Wagner, A. *Rule-Making and Industrial Peace.* Croom Helm Ltd., London, 1976 (RC).

Heneman, H. G. and Yoder, Dale. *Labor Economics,* 2nd ed., South-Western Publishing Co., 1965, Ch. 4, Appendix A.

*Hyman, Richard. *Industrial Relations: A Marxist Introduction.* London, Macmillan, 1975 (RC).

*Kochan, Thomas A. *Collective Bargaining and Industrial Relations: From Theory to Practice.* Richard D. Irwin, Homewood, IL, 1980, Chs. 1, 2. (RC).

Marshall, F. R., Cartter, A. M. and King, A. G. *Labor Economics: Wages, Employment and Trade Unionism.* Richard D. Irwin, Homewood, IL, 1976 (3rd ed.), Ch. 3.

Marx, Karl. *Capital.* Everyman's Library, Dutton, New York, Vols. 1 & 2, 1967, esp. p. v-xxv.

Mullins, Nicholas C. *Theories and Theory Groups in Contemporary American Sociology.* New York, Harper & Row, 1973, Ch. 1.

Parsons, Talcott and Shils, E. A., (Eds.) *Toward a General Theory of Action.* Harper Torchbooks, The Academy Library, Harper & Row, New York, 1951, pp. 30-44.

Plowman, D., Deery, S. and Fisher, C. *Australian Industrial Relations.* McGraw-Hill, Sydney, 1980, Ch. 1

*Poole, Michael. *Theories of Trade Unionism: A Sociology of Industrial Relations.* Routledge and Kegan Paul, London, 1981 (RC).

Samuelson, Paul A. *Foundations of Economic Analysis.* Cambridge, Harvard University Press, 1948, Ch. IX.

*Somers, Gerald (Ed.) *Essays in Industrial Relations Theory.* Iowa State University Press, Ames, IA, 1969, esp. Chs. 1-3, 12 (RC).

*Stephenson, G. M. and Brotherton, C. J. (Eds.). *Industrial Relations: A Social Psychological Approach.* John Wiley, Chichester, 1979, Ch. 1-K. F. Walker, 2-Faucheux and Rojot, 16-Strauss (RC).

*Walker, K. F. *Research Needs in Industrial Relations,* F. W. Cheshire for the University of Western Australia Press, 1964 (RC).

Walton, R. E. and McKersie, R. B. *A Behavioral Theory of Labor Negotiations.* McGraw-Hill, New York, 1965, esp. Ch. 1.

Webb, Sidney and Beatrice. *Industrial Democracy.* Longmans, Green & Co., 1902, pp. v-xiv, 173-221, 807-850.

Articles, Pamphlets, Reports, etc.

Adams, Roy J. "Bain's Theory of White Collar Union Growth: A Conceptual Critique," *British Journal of Industrial Relations,* Vol. XV, No. 2, 1977, pp. 317-331.

*Bain, Geo. and Clegg, Hugh. "Strategy for Industrial Relations Research in Great Britain," *BJIR,* Vol. XII, No. 1, 1974, pp. 91-113 (RC).

Blain, A. N. J. and Gennard, J. "Industrial Relations Theory: A Critical Review," *BJIR,* Vol. VIII, No. 3, 1970 (RC).

Blain, A. N. J. "Approaches to Industrial Relations Theory: An Appraisal and Synthesis," *Labour and Society,* Vol. 3, No. 2, April 1978 (RC).

Bray, Mark. *The Labour Process: A New Approach to the Study of Industrial Relations,* Dept. of Industrial Relations, University of New South Wales, May 1981.

*Clegg, Hugh A. "Pluralism in Industrial Relations," *BJIR,* Vol. XIII, No. 3, November 1975, pp. 309-316 (RC).

Dabscheck, Braham. "The Australian System of Industrial Relations: An Analytical Model," *The Journal of Industrial Relations,* Vol. 22, No. 2, June 1980, pp. 196-218.

Dabscheck, Braham. "Theories of Regulation and Australian Industrial Relations." *The Journal of Industrial Relations,* December 1981, Vol. 23, No. 4, pp. 430-446.

Dabscheck, Braham. "Of Mountains and Routes Over Them: A Survey of Theories of Industrial Relations," *The Journal of Industrial Relations,* December 1983, Vol. 25, No. 4, pp. 485-506.

Derber, Milton. *Strategic Factors in Industrial Relations Systems: The Metalworking Industry.* International Institute for Labour Studies, Research Series, No. 1, 1976.

Dunlop, John T. "Policy Decisions and Research in Economics and Industrial Relations," *Industrial and Labor Relations Review,* April 1977.

Fatchett, Derek. "Trends and Developments in Industrial Relations Theory," *Industrial Relations Journal,* Vol. 7, No. 1, 1976.

Flanders, Allan. Review of *Industrial Relations Systems* by John T. Dunlop, *Industrial and Labor Relations Review,* Vol. XIII, 1959-60, pp. 437-439.

*Fox, Alan. "Industrial Sociology and Industrial Relations," *Royal Commission on Trade Unions and Employers Associations,* Research Paper 3, London, HMSO, 1966 (RC).

Fox, Alan. "Collective Bargaining, Flanders and the Webbs," *British Journal of Industrial Relations,* (BJIR) Vol. XIII, No. 2, July 1975, pp. 151-174.

Geare, A. J. "The Field of Study of Industrial Relations," *The Journal of Industrial Relations,* Vol. 19, No. 3, September 1977.

Goodman, J. F. B. and others. "Rules in Industrial Relations," *Industrial Relations Journal,* Spring 1975, Vol. 6, No. 1, pp. 14–30.

Gulick, Charles A. and Bers, Melvin K. "Insight and Illusion in Perlman's *Theory of the Labor Movement,"* *Industrial and Labor Relations Review,* Vol. 6, 1953, pp. 501–31.

Howard, W. A., ed. *Perspectives on Australian Industrial Relations.* Longman, Cheshire, Melbourne, 1984, Ch. 3 (by Howard).

Hameed, S. M. A. "Theory and Research in the Field of Industrial Relations," *BJIR,* Vol. V, No. 2, 1967, pp. 222–236.

Hyman, Richard. "Pluralism, Procedural Consensus and Collective Bargaining," *BJIR,* Vol. VI, No. 1, March 1978, pp. 16–40.

Hyman, Richard. "Theory in Industrial Relations: Towards a Materialist Analysis." Reprinted in Boreham, Paul and Geoff Dow (eds.), *Work and Inequality,* Macmillan, 1980. (See Chapter 2 by Richard Hyman: "Theory in Industrial Relations: Towards a Materialist Analysis").

Kirkbride, P. S. "The Concept of Power: A Lacuna in Industrial Relations Theory? *The Journal of Industrial Relations,* September 1985, pp. 265–282.

*Kochan, Thomas A., "A review symposium of *Collective Bargaining and Industrial Relations* by Thomas A. Kochan. Comments by Orley Ashenfelter, L. L. Cummings, Milton Derber, Clark Kerr, George Strauss and Richard Hyman, with a reply by Kochan," *Industrial Relations,* Vol. 21, No. 1, Winter 1982, pp. 73–122 (RC).

*Laffer, Kingsley. "Is Industrial Relations an Academic Discipline?" *The Journal of Industrial Relations,* Vol. 16, No. 1, March 1974, pp. 63–74 (RC).

Laffer, Kingsley. "Industrial Relations, Its Teaching and Scope: An Australian Experience," *Bulletin of the International Institute for Labour Studies,* Nov. 1968, pp. 9–26.

Lumley, R. "A Modified Rules Approach to Workplace Industrial Relations," *Industrial Relations Journal,* Winter 1979/80, Vol. 10, No. 4, pp. 49–56.

*Margerison, C. J. "What Do We Mean By Industrial Relations? A Behavioral Science Approach," *BJIR,* Vol. VII, No. 2, 1969 (RC).

Marsden, Richard. "Industrial Relations: A Critique of Empiricism," *Sociology,* 7, Vol. 16, 1982, pp. 232–250.

*Maurice, M., Sellier, P. and Silvestre, J. "Rules, Contexts and Actors: Observations Based on a Comparison Between France and Germany," *BJIR,* Vol. XXII, No. 3, November 1984, pp. 346–363.

Milkovich, G. "Toward a System of Systems," *Manpower and Applied Psychology,* Vol. 3, No. 1 & 2, pp. 37–41.

Oostermeyer, Ignace. "Richard Hyman and Industrial Relations: A Radical Alternative or a Radical Dilemma?" Dept. of Industrial Relations, University of New South Wales, Research Paper No. 30, October 1978.

*Open University, Barrett, Brian and Beishan, John. *Approaches to Industrial Relations,* The Open University, p. 881, Unit 1, 1976 (RC).

Roberts, B.C., Flanders, Allan, *BJIR,* Vol. XI, No. 3, November 1973, p. 328.

Romeyn, J. "Towards a Motivational Theory of Arbitration in Australia," *The Journal of Industrial Relations,* Vol. 22, No. 2, June 1980, pp. 181–195.

Schienstock, G. "Towards a Theory of Industrial Relations," *BJIR,* Vol. XIX, No. 2, July 1981, pp. 170–189.

Singh, R. "Systems Theory in the Study of Industrial Relations: Time for a Reappraisal," *Industrial Relations Journal*, 7, 1976, pp. 59–71.

Singh, R. "Theory and Practice in Industrial Relations," *Industrial Relations Journal*, Vol. 9, No. 3, Autumn 1978, pp. 67–74.

Smith, David F. and Turkington, Don J. "Testing a Behavioural Theory of Bargaining: An International Comparative Study," *BJIR*, Vol. XIX, No. 3, November 1981, pp. 361–369.

Somers, Gerald. "The Integration of In-Plant and Environmental Theories of Industrial Relations," Unpublished paper presented at the International Conference on Trends in Industrial and Labor Relations, Tel Aviv, Israel, January 1972.

Walker, Kenneth F. "Workers' Participation in Management—Problems, Practice and Prospects," *Bulletin of the International Institute for Labour Studies*, No. 12 (1973), pp. 3–35.

*Walker, Kenneth F. "Towards Useful Theorising about Industrial Relations," *BJIR*, Vol. XV, No. 3, November 1977, pp. 307–321 (RC).

Winchester, David. "Industrial relations research in Britain," *BJIR*, Vol. XXI, No. 1, March 1983, pp. 100–114.

Wood, S. J., Wagner, A., Armstrong, E. G. A., Goodman, J. B. F. and Davis, J. "The Industrial Relations Systems Concept as a Basis for Theory in Industrial Relations," *BJIR*, Vol. XIII, No. 3, pp. 291–308 (RC).

3. GUIDELINES FOR SEMINAR PRESENTATIONS

The usual format for seminar presentations is as follows:

(1) A brief written abstract (approx. 1–2 typed pages) of a seminar paper is to be made available to all members, at the earliest opportunity prior to the relevant seminar. All class members are expected to prepare in advance so that they may participate effectively in group discussion.

Each abstract should contain a statement of:

    (a) main aim of seminar paper,

    (b) recommended reading—specify page numbers. Rank references in order of their usefulness,

    (c) main conclusion, and

    (d) suggested questions for further discussion in class.

(2) A specific time-period will be allocated for each presentation.

(3) Time will also be devoted to group discussion. All students should actively participate, as far as possible, by asking questions and making comments and constructive criticism. The speaker will be expected to respond to such comments and, when appropriate, to defend and expand on the paper.

(4) For planning and delivering their seminar presentation, course members should pay special attention to the following:

    (a) ensuring they adequately understand the topic,

    (b) reading as widely and as thoroughly as possible,

    (c) ensuring they have answered the question as fully and precisely as possible,

    (d) originality or independence of thought in evaluation of material,

    (e) lucidity in presentation and discussion and arguing their case convincingly,

    (f) effective use of technical aids such as the overhead projector,

    (g) clarity of abstract.

(5) Meeting with student who has queries or problems concerning the preparation of a seminar presentation.

4. SEMINAR TOPICS

(1) Discuss Professor K. F. Walker's definition of industrial relations:

Industrial relations will be taken to signify the systematic study of the various relations existing between managers and workers in industry, using the term industry widely to refer to any group of people engaged in the production of goods or services normally exchangeable on a market. "Managers" are those who have responsibility to organise the work of others; "workers" are those whose work is organised by managers. The relations between managers and workers, insofar as they show any degree of regularity, are governed by rules which vary in formality from laws to unwritten but recognised customs and traditions. These rules are the dependent variables which the study of industrial relations aims at explaining.

The above definition, which is essentially that of Dunlop (1958), makes industrial relations part of the study of human organisation. [Source: K. F. Walker, Research Needs in Industrial Relations (F. W. Cheshire for the University of Western Australia Press, 1964), pp. 2–4.]

(2) Discuss K. Laffer's definition of industrial relations:

. . . Industrial relations is concerned with the bargaining explicit and implicit between and among employers and employees over the making of the rules of work and with the factors that affect this bargaining. (Source: Kingsley Laffer, "Is industrial relations an academic discipline?" The Journal of Industrial Relations, Vol. 16, No. 1, March 1974, p. 72.)

(3) Discuss Bain and Clegg's definition of industrial relations:

In short, if these refinements are made to the Dunlop-Flanders approach, then the subject of industrial relations may be defined as the study of all aspects of job regulation—the making and administering of the rules which regulate employment relationships—regardless of whether these are seen as being formal or informal, structured or unstructured. (Source: G. S. Bain and H. A. Clegg, "Strategy for Industrial Relations Research in Great Britain," BJIR, Vol. XII, No. 1, March 1974, pp. 95–97.)

(4) Discuss J. Barbash's definition of industrial relations:

Industrial relations can be defined simply as the management of labor problems in an industrial society or, more operationally, as the theories, techniques and institutions for the resolution of contending money and power claims in an employment relationship. [Source: The Elements of Industrial Relations (Madison: Univ. of Wisconsin Press, 1984), p. 3.]

(5) Evaluate the following definition of a theory:

A theory is a statement, which can be falsified, about causal relationships between variables. Its purpose is to help us observe, understand, explain and predict phenomena. [Source: Brian Barrett and John Beishon, Approaches to Industrial Relations (The Open University, 1976), p. 19.]

(6) Does the following quotation encapsulate a "theory" as you would use the term from your standpoint as a student of Industrial Relations Theory?

The conventional theory on industrial relations is that when arbitration fails, a strike may be justified as a last resort. The reality is that some workers, especially those with special clout in key jobs, strike before all avenues of settlement have been explored, then go to arbitration. (Source: The Australian, 5/18/79.)

Justify your answer.

(7) Explain the following statement:

Karl Marx's views on trade unions are part of his general theory of capitalism. [Source: F. Ray Marshall, Allan M. Cartter and Allan G. King, *Labor Economics: Wages, Employment and Trade Unionism* (Richard D. Irwin, 1976), p. 98.]

(8) Do you agree with the following statement? Why?

And although "Industrial Democracy" did not establish industrial relations as a separate field of study, once the subject began to be established some fifty years later, this seminal work was recognized as its major and perhaps only classic. (Source: G. S. Bain and H. A. Clegg, "A Strategy for Industrial Relations in Great Britain," *BJIR*, Vol. XII, No. 1, March 1974, p. 98.)

(9) Discuss Selig Perlman's theory of the labour movement.

See Selig Perlman, *A Theory of the Labor Movement* (New York: Augustus M. Kelley, 1949).

(10) Explain and discuss the following:

In 1948 Clark Kerr, in an article entitled "The Model of the Trade Union," drew attention to the narrowness of approach to the analysis of trade unions, arguing that a combination of economics and politics would provide a more realistic understanding. (Source: A. N. J. Blain and John Gennard, "Industrial Relations Theory—A Critical Review," *BJIR*, Vol. VIII, No. 3, November 1970, p. 390.)

(11) What did J. T. Dunlop mean by an "Industrial relations system"? (See J. T. Dunlop, *Industrial Relations Systems* (New York, Henry Holt, 1958), Ch. 1, 2, 3, 4.)

(12) How useful was Dunlop's theory in explaining bituminous coal and building industrial relations systems? (Dunlop, Chs. 5 and 6.)

(13) How useful was Dunlop's theory in explaining the Yugoslav industrial relations system and the development of national industrial relations systems generally? (Dunlop, Chs. 7 and 8.)

(14) Do you agree with Dunlop that industrial relations discussion needed to be released from the preoccupation, if not obsession, with labor peace and warfare? (Dunlop, p. 380)

(15) Discuss the refinements proposed to Dunlop's theory by Blain and Gennard. (Blain and Gennard, *BJIR*, Vol. VIII, No. 3, November 1970, pp. 392–407.)

(16) Evaluate Craig's refined systems model. (See A. W. J. Craig, "A Framework for the Analysis of Industrial Relations Systems" in B. Barrett, E. Rhodes, J. Beishon (eds.), *Industrial Relations and the Wider Society: Aspects of Interaction* (London: Collier Macmillan, 1975), Ch. 1.)

(17) Explain and discuss the theoretical approach of Goodman, Armstrong, Davis and Wagner in their book *Rule Making and Industrial Peace* (London: Croom Helm Ltd., 1976.)

(18) Evaluate the theoretical framework developed by N. F. Dufty in his book *Industrial Relations in the Public Sector: The Firemen* (Brisbane: University of Queensland Press, 1979.).

(19) Evaluate Maurice, Sellier and Silvestre's theoretical refinements to "systems" theory. (M. Maurice, F. Sellier and J. J. Silvestre, "Rules, contexts and actors: Observations based on a comparison between France and Germany," *BJIR*, Vol. XXII, No. 3, November 1984, pp. 346–363.)

(20) Explain why Flanders' approach to industrial relations theory is known as an "institutional approach." Is his approach too narrow? (See Allan Flanders, *Management and Unions: The Theory and Reform of Industrial Relations* (London: Faber and Faber, 1975), pp. 83–128)

(21) Evaluate Flanders' theoretical analysis of collective bargaining, including his criticism of the Webbs. (See Allan Flanders, Ibid., pp. 213–240.)

(22) How does G. Somers' "Bargaining power" approach to industrial relations theory differ from that of other theorists? [See G. Somers (ed.), *Essays in Industrial Relations Theory* (Ames: Iowa State Univ. Press, 1969), Ch. 3.)

(23) What is meant by "unitary" and "pluralist" perspectives in industrial relations? (See Alan Fox, "Industrial Sociology and Industrial Relations," *Royal Commission on Trade Unions and Employer Associations* (London: HMSO, 1966); see also chapter by Sir Halford Reddish (Ch. 28) in B. Barrett, E. Rhodes and J. Beison (eds.), 1975.)

(24) What are the implications for industrial relations in modern society of Fox's radical assault on pluralism? (See A. Fox, *Beyond Contract, Work, Power and Trust Relations* (London: Faber and Faber, 1974), Ch. 5, 7; see also H. A. Clegg, "Pluralism in Industrial Relations," *BJIR,* Vol. XIII, No. 3, pp. 309–316.)

(25) Evaluate Margerison's view that the two major conceptual levels of industrial relations are at the intra-plant level and outside the firm. (C. J. Margerison, "What do we mean by industrial relations? A behavioural science approach," *BJIR,* Vol. VII, No. 2, 1969, p. 286.)

(26) To what extent is Hyman's book "Marxist"?

> In his introduction the author states ruefully that there is no simple and clear-cut Marxian theory of industrial relations. He therefore seeks to develop an analysis which is firmly anchored to a Marxist perspective, but which stems from one individual's insights and interpretations at a particular point in time. After this confession of idiosyncrasy it is perhaps not surprising that a great deal of this work owes little or nothing to Marx. (Source: B. C. Roberts's review of R. Hyman's *Industrial Relations—A Marxist Introduction, BJIR,* Vol. XIV, No. 2, pp. 236–237.

(27) How does Hyman use the concepts of "totality," "change," "contradiction" and "practice" to elaborate his Marxist approach?

(28) Do you agree with Hyman that, in defining the boundaries of industrial relations, it is misleading to "posit a (relatively) autonomous sphere of social relations involving bargaining and 'rule-making,' between unions and employers. . . ." (See David Winchester, "Industrial Relations Research in Britain," *BJIR,* Vol. XXI, No. 1, March 1983, p. 104.)

5. ESSAY

(a) Selection and Approval of Topics and Titles

Each student will write an essay and give a verbal presentation on it. Before commencing work on the essay, he or she should formulate a title in writing and submit it for confirmation that it is compatible with the requirements of the course. Please seek approval for any significant variations to the title.

(b) Length

(1) Essays should *not* exceed 4,000 words. It is important that, as part of academic rigour, you demonstrate an ability to present information and express ideas on complex questions concisely within a specified work limit.

(2) Please indicate clearly at the front of your essay the approximate length.

(c) Format

(1) The essay should be accompanied by a *brief abstract* (100 words or less) which succinctly summarises the main arguments and conclusions of your paper.

(2) Please state clearly the aims and conclusions.

(3) In marking essays, attention will be given to such factors as: whether or not the aim of the paper has been achieved, scope and depth of analysis, relevance to the topic,

length, footnoting and bibliography, structure (including the use of headings and subheadings), style and overall readability.

(d) Due Date

All essays should be handed in *on time*. A penalty will be applied for lateness.

(e) Explanatory Notes

The main purpose of the essay requirement is to enable you to demonstrate in writing that you can usefully apply industrial relations theory to achieve new understanding of, and insight into, industrial relations issues. The essay should integrate theoretical and empirical material; if appropriate, empirical material relevant to your own personal work experience can be used. Theoretical tools should be used as an aid in the analysis of an actual industrial relations issue of your choice.

6. ASSESSMENT (PRELIMINARY INFORMATION)

Methods of assessment will include: final examination, an essay and seminars. It is proposed, on the basis of previous experience, that the assessment be—examination 40%, essay 30%, seminar presentation 15% and participation in seminars 15%.

15

TOWARD A DIAGNOSTIC FRAMEWORK OF POWER IN UNION-MANAGEMENT RELATIONSHIPS ━━━━━━

ARIE SHIROM

Organization development (OD) work in unionized work settings must include union-management relations in its diagnostic efforts. Nonetheless, the literature hardly offers any diagnostic model that practitioners may apply in their diagnostic work in that context. The model developed in this paper is built upon a systems-theory-based conceptualization of the labor relations system (LRS). Three initial diagnostic phases are proposed and explained: (a) an evaluation of the balance of power resources in the LRS environmental contexts; (b) an identification of the prevalent type of power orientations in the LRS, considered as a structural characteristic of the LRS; and (c) an assessment of each of the parties' predisposition to use power relative to the range of issues resolved in the LRS. The third phase of the diagnostic model refers to the LRS inputs. The relevance of the proposed diagnostic model to organization development work is illustrated.

OD is often described as a systematic change strategy designed to increase the organization's effectiveness, a change strategy implemented by top decision makers assisted by skilled consultants who possess behavioral science knowledge.[1] OD consultants usually contribute their diagnostic skills to diagnose locations and causes of ineffectiveness[2] in the client system. In their diagnostic efforts, OD consultants may be guided by several diagnostic models.[3]

In unionized work settings, OD consultants must necessarily include the subsystem of union-management relations in their diagnosis; otherwise, they would provide the client system with a partial, probably biased assessment of the organization's effectiveness. There are several additional reasons for this. First, in some situations the immediate need for OD work has to do with a felt need for changes in union-management relations.[4]

226

Second, many issues resolved in union-management interactions actually arose in other subsystems of the organization or in its environment, and are indicative of problem areas in them. Third, most OD interventions affect traditional work rules (e.g., management by objectives), seniority systems (e.g., career planning), reward systems (e.g., behavioral modification), job classifications (e.g., job redesign and enrichment) or other issues at the heart of local unions' collective agreements with their respective management. This granted, it is rather surprising that since Kochan and Dyer's pioneering work,[5] the theory of OD interventions in unionized work settings has progressed so little,[6] providing only scant guidance on diagnosis and assessment of union-management relations.[7]

The major objective of this paper is to develop a diagnostic model for the initial diagnostic work on union-management relations in unionized work settings. Although not essential for the actual utilization of the proposed diagnostic model, it was developed for a unionized, profit-making manufacturing plant in which management bargains with the representatives of a single plant-level union; this local-level bilateral bargaining relationship is typical of the unionized sector of U.S. manufacturing industry.[8]

In the paper's first section, union-management relations are conceptualized on the basis of systems theory. Next, the resultant conceptual framework, dubbed the labor relations system (LRS), is used to describe relative power resources of the parties (i.e., union and management) and to identify the consequences of significant structural power imbalances for OD work. This constitutes the first phase of the diagnostic model. The second phase is intended to identify the prevalent type of power orientations in an LRS. The following section deals with union and management representatives' predisposition to use power relative to a range of LRS issues. This constitutes the third diagnostic phase. Finally, the last section reviews the model's major limitation and indicates directions for future development of the proposed model.

THE LABOR RELATIONS SYSTEM

The growth of OD as a new field of scientific research and, more markedly, a semi-profession, has its intellectual base in system theory or systems approach.[9] Therefore the conceptual framework of union-management relations adopted here, referred to as the labor relations system and abbreviated as LRS, rests on the theoretical pillar of systems theory. Because it has been fully described elsewhere,[10] only its bare outline is presented here. Each of the panels in Figure 15.1 represents a basic LRS component that is succinctly explained below, starting from the panel labeled 'Inputs' and proceeding toward the right. Last to be discussed is the component of the "Environmental Contexts."

Inputs

Inputs into the LRS consist of the representatives of the two parties directly involved in the employment relationship under consideration, that is, those local union and management officials who interact in an intergroup context to resolve labor relations issues, their orientations toward the resolution of labor relations issues, and the issues themselves. Participants in the LRS may interact in other relevant subsystems of the plant, for example, in the production subsystem. An operational definition of a labor relations issue would be a specific state or problem perceived by either participant as one that should necessarily be resolved in a bilateral decisionmaking process, that is, in the LRS process.

Processes

LRS processes include all the power interactions related to the resolution of labor relations issues and involving the participants. Thus the term "power interaction" refers to a participant's attempt to change the other participant's position in the direction of his own desired objectives. Through those power interactions, the participants influence each other's position and reach verbal or written agreements about the resolution of the LRS issues. The processes are referred to as collective bargaining negotiations when they are highly structured, take place periodically, and culminate in a written agreement defining the participants' future contractual relationships. However, LRS processes also include a variety of informal and unstructured power interactions.

Structure

An LRS structure consists of all forms of institutionalized behavior, that is, relatively stable, patterned and recurring interactions. Accepted practices and customs, such as those formalized as negotiation procedures outlined in a collective bargaining agreement, or as grievance committees, or as joint safety committees, are examples of elements of an LRS structure.

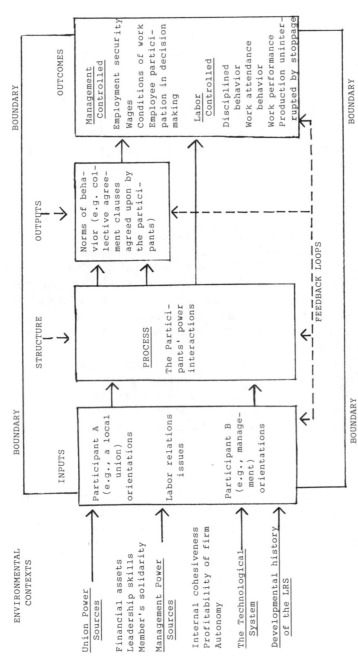

Figure 15.1. The components of the labor relations system.

Outputs

As represented in Figure 15.1, LRS outputs and outcomes are conceptualized as two distinct components of an LRS. LRS outputs are immediate and direct products of the participants' interactions: namely, agreed resolutions of labor relations issues articulated in the form of norms of behavior, which are usually contractually binding upon the respective constituency. In an LRS, outputs are likely to be formalized in a collective agreement, grievance committee decisions, or management regulations and policies that are decided upon bilaterally, but are issued by management.

Outcomes

The outcomes represent the needs and desires of each participant, or of the relevant constituency, the satisfaction of which depends partly upon the other participant's behavior. Therefore, each participant attempts to fulfill these needs and desires through LRS processes. This component is multidimensional because it includes economic, social, and psychological needs; and it is multilevel because the needs are defined on the individual level (e.g., the management spokesperson's personal need for achievement), group level (e.g., specific desires of certain occupational categories of union members, or needs of management as a group), and organizational level (e.g., the need for uninterrupted production). In Figure 15.1 the outcomes are located on the LRS boundary. This location reflects the proposition that LRS outcomes are, to a significant extent, influenced and shaped by other systems within the work organization and by the organization's environment.

Boundary

The boundary, which separates the LRS from its environment, shifts and is permeable in both directions, allowing the LRS to affect and be affected by its environment. An LRS boundary may be drawn so as to include the labor relations issues actually resolved in it.

Feedback Loops

The feedback loops, represented in Figure 15.1 by broken lines, continuously provide the participants with information about the consequences of their bilateral decisionmaking process.

Environmental Contexts

The elements in the LRS environment are referred to as environmental contexts. They represent other subsystems in the work organization under consideration, or in other systems, whose components generate labor relations issues and the participants' power resources. The contexts are not part of the LRS but a change in them may lead to a change in the participant's orientations or to the emergence of labor relations issues. The panel of environmental contexts in Figure 15.1 is not intended to provide an exhaustive list but only a few selected examples.

PHASE 1: THE BALANCE OF POWER RESOURCES

The deliberate and reciprocal acts of influence by means of which the participants resolve labor relations issues invariably involve the use of power resources. Power resources refer to the potential reservoir of valued and scarce resources that allow a participant to shape LRS issues and processes.[11] Power resources are often used by a participant to raise certain LRS issues or cause other issues to be ignored. The major premise of the first phase of the diagnostic model is that a systematic assessment of the balance of power resources in LRS is of crucial importance for the understanding of the LRS and its components, and should be the very first diagnostic work undertaken.

Following Pruitt,[12] power resources in an LRS are operationally defined as self-perceived and relational. (For other possible methods for measuring the power of the participants, see Pfeffer.)[13] That is, the power resources that each participant perceives to have relative to the other participant, evaluated in qualitative terms for each relevant resource and aggregated across all resources, would provide the required assessment of the balance of power resources. Unfortunately, industrial relations theoreticians who dealt with the participants' power resources, either from the perspective of management[14] or from that of the union[15] did not specify systematically relevant power resources, nor did they provide a method for the qualitative aggregation of those power resources identified in their work.

Table 15.1 was constructed as an initial attempt to specify the range of LRS relevant power resources. Table 15.1 follows the logic of French and Raven[16] classification of power bases, noted by Wood[17] to be the most widely accepted inventory of power resources.

Table 15.1 may provide OD practitioners with a stepping-stone necessary for the qualitative assessment of the balance of power resources. Admittedly, improved

Table 15.1. Potential Power Resources of LRS Participants

Type of Resource	Illustrative Forms	
	Union	Management
A. Intra-organizational:		
1. Coercive power	Strike	Lock-out
2. Reward power (Dubin, 1973)	Control of economic assets; participation in decision making; number of employees represented	Plant profitability; authority to offer rewards; availability of status rewards
3. Dependence power (French and Raven, 1959, p. 157)	Extent to which the local union represents irreplaceable employees: autonomy from the international union	Extent of dependence on suppliers of raw materials, bankers, or the board of directors; extent to which final product may be stored up
4. Location power (Crozier, 1983)	Strategically favorable position of represented employees	Proximity and accessibility of alternative workforce
B. Interorganizational:		
5. Connections power	Support of other union locals/internationals	Support of community group or of other employers
6. Information power (Pettigrew, 1975)	Access to information relevant to the LRS issues	Control of financial, marketing, and other information
7. Professional expertise	Availability of staff experts, e.g., accountants	Availability and access to experts
8. Referent power and symbolic power	Ascriptive characteristics which may induce identification and commitment of followers to leaders; such as charisma; and capability of using moral persuasion or shared ideology	

operationalization of each type of power resources is clearly needed, since available measures of power resources suffer from severe content validity problems.[18]

PHASE 2: THE PREVALENT TYPE OF POWER ORIENTATIONS

The second phase of the diagnostic model involves the identification of the prevalent type of power orientations in the LRS under consideration. In a classic contribution to the conceptualization of power, Riker[19] examined five well-known definitions of power (namely, those formulated by Shaply and Shubik, March, Dahl, Cartwright, and Karlsson) and distilled from them their common elements. As Riker[20] noted, the distinction between people and issues, as two alternative references of power interactions, was well establish-ed in the literature. In an LRS context, this distinction relates to the subject matter of the participants' power orientations (defined as an LRS input). When power orientations are tied to LRS issues, or when issue-power orientation prevails, one can expect substantial variance in a participant's predispositions to use power relative to a range of LRS issues. That is, par-ticipants presented with a list of LRS issues, would express varying predisposi-tions to use power depending on the issue at stake. In contrast, when power orientations are tied up to people, or when people-power-orientation prevails, one may expect only minimal differences among LRS issues in a participant's predispositions to use power relative to them.

Realistically, one may expect to find varying combinations of issue- and people-power orientations in any given LRS and for each participant. It is submitted, however, that when one locates an LRS in which a partici-pant's power orientations are predominantly tied up to people, the like-lihood that one can succeed in introducing an effective union-management cooperation scheme is scant. Power, under such circumstances, is viewed as a group possession, rather than a condition contingent upon the issue at stake.

The relative dominance of people-power orientations is considered as a structural characteristic of the LRS under investigation. This is because there is evidence indicating that whenever it exists, it tends to reflect well-ingrained sets of values of a participant, such as a view of the world as largely contain-ing competitors that have to be competed with,[21] or a basic unwillingness to accept the legitimacy of the other participant.[22] To illustrate: Within the limits imposed by available resources, management may develop a strategy of fierce and aggressive resistance to the union on any issue, because of an anti-union ideology it harbors. Ideologically rooted innate aggressiveness may lead a union to adopt militant policies towards management, irrespective of the subject matter discussed. (For a discussion of those strategies, see Good-man and Sandberg.)[23]

The suggested method for the identification of the prevalent type of power orientations in an LRS is explained in the next section, since it is similar to the one developed for measuring a participant's predisposition to use power relative to an issue. Table 15.2 illustrates how differing combinations of the participants' relative power and of their predominant power orientations may result in widely different characteristics of LRS processes.

Table 15.2. Balance of Power and Power Orientations in LRS

Balance of Power	Issue Power Orientation	People Power Orientation
Management has the upper hand	Very limited scope of issues resolved in the LRS; minimal interactions	Managerial paternalism or domination
About equal power of the participants	Integrative bargaining, or problem solving approach, likely	Distributive bargaining on every issue— continuous conflict
Management is the weaker party	Very broad scope of issues resolved in the LRS	Union is actively involved in the management of human resources (e.g. in hiring and training employees)

PHASE 3: PREDISPOSITIONS TO USE POWER

The third phase of the diagnostic model is an assessment of each of the participant's predispositions to use power relative to each labor relations issue. The term power predisposition is used here synonymously to the earlier term power orientation but connotes a closer proximity of the attitudinal component to actual behavior, or a behavioral intention. Following Frey and Bacharach and Lawler,[24] it is proposed that power interactions can meaningfully be studied only on an issue-by-issue basis. The choice of an issue affects the orientations of the participants and the combination of power resources they use.[25] A participant's predisposition to use power relative to an issue, abbreviated as PPI, probably reflects past experience with the solutions offered to the same or similar issues. The more reconcilable the past solutions offered by the participant to an issue, the lower the PPI score of that participant.[26] PPI probably also reflects the perceived importance or essentiality of the issue under consideration.[27]

Little is known about the range of issues dealt with in an LRS and about the participants' PPI associated with each. Content analysis of LRS processes may lead to an identification of the relative frequency of appearance of items or subject matters. Expert judges may then be used to cull similar items into meaningful issues. Several behavioral studies of bargaining used such issue-identification methods.[28]

Having delineated a list of issues resolved in an LRS, the next task is to measure the PPI of each participant relative to each issue. Having completed this measurement task, one can draw a graph such as the one illustrated by Figure 15.2, namely the PPI graph. The graph consists of two axes, the horizontal one representing the range of LRS issues and the vertical axis representing the mean PPI score of each participant. Figure 15.2 should be viewed as a pictorial example of a presumed rank order of PPI obtained respectively from management and from union representatives. The total area enclosed by each of the two curves in Figure 15.2 may represent potential conflict in the LRS from the viewpoint of the respective participant.

Five zones of issues were identified in Figure 15.2, using the fictitious data in it for illustrative purposes. The extreme left- and righthand zones, separated by a dividing line from the other three zones, represent LRS boundaries, because for each of the issues in them, one of the participants has an extremely high PPI score and the other a PPI score close to zero. Adjacent to the two boundary zones are zones in which the two participants' PPI scores are either uniformly high—designated as the zone of conflictive issues—or uniformly low—designated as the zone of participatory issues. Again, the genotypic nature of the illustrative issues listed in each zone is subject to future confirmation in empiric research.

The middle zone, designated as the zone of indeterminate issues, represents a cluster of issues for which the participants' PPI lack closure. Therefore, they cannot be classified either with the conflictive or participatory issues. These issues probably reflect the influence of system specific characteristics, such as technology, on the PPI scores of one of the participants.

There are some similarities between the PPI graph and Tannenbaum's control graph;[29] for a review of studies using the control graph, see Tannenbaum and Cooke.[30] The control graph represents the amount of control exercised by each of the hierarchical echelons of an organization, and therefore represents a uniquely organization-level description of the distribution of control. Similarly, the PPI graph offers a holistic characterization of the power predispositions of each LRS participant. Both graphs are subjective, perceptual, conceived with survey methodology in mind, and face the difficulty of averaging noncorresponding responses obtained from same groups of respondents. There are, however, two noteworthy dissimilarities. First, the control graph respondents assess on a posterior basis the amount of relative control possessed by each organizational layer, although the PPI graph respondents are requested to assess only their own behavioral intentions. Second, although both graphs' respondents are guided by a very general work-

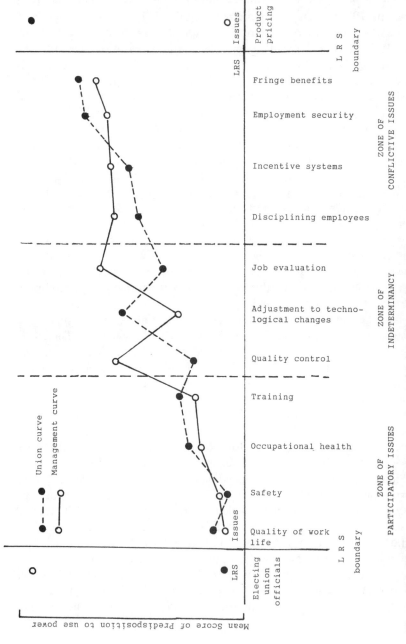

Figure 15.2. Union and management representatives' predispositions to use power relative to LRS issues (PPIs graphs).

ing definition of control or power, the construction of the PPI graph entails directing respondents to each issue—a very specific frame of reference.

The PPI graph completes the initial diagnosis of the LRS under consideration. Its uses may be illustrated by the following example. As noted, mutually low PPI scores measured for a set of issues may reflect the participants' expectations that mutually beneficial outcomes can be gained from the resolution of each issue. It is suggested that when the OD consultants feed back this information to the participants (and possibly also to their respective constituency) as objective facts, this may set in motion a self-fulfilling prophecy and increase the likelihood that a union-management participative scheme, designed solely for the resolution of those issues, would prove effective.

DISCUSSION

A limitation of the diagnostic model is that it is not concerned with the problem of ill defined issues.[31] Throughout the presentation it has been assumed that LRS issues are relatively well-defined; it was suggested that effective OD consultants should start out by identifying those issues, much like the way that effective mediators function.[32] However, some issues may disappear when reality-tested (e.g., a misattributed conflict, such as the disagreement of a union representative with a management's policy that actually does not exist) or when their underlying latent issue are uncovered (e.g., an addressed issue is but a manifest expression of another one). Filley[33] has suggested several mechanisms to adjust or redefine such issues; nonetheless, much additional research on them and on the relative efficacy of the techniques proposed to deal with them is needed.

The hypothesized proximity of the participants' PPI scores in the zones of conflictive and participatory issues has been explained above in terms of the participants' learning from past experiences. Yet another explanatory factor is the importance or relevance of the issue under consideration to a participant's critical objectives. It may be that issues categorized in the zone of participatory issues are less likely to be critically important to either of the participants. Carrying this line of reasoning a bit further, it may be that issues in the zone of indeterminacy are characterized by significant differences between the two participants in their assessment of each issue's relevancy to them. Thus quality control may be very important to management representatives but not so important to the union representatives.

For the purpose of simplifying the presentation, it was assumed that the representatives of the parties actually represent their constituency, that is, that they mirror in their attitudes and behaviors the preferences and desires of their respective constituency. As seen in surveys of the literature,[34] this assumption is probably too simplistic. As an example, Derber and his associates[35] found a correlation of .90 on attitudes toward the company between union officials and rank-and-file members, but a correlation of only .50 between top managements' and foremen's attitudes toward the union. Relaxing this assumption means that "a participant" will be replaced by "a party"—namely, the representatives and their constituency or a representative sample thereof— in future attempts to apply the proposed diagnostic model. Such a change of focus in defining the universe of content poses several methodological difficulties. As an example, suppose the PPI scores of union representatives and their rank-and-file followers relative to a given issue are widely incongruent. How should one weigh the mean score of the "party"? Similar group reliability problems were shown by Markham et al.,[36] to exist in the control graph approach.

In sum, the proposed diagnostic model dealt, in its three phases, with the LRS environmental contexts (the assessment of the relative power resources of the participants), structural characteristics (the predominant type of power orientations of the participants) and inputs (the predisposition to use power relative to an issue). The model needs to be further developed to allow for the diagnosis of the other components in an LRS, including its processes and outcomes.

NOTES

1. W. W. Burke, *Organization Development: Principles and Practices* (Boston: Little, Brown & Co., 1982).

2. K. S. Cameron, "The Effectiveness of Ineffectiveness" in B. S. Staw and L. L. Cummings, eds., *Research in Organizational Behavior* (Vol. 6; London: JAI Press, 1984), pp. 235–285.

3. E. E. Lawler, D. A. Nadler and C. Cammann, eds., *Organizational Assessment: Perspectives on the Measurement of Organizational Behavior and the Quality of Work Life* (New York: John Wiley & Sons, 1980).

4. J. A. Drexler, Jr. and E. E. Lawler, III, "A Union Management Cooperative Effort to Improve the Quality of Work Life," *Journal of Applied Behavioral Science,* 13 (1977), pp. 373–387.

5. T. A Kochan and L. Dyer, "A Model for Organizational Change in the Context of Labor-Management relations," *Journal of Applied Behavioral Science,* 12 (1976), pp. 59–78.

6. Cf. George Strauss, "Can Social Psychology Contribute to Industrial Relations?" in G. M. Stephenson and C. J. Brotherton, eds., *Industrial Relations: A Social Psychological Approach* (Chichester, England: John Wiley & Sons, 1979), pp. 383–385.

7. R. J. Bullock, B. A. Macy and P. M. Mirvis, "Assessing Unions and Union-Management Collaboration in Organizational Change," in S. E. Seashore, E. E. Lawler, III, P. H. Mirvis and C. Cammann eds., *Assessing Organizational Change* (New York: John Wiley & Sons, 1983), pp. 369–413.

8. J. L. Koch and C. L. Fox, "The Industrial Relations Setting Organizational Forces and the Form and Content of Worker Participation," *Academy of Management Review,* 3 (1978), pp. 572–583.

9. T. E. Cummings, ed., *System Theory for Organization Development* (Chichester, England: John Wiley & Sons, 1980).

10. A. Shirom, "Toward a Theory of Organization Development Interventions in Unionized Work Settings," *Human Relations,* 36 (1983), pp. 743–764,

11. K. S. Cook, "Exchange and Power in Networks of Intrerorganizational Relations," *Sociological Quarterly,* 17 (1977), pp. 62–68.

12. D. G. Pruit, *Negotiation Behavior* (New York: Academic Press, 1981), pp. 87–88.

13. J. Pfeffer, *Power in Organizations* (Boston: Pitman, 1981), pp. 43–61.

14. T. A. Kochan, *Collective Bargaining and Industrial Relations* (Homewood, IL: Irwin, 1980), pp. 193–200.

15. M. Poole, "A Power Analysis of Workplace Labor Relations," *Industrial Relations Journal,* 7 (1976), pp. 31–43.

16. J. R. P. French, Jr. and B. Raven, "The Bases of Social Power" in D. Cartwright and A. Zander, eds., *Group Dynamics* (2nd ed., New York: Harper & Row, 1960), pp. 607–624.

17. M. T. Wood, "Power Relationships and Group Decision Making in Organizations," *Psychological Bulletin,* 79 (1973), pp. 280–293.

18. P. M. Podsakoff and C. A. Schriesheim, "Measurement and Analytic Shortcomings in Field Studies of French and Raven Bases of Social Power," in J. A. Pearce and R. B. Robinson, Jr., eds., *Proceedings of the Academy of Management Forty-Fourth Annual Meeting* (1984), pp. 227–231. (Columbia, SC: Academy of Management).

19. W. H. Riker, "Some Ambiguities in the Notion of Power," *American Political Science Review,* 72 (1964), pp. 262–274.

20. Ibid.

21. B. R. Schlenker and H. J. Galman, "Cooperators and Competitors in Conflict," *Journal of Conflict Resolution,* 22 (1978), pp. 393–410.

22. D. Knight and J. Roberts, "The Power of Organization or the Organization of Power?" *Organization Studies,* 3 (1982), p. 49; see also T A. Kochan, *Collective Bargaining and Industrial Relations* (Homewood, IL: Irwin, 1980), pp. 183–191.

23. J. P. Goodman and W. R. Sandberg, "A Contingency Approach to Labor Relations Strategies," *Academy of Management Review,* 6 (1981), pp. 145–154.

24. F. Frey, "Comment: On Issues and Non-Issues in the Study of Power," *American Political Science Review,* 65 (1971), pp. 1081–1101; see also S. B. Bacharach and E. J. Lawler, *Power and Politics in Organizations* (San Francisco: Jossey-Bass, 1980).

25. B. Goodstadt and D. Kipnis, "Situational Influences on the Use of Power," *Journal of Applied Psychology,* 54 (1970), pp. 201–207.

26. R. M. Krauss, "Structural and Attitudinal Factors in Interpersonal Bargaining," *Journal of Experimental Social Psychology,* 2 (1966), pp. 42–44.

27. R. E. Walton and R. B. McKersie, *A Behavioral Theory of Labor Negotiations* (New York: McGraw-Hill, 1965).

28. I. E. Morley, "Behavioral Studies of Industrial Bargaining," in G. M. Stephenson and C. J. Brotherton, eds., *Industrial Relations: A Social Psychological Approach* (Chichester, England: John Wiley & Sons, 1979), pp. 215–216.

29. A. S. Tannenbaum, *Control in Organizations* (New York: McGraw-Hill, 1968), pp. 31–45.

30. A. S. Tannenbaum and R. A. Cooke, "Organizational Control: A Review of Studies Employing the Control Graph Method," in C. J. Lammers and D. J. Hickson, eds., *Organizations Alike and Unlike* (London: Routledge and Kegan Paul, 1979), pp. 183–210.

31. A. C. Filley, "Problem Definition and Conflict Management," in G. B. J. Bomers and R. B. Peterson, eds., *Conflict Management and Industrial Relations* (The Hague, Netherlands: Nijhoff, 1982), pp. 79–96.

32. T. A. Kochan and T. Jick, "The Public Sector Mediation Process: A Theory and Empirical Examination," *Journal of Conflict Resolution,* 22 (1978), pp. 209–240.

33. Filley, op. cit., pp. 79–96.

34. A. S. Tannenbaum, "Unions" in J. G. March, ed., *Handbook of Organizations* (Chicago: Rand McNally, 1965), pp. 717–719.

35. M. Derber et al., *Labor Management Relations in Illini City* (Vol. II, Champaign: University of Illinois Press, 1954).

36. W. T. Markham, C. Bonzean and J. Corder, "Measuring Organizational Control: The Reliability and Validity of the Control Graph Approach," *Human Relations,* 37 (1984), pp. 285–286.

ADDITIONAL REFERENCES

Bacharach, S. B. and Lawler, E. J. *Bargaining.* San Francisco: Jossey-Bass, 1981.

Crozier, M. "The Problem of Power," *Social Research,* 40 (1973), pp. 211–228.

Dubin, R. "Attachment to Work and Union Militancy," *Industrial Relations,* 12 (1973), pp. 51–65.

Pettigrew, A. "Toward a Political Theory of Organizational Intervention," *Human Relations,* 28 (1975), pp. 191–208.

16

INDUSTRIAL RELATIONS AS AN ACADEMIC FIELD: WHAT'S WRONG WITH IT? ————————

GEORGE STRAUSS

Ten years ago Peter Feuille and I wrote "Industrial Relations Research: A Critical Analysis" (Strauss and Feuille, 1978, 1981) in which we analyzed the development of academic Industrial Relations (IR) up to that time. We ended on the upbeat: although IR had been going through the "Doldrums," it might be on the verge of a "Renaissance."

What has happened since then? From my biased point of view, the news is more bad than good. Academic IR's problems naturally reflect the problems of IR in the real world. As union density has declined, so has the social significance of IR classes, centers, and research. In a nut shell, although hard data are lacking, enrollment in courses dealing with labor-management relations appears to have declined substantially from earlier periods, especially in business schools. On the other hand, enrollment in human resources courses is doing well. The funding and even continued existence of many industrial relations centers and institutes (including my own) has come under serious attack, with opponents arguing that these centers were designed to respond to the agenda of the 1940s and are now obsolete. The good news is that so far the attacks have been beaten off (and new centers established at Columbia, South Carolina). However, this often has been at the cost of reduced budgets, staffs and course offerings. Research has become more quantitative, rigorous, and narrowly confined to union-management relations. With notable exceptions (e.g. Kochan, Katz and McKersie, 1986) mainstream IR scholars have ignored the big picture—the rapid decline of unions and collective bargaining. Meanwhile, economists, sociologists and historians have been making significant contributions to understanding work relations, but little of this has been integrated into mainstream IR research.

241

My discussion below deals generally with IR's plight.[1] As before, I end on the upbeat, with some modest suggestions for making IR more relevant to the needs of the 1990s. But first let me place contemporary IR in historic context.

ACADEMIC IR: A BRIEF HISTORY

In 1978, Feuille and I divided the history of academic industrial relations to that time into three periods, the early days (up to the mid-1930s), the golden age (from the mid-1930s to the mid-1950s), and the doldrums (roughly from 1957 to 1975).

The Early Days

The leaders during this period, Commons, Perlman, and Witte, among others, called themselves "institutional economists." Their two main concerns were the description, explanation, and legitimation of the then struggling labor movement and the enactment of social legislation dealing with such subjects as social security and child labor.

The Golden Age

During the thirties and forties, as unions and collective bargaining spread rapidly, IR became the focus of national attention. The strike wave after World War II made IR the country's social problem—or so many Americans thought, including a large cohort of returning veterans (such as myself), who entered graduate study of IR courtesy of the GI Bill. During much of the period it was an open question as to whether union-management strife could be contained within socially manageable levels. The professors who date their Ph.D.s from this zesty era constituted the core of most academic IR groups, at least until recently.

Responding to student and public demands, schools and institutes of industrial relations were widely established. Enrollments in IR courses boomed; in some business schools at least one IR course was required for graduation.

Most early IR scholars were economists; however, the field also drew sociologists, psychologists, political scientists, and lawyers. But background meant little because the main focus of this interdisciplinary crew was applied—problem-oriented—not theoretical. (Many academicians also worked as arbitrators.) There were numerous case studies dealing with labor relations at the shop, plant, and company levels, but there was little quantification. People trained as economists also wrote about law, history, and personnel.

Consistent with the emerging reality of the period, IR people began to accept a set of pluralist assumptions made explicit by Dunlop (1958).[2] These assumptions are that though the parties have important conflicts of interest, they basically accept the system. Thus they can reconcile their differences through bargaining, and a dynamic equilibrium will emerge. This contrasts with what Fox (1971) has called the unitary assumption that the interests of the parties are basically similar and that differences that do emerge can be easily resolved through better management. It also conflicts with assumptions of radical critics (Hyman, 1975) that the differences between the parties are fundamentally irreconcilable and that the whole Dunlop approach is designed to legitimate the status quo.

Two partly legitimate offshoots from mainstream IR, Personnel and Human Relations, dealt with such issues as recruitment, discipline, motivation, and compensation. These fields were considered subsidiary to mainstream IR; nevertheless they were commonly included in IR's jurisdiction.

The Doldrums

IR research seemed to lose much of its former excitement during this period. Collective bargaining had become routinized. Indeed, during the turbulent sixties the industrial relations system was one of the few stable institutions in American life. Other issues such as poverty, race and gender relations began to excite socially conscious students who once might have been IR majors. Production of Ph.D.s dropped off, and IR suffered a "lost generation."

Meanwhile, in most of the social sciences the pendulum was swinging from interdisciplinary research, raw empiricism, and application to theory making, theory testing, and quantification (in part the result of computers and money to operate them). As a consequence IR's old interdisciplinary amalgam began to fall apart. Economists, lawyers, historians, psychologists and sociologists all began writing in their own disciplinary journals and in terms of their disciplinary paradigms. IR suffered too because it was among the last social science fields to become quantified.

While IR stagnated, a new field, Organizational Behavior (OB—often called Management), in some ways an offshoot of Human Relations, emerged and flourished. In many places, such as Berkeley, it grabbed IR's slot as the compulsory, people-oriented course and it even took over its faculty positions.[3]

In the hard competition for space in the business school core, OB had two major advantages over IR: (1) it had a better claim to be a basic science; at least it began quantitative hypothesis testing earlier than did IR, and (2) it claimed jurisdiction over all work-relations; IR concerned itself primarily with an ever-decreasing unionized minority.

RELATED FIELDS

Defining IR has become increasingly difficult. A broad definition might cover all the subjects encompassed in the field during the Golden Age, including issues as diverse as unemployment, testing, and group structure. A narrow definition confines IR to union-management relations. As the years went by, the more peripheral fields drifted away and the work of people who call themselves IR specialists became increasingly narrow, making the more restrictive definition of what I will call mainstream IR increasingly appropriate.[4]

Other fields have not ignored IR phenomena, whether broadly or narrowly defined; quite the contrary. Important work on IR topics is being done by economists, historians, sociologists, and the like, but few of these people call their research industrial relations. More tragic, mainstream IR scholars are largely unaware of this work. Some cross-fertilization occurs, particularly by people whose work overlaps IR and economics or IR and OB.

The fragmentation of the field is illustrated by a host of new academic and quasi-academic journals including *Journal of Labor Economics, Journal of Labor Research, Industrial Relations Law Journal, Negotiations Journal, Labor Studies Journal, Employee Responsibilities and Rights Journal,* and *Journal of Collective Bargaining in the Public Sector* (not to mention the many new journals in Human Resources and OB). As the references in these journals suggest, their contributors are generally quite parochial in their reading. Only the *Journal of Labor Research* has pretensions of covering IR broadly.

Great progress has been made in these related fields. Let me assess their possible contributions to the mainstream. I deal with both full-scale disciplines, such as law, and more informal interdisciplinary groupings, such as bargaining and radical criticism.

Labor History

Though largely ignored by mainstream IR, this flourishing field is making significant contributions to our understanding of IR, whether narrowly or broadly defined. Labor history today is no longer primarily concerned with the history of unions. Instead labor historians examine the history of work and of workers, as well as the development of various forms of labor markets and personnel systems (both union and nonunion). Their research is closely linked to studies of management history. Although sociologists are integrating labor history into their research, mainstream IR is largely ahistorical. Two important exceptions are Jacoby (1985) and Piore and Sable (1984) whose contributions do much to place contemporary IR in perspective.

Sociology

The new organizational sociology has little to do with old industrial sociology, but there is interest on the part of sociologists in such issues as internal labor markets, career ladders, and wage levels and distribution (Berg, 1981; Granovetter, 1984; Pfeffer and Davis-Blake, 1987). These are IR issues, at least broadly defined. Sociologists are generally aware of IR research—or so their footnotes indicate—but the reverse is not true.

Left-wing sociologists have interests and methodologies more akin to those of the industrial sociologists of the 1940s. They actually talk to real workers (e.g., Burawoy, 1979)

Psychology

Aside from some studies of membership commitment to unions (e.g., Gordon et al., 1980), psychologists have shown little interest in narrowly defined IR. On the other hand, they have made many contributions to HR and OB and have done notable work on bargaining. A small number of psychologically trained people with interests in OB and IR have used questionnaires to study why workers vote for unions in National Labor Relations Board (NLRB) elections.

Further, as a recent symposium (Lewin, 1988) illustrates, a growing number of IR people are using tools, methodologies and concepts borrowed from sociology and psychology, especially the latter. Indeed it is no longer a great rarity to find psychological and economic literature cited in the same articles, and IR people are making increasing use of experiments and attitude surveys. This is all to the good.

Law

Labor law was once concerned primarily with union-management relations, but the hot areas since the 1970s have revolved around such subjects as equal employment and unfair dismissal. Mainstream IR scholars (an exception is

Leonard, 1984) have largely ignored these topics except as they impinge on collective bargaining. Although IR people have been concerned with the impact of the law on union decline, lawyers have been concerned chiefly with legal niceties rather than the big picture (an exception is Weiler, 1983). There has been little overlap between lawyers and IR people.

Radical Critics

I come now to a group of historians, sociologists, lawyers and economists (some of whom identify themselves as political economists) who might be called radical critics. A few—but only a few—call themselves Marxists. This group is relatively smaller in the United States than it is in Europe.

By contrast with their more conservative colleagues, radical scholars tend to question the pluralist assumption that the differences between labor and management are relatively minor and can be resolved through collective bargaining. Instead these scholars argue the IR disputes are rooted in basic societal differences, some related to class.

Radical scholars are at least as interdisciplinary in their interests as their mainstream counterparts were during the Golden Age. They are particularly aware of history. Some, for example, argue that "the New Deal structure of industrial relations," including the Wagner Act (Kochan et al., 1986), was designed in part to coopt workers (for an example from "critical labor law theory," see Klare, 1978).

Among the topics of special interest to radical scholars today are (1) labor market segmentation, (2) techniques for controlling workers (more conservative scholars might be more comfortable with the word motivating), and (3) technology (labor process).

Some radical scholars are narrow in their analytic framework and off-putting in their terminology. (But neo-classical economists are even more so—and they lack the radical's interdisciplinary breadth.) Radical work is largely ignored by mainstream IR, which is a pity.

Bargaining and Conflict Resolution

Courses on bargaining and conflict resolution are booming in business and law schools. Mediation and alternate dispute resolution have become almost a fad, being prescribed for everything from family and landlord-tenant relations to pre-trial negotiations.

In business schools, bargaining courses are being taught by faculty from a large number of backgrounds, but more often by OB people than by IR people, this despite the fact that bargaining and mediation are at the heart of traditional IR and many of the concepts were originally developed in an IR context. With notable exceptions,[5] IR people have been too parochial to see the broader applications of their discipline.[6] So IR missed the boat.

The typical bargaining course relies heavily on game-theory economics and psychological laboratory experimentation. Both are individualistic approaches that simplify the reality of real-life bargaining, especially when this occurs in organizational contexts. IR could offer a lot. Unfortunately there is little current IR research on the process of bargaining or conflict resolution (an exception is Kolb, 1983).

The Society of Professionals in Dispute Resolution (SPIDR), the new field's practitioner association, is growing rapidly. About half of its members and half of its annual conference sessions deal with IR. Much of this discussion might have taken place at the IRRA, which sadly has run few sessions on bargaining theory.

Labor Studies

During the 1970s labor education specialists began thinking of Labor Studies as a separate academic field and to develop a professional association and their own *Labor Studies Journal.* Two factors were responsible for this move towards professionalization. In the first place, a demand arose to expand university labor education offerings beyond short courses and conferences to full fledged associate and bachelor (and even Ph.D.) degree programs. Many of the new associate-level courses were sponsored, not by established university IR centers but by community colleges. Second, university extension staffs began asking for regular faculty status rather than being treated as second class citizens. But to justify this status universities increasingly began requiring that their staffs have masters or doctoral degrees.

Labor Economics

At one time Labor Economics and Industrial Relations were almost interchangeable terms. Gradually they grew apart (from 1966 to 1984 the percent of members of the national Industrial Relations Research Association calling themselves labor economists fell from 23 to 7 percent).[7]

Early texts combined the two fields (for example, Reynolds, *Labor Economics and Labor Relations,* 1954). These texts served the field well for over a quarter century. But by the late-1970s some new purely labor economics texts appeared, some of which hardly mentioned unions at all. Meanwhile numerous purely IR texts were published. These dealt almost exclusively with union-management relations and gave little space to economics. Important work continues to be done linking IR and labor economics. Freeman and Medoff's *What Do Unions Do?* (1984) has been justly praised, even though some of it is based on pre-concession-bargaining data and so needs redoing. Nevertheless this landmark study hardly represents the mainstream of labor economics today.

The mainstream has become heavily theoretical or quantitative. Much of its effort has been to explain, in neo-classical economic theory, regularities that economists find disturbing[8] but which mainstream IR people feel they have understood all along, for example, (1) why the wage rates for any given occupation differ so widely in the same community or (2) why employers are prepared to pay wages higher than the market-clearing rate. Little of this research has practical application; most of it ignores collective bargaining.

Nevertheless, work of this sort helps integrate labor economics with economic theory and so raises labor economics' status. In so doing it makes use of a tremendous variety of innovative new concepts, such as efficiency wages, agency theory, gift exchange, moral hazard, implicit contracting, shirking, and the like.

I find the *Journal of Labor Economics* fascinating, if weird. Even when labor economists merely restate old verities, they do so with a precision that makes new insights emerge. Long before Newton, people knew that apples fell. But by explaining gravity in mathematical terms, Newton laid the groundwork for modern physics.

My main reservation is that many of the assumptions made by contemporary labor economists are wildly unrealistic.[9] Even where these assumptions are not wholly wrong, they sometimes abstract away such large portions of reality that they end up being more wrong than right. I am distinctly uncomfortable, for example, with the assumption that all unemployment is voluntary or that an institution's behavior should be analyzed as if it were determined by the sum of its members' preferences (or those of its median and even marginal member).

Human Resources

Personnel, renamed Human Resources Management, has been booming. In most schools, demand for HRM courses is considerably greater than it is for traditional courses in collective bargaining, labor economics, and labor law. As the director of a leading IR center put it, "All our students want is HR, all our faculty want to teach is IR."[10] Thus there have been many more recent academic openings in HRM than in traditional IR.

Although, HRM faculty, as a group, are closer to OB or to psychology than they are to IR or economics, nevertheless IR has a historic claim over Personnel. Thus, reacting to market pressures, some IR departments have renamed themselves HRM or at least incorporated HRM in their name.

The switch to HRM reflects changes in employment opportunities.[11] At Cornell, for example "of those ILR School graduates who enter directly into the job market . . . fewer than 25 percent obtain positions that bring them into contact with union-management relations. The other 75 percent obtain jobs where they are involved in the management of non-union personnel systems" (Rehmus, 1985).

Symptomatic of this trend, the Industrial Relations Center Directors (a hitherto informal group that meets with the IRRA) recently decided to formalize themselves and tentatively to adopt a new name, the Association of Industrial Relations and Human Resources Programs.[12]

The annual meeting of the Personnel/Human Resources Division of the Academy of Management offers approximately as many sessions as the IRRA and its attendance may be about the same.[13] Certainly the average age of those who attend is younger.

Regardless of its broader pretensions, HRM's heart, at least as it is taught in most schools and covered in most textbooks, is still what used to be called Personnel. For my taste the field is too narrow, specifically in the following areas.

(1) Its texts are too cookbooky—they tell you what to do or what the alternatives are—but they pay little attention to the political problems of implementation.

(2) The various parts of the field are poorly integrated: there is little discussion of the possibility, for example, that if you use profit sharing rather than piecework you might also want a different kind of selection and induction system. In short, it is more concerned with tactics than with strategy.

(3) Many of the same criticisms may be directed to its research. The typical research project is concerned with the development of techniques and instruments for use in such functions as testing and performance evaluation. Typically it makes careful use of control and experimental groups (often of students). But there is little research on how to implement these techniques effectively.

(4) The field is too psychological. It ignores development in the world at large, such as changes in technology.

(5) The field seems directed toward staff specialists rather than line managers.

As a last ironic point, several well-known labor economists (eg., Edward Lazear, Daniel J. B. Mitchell) are currently trying to develop an "economics of personnel." Indeed we are beginning to see a multidisciplinary approach to what I would call "the IR of the nonunion sector," but the practitioners of this new approach are more likely to call it economics or human resources than industrial relations. Again IR is being bypassed. In short, the real intellectual excitement today is in history, labor economics, and radical studies while HRM is taking away our students.

MAINSTREAM IR

Narrowly defined, IR has made some important advances over the last ten years. For example, in addition to the important research summarized in Freeman and Medoff (1984) and Kochan et al. (1986), we now know a lot more about public sector bargaining.[14] Nevertheless, with important exceptions, IR research is narrower than it was 30 years ago. The focus of both its research and its teaching (as reflected in its major new texts) is primarily on union-management relations, at a time when these are declining in importance.

There has been a marked change in IR research style since the early 1970s. From my point of view this has both advantages and disadvantages. My analysis is heavily influenced by Cappelli (1985).

Older Research Methodology

Institutional economics, modern IR's main forebear, stressed its atheoretical nature. Early IR research tended to be inductive, looking first at the problem in rich detail, then drawing generalizations from these data. It was based on micro-case studies or macro-policy issues; much of it was anecdotal. (Research in Great Britain still largely follows this model.) As suggested earlier, IR was late to make use of computers. Finally, older research tended to be applied, making possible, for example, an Industrial Relations Research Association in which both academicians and practitioners participated.

Current Research Methodology

IR research today is rigorous and quantitative. Further, it is deductive, frequently drawing hypotheses (or models) from economic and psychological theory, and then testing these hypotheses with available data, even though these data may be only imperfect proxies for the dimensions that they are supposed to represent. Indeed the easy availability of the computer may be a curse as well as a blessing.

By contrast with earlier studies, little current research involves talking to real workers or managers (at the most there are lab experiments and written questionnaires, Lewin, 1988). The most common current sources of data are already available in libraries or on computer tapes. Further, deductive research, which yields general laws rather than explanations of individual cases, is less likely to be policy-oriented. This may have contributed to the decline of the national IRRA meetings as a forum for interchange between academicians and practitioners.

Also as Cappelli has pointed out, the emphasis in IR research has switched from the institutional and social levels to the individual.[15] This individual level is the one on which economics and micro-OB are primarily based. Unions are assumed to represent the interests of the median voter, with purely institutional interests being largely ignored (by contrast some current schools of sociology view institutions as almost having a life of their own). There is little interest in groups or institutions as such. Consequently sociology or political science has little current impact on IR (a notable exception is Piore and Sable, 1984). There is little use of theories of collective action from sociology, though these are obviously relevant. IR's disregard of its institutional heritage may have contributed to its failure to make new contributions to the growing bargaining-conflict resolution field. Finally, though IR research may provide more implications for practice than does most research in economics or OB, it is considerably less applied today than it was during the Golden Age. Rigor has displaced relevance.

Research Topics

Although contemporary IR draws heavily from the other social sciences for its methodology, in choice of questions to be asked it is largely bound by the Dunlop paradigm. The pluralist assumptions, which largely reflected the realities of "the New Deal industrial relations system" (Kochan, Katz and McKersie, 1986) during the fifties and sixties, have been rejected by an increasing number of companies that are now operating under unitary assumptions.

Current IR research is concerned chiefly with union-management relations, not with other relations between managers and employees, or relations among employees or among managers. Yet the scope of collective bargaining and arbitration has gradually been eroded. Many of the IR innovations today come from non-union management, the women's movement, and the government.

Rights derived from Equal Employment Opportunity (EEO), Employee Retirement Income Security Act (ERISA) and Occupational Safety and Health Administration (OSHA) laws may be more important than the contract.[16]

Further, contemporary IR has largely ignored the changing nature of the context within which real-world IR occurs. Research has focused on the relationships between a small number of independent and dependent variables. It has examined in exquisite detail the impact of unions on almost everything, but has done so for the most part using pre-1980 data, so this research today has chiefly historic interest. It has looked endlessly at various forms of final offer arbitration, determinants of strikes, union growth and decline, and the like, but with the notable exception of the MIT group it has largely ignored the big picture. It is like studying passenger menu preferences while the *Titanic* sinks.[17]

For example, with significant exceptions (chiefly at MIT) IR scholars have paid little attention to important but contradictory trends such as the growth of "high commitment" labor policies in such firms as Hewlett-Packard and IBM, and widespread layoffs of white collar, professional, and managerial employees who had previously viewed themselves as enjoying virtual lifetime employment.

If IR keeps itself this narrow it will inevitably lose much of its remaining research and student interest. True, there is much that is interesting and study-worthy as unions decline, but decline is rarely as exciting and always more depressing than growth. Unions may revive again, but there may be a long wait until this occurs; perhaps Jacoby is right: 1940 to 1980 was a great exception to the US norm, which is for firms to be militantly nonunion.

THE INDUSTRIAL RELATIONS RESEARCH ASSOCIATION

Developments within the IRRA, the field's professional organization, reflect predicaments faced by the field generally. Formed in 1948 by "rebels" grumbling over "the neglect of labor economics" by the American Economic Association (Kerr, 1984, p. 14), the new organization sought to bridge the gap between practitioners and scholars and among scholars from various disciplines. As professors who moonlighted as arbitrators, most of its early leaders were both practitioners and academicians.

At first it succeeded reasonably well in its bridging function, but gradually it began suffering from previously mentioned ills. Despite continuing (though sometimes perfunctory) efforts to draw labor economists, OB people and occasionally historians to its annual meetings, scholars from these fields reserve their best work for their own disciplinary societies. The IRRA paid little attention to new scholarly development outside economics and mainstream IR. To my knowledge, no radical critic has ever presented an IRRA paper. Bargaining academicians spent some time looking for a new home and finally were granted a special section in the Academy of Management, not the IRRA.

In part because of the "lost generation," the IRRA's leadership and much of its participation has been disproportionally concentrated among those who received their Ph.D.s prior to 1955. Many younger mainstream scholars feel their contributions are more welcome at the Academy of Management, especially since IRRA papers are selected primarily by invitation rather than through open competition.

IRRA continues to seek out practitioner participation. A majority of its executive board and forty percent of its recent presidents have been practitioners. Yet few practitioners attend or give papers at its annual meetings.[18] On the other hand, membership in the practitioner-oriented local chapters has been increasing much faster than national membership.

IRRA's dilemma is that if the organization tries too hard to draw in a broad range of academicians from various disciplines as well as practitioners, it might instead repel them all. Compared to the situation 40 years ago, the major parties are less interested in hearing each other.

Teaching

Faced with declining student interest in straight IR, business schools such as Harvard, MIT, Columbia, and Northwestern have been experimenting with courses that combine IR and HRM (with perhaps some labor economics). Harvard has already produced a casebook (Beer et al, 1985) with a heavy emphasis on how human resource problems are handled in unionized companies. At MIT Kochan and Barocci have written a text with many cases, *Human Resources Management and Industrial Relations* (1985).

There are some problems with this approach if done too mechanically. Viewing the course as half one thing and half another will not work; there must be some integrating scheme. Further, traditional Personnel or HRM people tend to be psychologists, IR people are often economists; to date few people have been trained to teach both halves of the course. There is a danger that ex-IR people and ex-HRM people will excessively emphasize the technical aspects of their former fields. At least on the HRM side the elements of these courses I have seen have been too concerned with tactics rather than strategy.

WHERE DO WE GO FROM HERE?

Given the foregoing it should be no surprise that I think IR should seek to restore some of the ties that existed with allied fields during the 1950s and that it should broaden its scope beyond union-management relations.[19]

IR has been defined formally as something broader than merely labor-management relations. Perhaps it ought to exercise more vigorously the domain it has set for itself.

As far as research is concerned I think the MIT group provided a model for us all. I applaud the catholicity of its research methods—institutional descriptions, case studies, and careful quantitative hypothesis testing. I also like the range of subjects with which it deals. But let me be a bit more specific as to the kinds of questions IR should cover in both its research and its teaching.

1. We should recognize that for the near future management will be the primary initiating party in IR, with the government and the women's movement playing roles perhaps as important as unions. This means, for example, that we need much more research (including case studies) on managerial IR decisionmaking procedures, perhaps as much as we once devoted to union decisionmaking and governance.

2. We should recognize that management must make a range of strategic choices, not just whether to accept or oppose the union. It may pursue a high commitment strategy, including virtual lifetime employment, loosely defined jobs and high levels of participation (a policy followed at Hewlett-Packard and increasingly at GM plants). Or its policy may be one of narrowly defined jobs, rigid promotional ladders, and well established work rules (as in unionized manufacturing and bureaucratic organizations generally). Still another alternative is to rely on temporary workers and subcontractors (already the pattern in construction and entertainment). Or it may offer life-time employment to core employees, with temporary employees handling peaks of demand (a common practice in Japan). Management's success in following each of these strategies may depend on a variety of factors, all of which are worth studying and teaching.

3. We should devote more attention to the impact of technology and especially computers in both the office and the factory (e.g., robots and computer-controlled machine tools), recognizing that technology is not purely an exogenous force. Management can choose the forms of technology to in-

troduce and whether to utilize them so as to increase or decrease worker autonomy.

4. Researchers should return to the shop. We need to reexamine what is happening to shopfloor labor relations during the concession bargaining era. Besides the kinds of work done by the MIT group, we need systematic surveys of shop-level practice such as those now common in Great Britain (e.g., Batstone, 1984; Milward and Stevens, 1987)

5. We should study the new forms of compensation, such as profit-sharing, Employee Stock Ownership Plans (ESOPs), knowledge-based pay and the like. We should be concerned with their macro-implications (e.g., the Weitzman plan) as well as their micro-impacts.

6. IR was relatively static for twenty-five years (1950–1975), thus works such as Kochan (1980) and Freeman and Medoff (1984) could afford to ignore history. We cannot do this today. The new labor history belongs in our courses. They should examine the history of work, workers, and authority, as well as unions.

7. IR needs to be better integrated with OB. The distinction between these fields is less clear than it once was. At one time, among the differences between the two fields was that IR was pluralist in its assumptions and OB unitary. This is much less the case today as OB looks increasingly at conflict and conflict resolution and mainstream IR investigates forms of union-management collaboration.

Comparative IR

Finally, a plug for comparative IR. By rights, this field should be at IR's heart. The question of why industrial relations varies so greatly among the nations of the world is among the most challenging and interesting problems we have. One gets a much better perspective on one's own IR system (and of the essential nature of IR generally) by considering the main alternatives elsewhere. Certainly if an IR theory is to be developed, it will be on a comparative base.

Years ago American scholars contributed numerous insightful analyses of industrial relations in other countries (e.g. Ross and Hartman, 1960: Kerr et al, 1960). Recently, however, there have been few attempts by Americans to analyze and explain differences among countries in systematic and predictive ways. The few recent theory-oriented U.S. studies have been conducted by political scientists (Hibbs, 1976; Wilensky and Turner, 1987), sociologists (e.g., Snyder, 1975) and economists (Flanagan et al., 1983).

Comparative IR flourishes in the rest of the world (e.g., Phelps-Brown, 1983;

Clegg, 1976; Poole, 1986; Bean, 1985; and Korpi and Shalev, 1979). The field has moved beyond comparative description to the empirical testing of hypotheses. There have been a number of significant empirical cross-national studies involving standardized research designs developed for use by teams from a variety of countries, (e.g., IDE, 1981). Almost none of these studies have involved the United States.

To give an example of comparative IR's value: it is common for U.S. IR scholars to ascribe a large share of the responsibility for the decline in our country's union density to changes in labor force structure (e.g., less employment in manufacturing), however, as Lipset (1986) points out, if we look internationally, we see only a weak correlation between structural changes and decline in union density. "American exceptionalism" should be reexamined.

Certainly there are numerous variables worth investigating. Some relate to the collective bargaining process, for example, union density, strike rates, centralism, scope of bargaining, and formality of agreements. Others relate to the environment in which bargaining occurs: corporatism, national politics, various national policies (active labor market, industrial, income, social), class consciousness, technology, levels and rates of economic development. Some of these variables are more concrete than others, yet weights can be assigned to most of them.

The relationships among these variables cry out to be analyzed. Hopefully the analysis will not be as mechanistic as some analyses in Economics and OB.

CONCLUSION

Ten years ago Peter Feuille and I predicted a Renaissance in academic IR. This would consist of four elements: (1) a greater use of quantitative techniques; (2) a resurgence of interest by other social disciplines in such topics as union participation, strikes, and union-management cooperation; (3) renewed cross-fertilization among fields; and (4) greater application of IR insights to other fields, for example, to race relations and international relations. Our first two predictions proved largely right, especially the first one. There has been some cross-fertilization, though more affecting radical critics than mainstream IR people. Old IR insights are influencing the new field of bargaining, although the two fields are developing separately.

What we had not predicted was the weakening of collective bargaining. The impact of this has been to decrease significantly the number of students and job openings in mainstream IR. Younger scholars may face the choice of converting themselves to HR teachers (something they are reluctant to do) or adopting the kind of teaching and research agenda I outlined above. Short of an unexpected resurgence of union victories academic IR will have to make major adjustments. Otherwise it may follow the example of the Cigarmakers and the Sleeping Car Porters, both leaders in their time.

NOTES

1. Note carefully: I am concerned with academic IR in the United States; developments elsewhere have been quite different.

2. Harris (1985) argues that pluralist, Wisconsin school assumptions did much to shape real-world labor relations.

3. In 1986 in schools affiliated with the American Association of Collegiate Schools of Business there were 1,969 faculty in Management/Organizational Behavior and 367 in Industrial Relations (and this later figure may include some people teaching personnel). In the same year these schools granted 121 doctorates in Management/OB and only 8 in IR. *AACSB Newsletter,* Vol. 17, no. 4 (April 1987), p. 4.

4. There is an element of arbitrariness in my distinction between mainstream and related IR fields. I recognize that there is a certain tautology in defining IR as dealing with just union-management relations and then criticizing IR people for being so restrictive in their interests. My point is that the Golden Age predecessors would have been more catholic.

5. These are chiefly associated with MIT. In notable articles, Kochan and Bazerman (1986) and Kochan and Verma (1983) apply lessons from IR research to negotiations and organizational behavior. Robert McKersie chairs the *Negotiation Journal*'s Editorial Policy Committee and Deborah Kolb is a member, but they are the only IR people on the eighteen person committee.

6. During the student unrest of the 1960s many of the key negotiators and mediators had IR backgrounds. Yet their attempts to resolve conflict failed, perhaps because their techniques were too IR-specific (Strauss, 1982). Broader concepts are needed.

7. In most departments today the percentage of graduate students with undergraduate psychology degrees is increasing. Their counterparts, years back, were economists.

8. I cannot help wishing that economists would spend less time solving economists' problems and more time solving those of society. Economists appeared less concerned with unemployment in 1983, when the figure was pushing 10 percent than they were twenty years earlier, when it was half that amount.

9. For example, "The uncertainty hypothesis is tested using measures of investor uncertainty over the firm's future profitability as a proxy for the union's uncertainty" (Tracy, 1987, p. 150).

10. Meanwhile the typical undergraduate background of graduate IR students in many programs has shifted from economics to psychology and the percentage of women has increased dramatically.

11. There is a tendency for student groups, which once might have formed chapters of the IRRA, to ally themselves with the American Society for Personnel Administration. As a faculty advisor put it, "ASPA provides better job contacts than IRRA."

12. Name changing is becoming common. The *Industrial Relations News* now calls itself the *Human Resources News.* Numerous companies in which the top department was called In-

dustrial Relations, with Personnel a subsidiary division, have now reversed the roles, with HR being given the top listing with IR being made subordinate to it.

13. Consistent with HR's claim to be the broader field that encompasses IR, the Personnel/HR Division runs sessions on mainstream IR topics such as "American Unions in a Changing Environment." Quite a number of younger scholars attend both IRRA and Academy of Management meetings.

14. Specifically, (1) collective bargaining works well in the public sector, but (2) bargaining power is expressed differently, particularly (3) third party dispute resolution procedures play an important role. Finally (4) unions can affect wages in the public sector, but less so than in the private sector. I am indebted to Peter Feuille for this brief summary, as well as for comments generally.

15. "The continued focus of research on the individual level has meant that all that is unique about industrial relations—the institutions and their relations with each other and individuals—is ignored." (Cappelli, 1985, p. 104).

16. Standard IR courses used to deal with unemployment and inflation. Now these are covered in separate courses on economics.

17. Earlier scholars rarely forgot the big picture. Perhaps the best "big picture" study was Kerr et al., 1960.

18. Two of the announced papers at the 1986 national IRRA meetings came from management, four from labor, and over a hundred from academicians.

19. My agenda is much like that proposed by Ross (1964) a quarter century ago.

REFERENCES

Batstone, Eric. *Working Order: Workplace Industrial Relations Over Two Decades.* Oxford: Basil Blackwell, 1984.

Bean, R. *Comparative Industrial Relations.* London: Croom Helm, 1985

Beer, Michael, Bert Spector, Paul Lawrence, D. Quinn Mills, and Richard Walton. *Human Resources Management: A General Manager's Perspective.* New York: Free Press, 1985.

Berg, Ivar, ed. *Sociological Perspectives in Labor Markets,* New York: Academic Press, 1981.

Burawoy, Michael. *Manufacturing Consent: Changes in the Labor Process under Monopoly Capitalism.* Chicago: University of Chicago Press, 1979.

Cappelli, Peter, "Theory Construction in IR and Some Implications for Research." *Industrial Relations.* Vol. 24, No. 1 (Winter 1985) pp. 90–112.

Clegg, Hugh A. *Trade Unionism under Collective Bargaining: A Theory Based on a Comparison of Six Countries.* Oxford: Basil Blackwell, 1976.

Dunlop, John. *Industrial Relations Systems.* New York: Henry Holt, 1958.

Flanagan, Robert, David Soskice, and Lloyd Ulman. *Unionism, Economic Stabilization and Incomes Policies: The European Experience.* Washington, DC: Brookings Institution, 1983.

Fox, Alan. *A Sociology of Work in Industry.* London: Collier-Macmillan, 1971.

Freeman, Richard and James Medoff. *What Do Unions Do?* New York: Basic Books, 1984.

Gordon, Michael, J. W. Philpot, R. Burt, C. Thompson, and W. Spiller, "Commitments to the Union: Development of a Measure and Examination of its Correlates," *Journal of Applied Psychology,* Vol. 65, No. 4 (August 1980), pp. 479–499.

Granovetter, Mark, "Small is Beautiful: Labor Markets and Establishments," *American Sociological Review,* Vol. 49, No. 3 (1984), pp. 323–334.

Harris, Howell. "Politics, Law and Shopfloor Bargaining, and the Shaping of Federal Labour Relations Policy in the U.S., 1915–47," in Stephen Tolliday and Jonathan Zeitlin, eds. *Shop Floor Bargaining and the State.* Cambridge: Cambridge University Press, 1985.

Hibbs, Douglas, "Industrial Conflict in Advanced Industrial Societies," *American Political Science Review,* No. 70 (1976), pp. 1033–1058.

Hyman, Richard, *Industrial Relations: A Marxist Introduction.* London: Macmillan, 1975.

IDE. *Industrial Democracy in Europe.* Oxford: Clarendon Press, 1981.

Jacoby, Sanford M. *Employing Bureaucracy.* New York: Columbia University Press, 1985.

Kerr, Clark. "A Perspective on Industrial Relations Research—Thirty-six Years Later." *Proceedings of the Thirty-Sixth Annual Meeting,* Industrial Relations Research Association. Madison, 1984.

Kerr, Clark, John Dunlop, Fred Harbison, and Charles Myers. *Industrialism and Industrial Man.* Cambridge: Harvard University Press, 1960.

Klare, Karl E. "Judicial Deradicalization of the Wagner Act and the Origins of Modern Legal Consciousness, 1937–41", *Minnesota Law Review.* Vol. 62, No. 3 (March 1978), pp. 265–339.

Kochan, Thomas. *Collective Bargaining and Industrial Relations.* Homewood, IL: Irwin, 1980.

Kochan, Thomas and Tom Barocci. *Human Resources Management and Industrial Relations.* Boston: Little, Brown, and Co., 1985.

Kochan, Thomas and Max Bazerman. "Macro Determinants of the Future of the Study of Negotiations in Organizations." In Roy Lewicki, Blair Sheppard, and Max Bazerman, eds. *Research in Negotiations in Organizations.* Vol. 1 (Greenwich, CT: JAI Press, 1986).

Kochan, Thomas, Harry Katz, and Robert McKersie. *The Transformation of American Industrial Relations.* New York: Basic Books, 1986.

Kochan, Thomas and Anil Verma. "Negotiating in Organizations: Blending Industrial Relations and Organizational Behavior Approaches." In Max Bazerman and Roy Lewicki, eds. *Negotiating in Organizations.* Beverly Hills: Sage, 1983.

Kolb, Deborah. *The Mediators.* Cambridge: MIT Press, 1983.

Korpi, Walter and Michael Shalev. "Strikes, Industrial Relations and Class Conflict," *British Journal of Sociology,* Vol. 30 (1979), pp. 164–187.

Leonard, Jonathan. "The Impact of Affirmative Action on Employment," *Journal of Labor Economics,* Vol. 2, No. 4 (October 1984), pp. 439–463.

Lewin, David, ed. "Behavioral Research in Industrial Relations," *Industrial Relations,* Vol. 27, No. 1 (1988).

Lipset, Seymour Martin. "North American Labor Movements: a Comparative Perspective," in Seymour Martin Lipset, ed. *Unions in Transition.* San Francisco: ICS Press, 1986.

Milward, Neil and Mark Stevens. *British Workplace Industrial Relations, 1980–84.* Aldershot: Gower, 1987.

Pfeffer, Jeffrey and Alison Davis-Blake. "Understanding Organizational Wage Structures: a Resource Dependence Approach", *Academy of Management Journal,* Vol. 30, No. 3 (September 1987), pp. 437–455.

Phelps-Brown, Sir Henry. *The Origins of Trade Union Power.* Oxford: Clarendon Press, 1983.

Piore, Michael and Charles Sable. *The Second Industrial Divide.* New York: Basic Books, 1984.

Poole, Michael. *Industrial Relations: Origins and Patterns of National Diversity.* London: Routledge & Kegan Paul, 1986.

Rehmus, Charles. "Report from the Dean," *ILR Research.* Vol. 22, No. 2 (Spring 1985), p. 3.

Reynolds, Lloyd. *Labor Economics and Labor Relations.* Englewood Cliffs, NJ: Prentice-Hall, 1964.

Ross, Arthur M. and Paul T. Hartman, *Changing Patterns of Industrial Conflict* (New York: John Wiley & Sons, 1960).

Ross, Arthur. "Labor Courses: The Need for Radical Reconstruction." *Industrial Relations.* No. 4 (October 1964), pp. 1–17.

Snyder, D. "Institutional Setting and Industrial Conflict: Comparative Analyses of France, Italy, and the United State," *American Sociological Review.* No. 70 (1975), pp. 259–278.

Strauss, George. "Bridging the Gap Between Industrial Relations and Conflict Management," in Gerard Bomers and Richard Peterson, eds. *Conflict Management and Industrial Relations.* Boston: Kluwer Nihoff, 1982.

Strauss, George and Peter Feuille. "Industrial Relations Research: A Critical Analysis," *Industrial Relations,* Vol. 17, No. 3 (October 1978), pp. 259–277.

_____. "Industrial Relations Research in the United States," in Peter Doeringer, ed., *Industrial Relations in International Perspective.* London: Macmillan, 1981.

Tracy, Joseph. "An Empirical Test of an Assymetric Information Model of Strikes," *Journal of Labor Economics,* Vol. 5, No. 2 (April 1987), p. 149.

Weiler, Paul. "Promises to Keep: Securing Workers' Rights to Self-Organization Under the NLRA," *Harvard Law Review.* Vol. 96, No. 8 (June 1983), pp. 1769–1827.

Wilensky, Harold and Lowell Turner. *Democratic Corporatism and Policy Linkages.* Berkeley: Institute of International Studies, University of California, 1987.

INDEX